The Travelers' Guide to
LATIN AMERICAN
CUSTOMS and MANNERS

Also by the authors:

The Travelers' Guide to European Customs and Manners
The Travelers' Guide to Asian Customs and Manners

The Travelers' Guide to

LATIN AMERICAN

CUSTOMS and MANNERS

Elizabeth Devine

and

Nancy L. Braganti

St. Martin's Press • New York

Maps by Vantage Art Inc.
Illustrations by Raquel Jaramillo

Library of Congress Cataloging-in-Publication Data

Braganti, Nancy L.
    The travelers' guide to Latin American customs and manners/Nancy L. Braganti and Elizabeth Devine.
        p.   cm.
    ISBN 0-312-02303-0
    1. Latin America—Description and travel—1981-   —Guide-books.
2. Latin America—Social life and customs.   3. Etiquette—Latin America.   I. Devine, Elizabeth.   II. Title.
F1408.29.B72   1988
918'.0438—dc19   88-18243

10 9 8 7 6 5 4 3

To Jerry and Cheryl
and to Frank
with love and gratitude

E.D.

To my daughter Tanya
with love and appreciation

N.L.B.

Acknowledgments

We wish to thank the following people for their help in this book, and we wish to thank those who assisted but who preferred to remain anonymous: Marta Alemán, Antonio Ayala, Marcel Baković, David Ball, José J. Banús, Alice Barron, Sally Barron, Beverly Brenner, Denia Butler, Noela Cabrera, Ellen Caldwell, Susy Cárdenas, Roberto Carvalho, Juan Crespo, Evelyne DeLori, Olga Dentler, Annette Dumbach, Silvia Faiguenbaum, Bernardo Fernandes, Alegría Freedman, Joan Freeman, Jennifer George, Skye and Ricardo Glade, Antonio Gómez, Peter Greiff, Roger Haddad, Claudio Heckmann, Sandra Herrera, Sara Hoffmann, Bonnie Howard, Donald Howard (Senior Vice President, Gray-Judson & Howard), Teresa Huyck, Clarine Johnson, Susana A. Johnston, Elsa Khwaja, Sylvia Kywi, Hedy Laskie, Mario León, Emma LoGuzzo, Carmen López-Blumenkron, Terry McCoy, Richard Mackler, Tina Mahler, Francesco Marchetti, Patricia Márquez, Ernesto Martelo, Carlos Mendoza, Richard Miller, Martha Montero, Karen Nurick, Dr. Raquel Ojeda, Julio Raúl Pabón, María Beatriz Plaza, Massimo Porciani, Irene Quinn, Alex and Beatriz Quiroga, Caitlin Randall, Diana Reynolds, José Ricardo-Gil, Alan Robinson, Barbara and Román Romero, James Samiljan, Dr. Guillermo Sánchez, Lionilda Santos, Elizabeth Schuster, Sylvia Seidenman, Jan Smith, D. V. Springgate, Leah Steimel, Pasquale Tató, Maria Van Dusen, Lucía Velásquez, Dr. Juan Carlos Vera, Felicidade Vieira, Alejandro Mora Viera, Ulrike Welsch, Nora Fonseca Zabriskie.

Contents

❦

The Travelers' Guide to
LATIN AMERICAN
CUSTOMS and MANNERS

Introduction

About travel, Mark Twain wrote, "A round man cannot be expected to fit in a square hole right away. He must have time to modify his shape."

When traveling to another culture, we often feel like round pegs trying to jam ourselves into square holes (or vice versa). If we leave the protective umbrella of the escorted tour, we worry that we won't know how to deal with people and won't correctly interpret their behavior.

For the increasing number of people traveling to Latin America, we offer a guide to help you feel confident that you're doing the right thing, whether as a businessperson or as a visitor. We hope this guide will minimize the amount of time it takes you to "modify [your] shape."

For easy reference, we have divided each chapter into a series of topics:

Greetings: To make a good impression, it's often important to know how you will be greeted and to react properly. In many parts of Latin America, greetings are rather effusive. People sometimes shake hands and sometimes kiss or embrace. In some places single women will be kissed three times on the cheek—twice in greeting and once as a wish for marriage.

Remember that most people use the family names of both parents in their surname, the father's first. José Díaz Rodríguez, for example, can be referred to or addressed formally as "Señor Díaz Rodríguez" or, more commonly, simply as "Señor Díaz."

Conversation: A few things to keep in mind. People from English-speaking countries often believe in being open, frank, and direct. Latin Americans take pride in being tactful and diplomatic. In both speech and writing they may be indirect, elaborate, and complimentary. Follow suit to avoid giving offense.

Try to learn before you go. A visit to any country is richer when you know something about it in advance, but to make a good impression in business or to strike up an acquaintance, it's essential to know something about the other person's world. Learn about soccer, a sport that is an obsession in most of Latin America. (In some sections of the U.S., your best sources will be kids in grammar school and high school who have taken up soccer enthusiastically.) It would be helpful to learn something about bullfighting, especially if you're visiting Mexico, Peru, Venezuela, or Colombia, where it is regarded as an art.

Remember that few people can resist the flattery of being asked for their opinion about sights to see, things to do, and places to eat. (We have one friend who, at the drop of a question, prepares a five-page mini-guide to her area.)

While people will usually enjoy discussing their country, resist the temptation to offer comparisons to your own country's wealth, employment rate, housing, traffic, roads, and so forth.

Also note that, while people of course have a national identity, there is also a strong identification with Latin America, rather than with Spain. And that Latin Americans think of themselves as Americans (*americanos*)—inhabitants of the Americas—and might resent people from the U.S. using that term solely for themselves.

Finally, don't be insulted if someone refers to you as a *gringo*. The word doesn't necessarily have negative connotations. For instance, in Peru it refers to a blond, fair-skinned person.

Telephones: Expect to find a wide range in the efficiency of telephone service—from the very modern service in Uruguay to the almost useless one in Argentina.

We've tried to take some of the mystery out of dealing with public telephones in the places where they can be found and to suggest alternatives where they can't.

If you're planning to make long-distance or overseas calls and would like to make them from your hotel (rather than from the telephone company office), be sure first to inquire whether the hotel imposes a surcharge and, if so, how much.

In some cases, it's much cheaper to call into the country from abroad than to call out of the country, and you might want to arrange to have business associates or family and friends phone you at prearranged times.

In Public: Some public manners and gestures don't travel. You may offend when you least intend to. For example, in conversation Latin Americans naturally tend to stand very close. Don't back away, or you might be considered snobbish and aloof. In some countries, you'll see men walking down the street arm in arm. The gesture has no sexual meaning.

Be careful about talking with your hands. Gestures mean different things in different countries. An illustration: the cheerful "okay" sign with thumb and index finger of the right hand in a circle is obscene in most Latin American countries.

Once again, in the desire not to offend, in some countries in Latin America, people will often tell you what they think you want to hear rather than the truth. If you ask someone, "Is the post office down that street?" he or she is likely to say "Yes," whether it is or not. Similarly, if you invite people to dinner, they may accept, whether or not they have any intention of coming. After enough time in Latin America, you'll develop a sixth sense about whether people mean what they say.

Remember that life in Latin America centers on the family and extended family. You'll find children at social occasions everywhere. One of the great occasions in a family's life is a girl's fifteenth birthday. You may be lucky enough to be invited to a great ball held in honor of the young woman, marking her entrance into the adult world.

Women especially should be sensitive to the local standards of behavior. If you are in one place—even a large city—for a long time, you will come under scrutiny. This holds true particularly in more conservative or traditional areas. If you engage in behavior that could be construed as disreputable—e.g., going out alone or associating with married men—you'll be the subject of gossip and your company avoided. If you're staying with a family, your behavior will reflect on them.

A few words about the less fortunate: In most of Latin America, there are no extensive welfare programs such as those found in the U.S. and Europe, so even local people usually give to beggars. And at the many markets, if you buy from women vendors, you can be sure that the money will be used for their children.

Dress: One of the easiest ways to offend is to dress inappropriately. North Americans are pretty much used to wearing whatever they want, but dress that is too casual, or in the case of women too revealing, is very offensive in some areas of Latin America. When selecting your traveling wardrobe, remember that you rarely err by being on the conservative side.

Before packing, be sure to check on the altitude of the areas you'll be visiting. You'll need warm clothing for the many places at high altitudes.

If your shoe size is a large one, be sure to bring an extra pair, as it will be difficult for you to find shoes in your size.

Meals: First, we'll tell you at what times people eat and what foods are usually served. For quick reference, in most Latin American countries, breakfast is *el desayuno* (el deh-sah-yoo-noh), lunch is *el almuerzo* (el ahl-mwehr-soh), and dinner is *la cena* (lah seh-nah) or *la comida* (lah koh-mee-dah). This is an area of some regional variation. For instance, in Mexico breakfast is *el desayuno* or *el almuerzo,* lunch is *la comida,* and supper is *la cena.* In many places you'll find that the main meal is at noon, followed by a siesta. At high altitudes, it's a good idea to have your heaviest meal at noon, because it will be easier on your digestive system. Also, avoid alcoholic beverages at high altitudes.

Next we take up the meal itself—where you'll probably sit, how the meal will be served, and how long you should stay after dinner at a person's home. And we also identify in this section table manners generally observed by people of each country. We should note here, though, that there is a great deal of variety in this area. Depending on the context of the meal or of the people involved, you can see everything from formal table manners in a pure, upper-class European fashion, to eating without silverware, with the ubiquitous *tortilla* taking its place (it's the spoon you can eat!). In general, though, in more formal settings, Latin Americans eat in the continental style, with the knife in the right hand and the fork in the left, using the knife to push food onto the fork. Also, the custom of keeping the left hand on the lap is not observed; keep both hands above the table.

Then we cover one of the major reasons many people travel—the wonderful variety of the world's cuisines. Latin America is especially rich in diverse cuisines, both from the many ethnic groups that have immigrated to Latin America, and from the ancient cultures native to the American continent. We also cover the different kinds of eating establishments available and the kinds of fare you'll likely find there. A word of caution: street bars in Latin America can tend to be rather sleazy. The local women usually do not go to these bars. The traveler, man or woman, would probably do well not to do so either.

We can't emphasize too strongly the importance of being *very* cautious in matters of food and drink. If you have even the slightest doubt about an item, don't eat or drink it. In most places, you must avoid raw vegetables, unpeeled fruit, and raw shellfish. Drink only bottled water, and don't drink fruit juices made with tap water. Don't use ice cubes made from tap water. Always ask for drinks *sin hielo* (seen yeh-loh), "without ice."

Hotels: While we don't recommend specific hotels, we try to describe different types of hotels available. Some countries offer interesting and agreeable alternatives to luxury hotels.

A caution about using water in bathrooms, both in hotels and in private homes: C stands for *caliente,* meaning hot, *not* cold. (In Brazil, Q stands for hot.) Pay close attention to the instructions for operating showers both in homes and in hotels. Turning on the water and electric heating unit in the wrong order can lead to disaster. Sometimes, you may not find soap in your room. If you call the bellboy, he will bring some, but you'll be charged for it. It's best to have a bar or two in your luggage.

Many travelers like to use one hotel as their base and fan out for one- or two-day trips. Most hotels, even small ones, have a luggage storage area that you can use if you've been a guest. Don't leave your luggage unless you're sure that the area is locked, and be sure to label the luggage carefully.

Tipping: Who *isn't* mystified by tipping? We've given advice on the amount to give people you're accustomed to tipping (porters, taxi drivers, etc.) and others you may not be accustomed to tipping, such as gas station attendants and ushers. Keep a supply of dollars for tipping. People everywhere appreciate being tipped in dollars. In many countries the rate of inflation is so high that it renders precise amounts obsolete in a matter of days. So we often provide amounts in U.S. equivalents.

Private Homes: Especially once you begin to establish a friendship with people, they are likely to invite you to their homes. Nothing gives a better insight into a culture than such a visit. On the other hand, it can turn into an awkward situation if you are not—in general—aware of what is expected of you or of what you might expect from your hosts.

We've given advice on how to behave when staying with a family.

Most of us aren't used to having servants to perform such chores as laundry, but many Latin American families, even in the middle class, do.

Note that some families are more traditional than others; try to fit in with the customs of the family with whom you're staying. For example, traditional families expect everyone to eat together and be on time for meals. Less traditional homes are more flexible about such matters.

If you're staying with a family for a few days and buy some food, be sure to share it with the family. Don't put it in the refrigerator and say, "This is mine."

To endear yourself as a guest, observe these rules when using the bathroom: 1) Hang your towels in the patio area rather than in the bathroom. Keep your toilet articles in your room. 2) Be sure to leave the bathroom floor dry after you've taken your shower or bath. 3) Women should never throw sanitary napkins or tampons down the toilet. Wrap them and put them in a wastebasket.

Again, single women especially should keep in mind that your behavior will be fairly closely observed by the community. Your actions will reflect on the family you're staying with. You should be considerate of your hosts, particularly in the more conservative or traditional homes.

In this section, there's also advice about good gifts to bring. Electronic items are often a good choice. For young people, illustrated T-shirts and cassette tapes are popular.

Business: In this section we start off by providing basic data about hours for businesses, government offices, banks, and shops, and the national currency. Then we provide information about business practices. Succeeding in business can be really trying if you don't know a few of the ground rules. Most important, if you're not willing to put the time into establishing a personal relationship before getting down to business, don't even consider doing business in Latin America. You'll have to spend a long time talking about yourself, your family, your background, and so on. Personal friendship and the accompanying feeling of trust is the strongest possible underpinning for business success.

You'll make a good impression if you study the politics, culture, and economy of the country so that you can participate in a conversation on those subjects.

Remember that you don't just get in touch with someone and plan to do business. Contacts are essential. We've tried to suggest some avenues for gaining contacts if you don't have any. If you're a member of an international organization (e.g., Rotary Club International or Lion's Club International) you may find business contacts through them. When you arrive at your destination, arrange to attend a meeting. (One business-man, whose flight home from Caracas was canceled and who faced being stranded for days, was given a seat on the next plane, thanks to the influence of a man he had met at a Rotary Club meeting and who happened to be at the airport also.)

In searching for contacts through an embassy, you needn't confine yourself to your own. Seek out the commercial division of the British, Canadian, U.S., and French embassies. Try to arrange an invitation to one of their cocktail parties. Such parties are an excellent way to obtain information from government officials—information for which otherwise, you'll spend hours waiting in offices to see people.

If you receive a letter in Spanish, be sure to answer in Spanish.

Try to develop as large a network of contacts as possible. There are many subtle political changes occurring with great frequency in Latin American countries, and contacts can often help you understand what is going on.

Be sure that you always deal with the very top people in a company, since they are the ones who make the decisions.

Even if you have established a personal relationship with people at a company, always have a lawyer and an accountant in the country where you'll be doing business. Major law firms in your country will probably be able to recommend a lawyer. Send copies of any agreements to her or him. In Latin America, a major difference in this area is the existence of the *notario*. Although the name translates as "notary," the *notario*'s is a full-fledged profession which requires four years of college work, and which ranks barely below that of lawyer. In fact, a *notario* is authorized to handle many matters that in the U.S. could only be handled by a lawyer.

Keep in mind that top-level officers usually speak English, so you won't need an interpreter when dealing with them. In fact, the manage-ment of a Latin American company might well be reluctant to do business in the presence of an outside party. The company will usually have a bilingual lawyer or *notario* available to do any necessary interpreting.

A few other cultural differences that are pertinent to business affairs: (1) The metric system reigns in Latin America, and should be used in any size and weight specifications. (2) Latin Americans write dates in the European style—first the day, then the month, and then the year, so 2/4/89 is April 2, 1989. (We had a person refuse to honor a travelers' check which was dated U.S. style.) (3) In some countries, when people write out amounts of money, periods distinguish thousands and commas denote fractions. Example: C$5.000,50 is 5,000 Chilean *pesos* and 50 cents. (4) The hours of the day are often written out on the basis of the full 24 hours of the day, not on that of the two 12-hour periods. In this system—familiar to many of us as "military time"—for example, 2:00 A.M. is 0200, and 2:00 P.M. is 1400. You'll find this usage especially prevalent in the case of train and plane schedules.

There are some abbreviations to know: S.A. = incorporated, Cía. = company, A.C. = a nonprofit organization, EE.UU. = United States, ENTEL = National Telecommunications Enterprise, F.F.C.C. = railroads.

Remember that a Latin American's sense of priorities may be different. If someone has an appointment with you, and a friend drops in, he or she will never say to the friend, "I'm sorry. I can't see you now. I have an appointment." Friends always come first, even if they stay three hours.

Small tips for business meetings: (1) In an elevator, realize that *PB* stands for *Planta Baja,* the ground floor, while *1* is the U.S. second floor. (2) In most countries, people are less than compulsive about getting to a meeting precisely on time. (3) Always exchange business cards immediately when you meet someone, and keep the cards.

When phoning people in Latin America from abroad, always call person-to-person. You'll waste less time, especially if secretaries don't speak your language. You should note that many businesses in Latin America, especially those involved in international commerce, make regular use of telex.

Etiquette for business gifts is a little different in Latin America: (1) Don't bring business gifts until a friendly relationship has been established. (2) If you're planning several trips to the country, it's appropriate to ask colleagues what sort of gift they would like from abroad. (3) Don't give gifts in a business environment—wait until the setting is social.

For women traveling on business, see also the advice, "Some Special Words for Women," later.

Holidays: If you're on a pleasure trip, you may want to plan it around a holiday, but if you're on a business trip, you may want to avoid holidays. Be sure to have an adequate supply of local currency before a holiday begins, because you probably won't be able to find many places to change travelers' checks.

Be sensitive to the many religious festivals in Latin American countries. Don't drive through parades or photograph festivals without permission of the participants.

One special religious festival you'll notice is celebrated widely in Latin America is the Feast of the Epiphany, on January 6. This is called *el Día de los Reyes Magos* (the Feast of the Magi) and commemorates the visit of the magi bearing gifts for the infant Jesus. In many places, children receive gifts on this day rather than on Christmas.

Transportation: We've covered both public transportation and driving. In the same country, you may find modern subways and first class, four-lane roads, together with the most primitive transportation. In cities, the best advice is to take taxis. Though the ones around hotels are generally the most expensive, they're also usually the most reliable. And, in many cases, the drivers know some English. When dealing with train and bus schedules, remember that these are usually posted in military time.

In some places, it's possible, and convenient, to rent a car. (Remember that gas is sold by the liter in most countries of Latin America.) But, unless you have experience driving through herds of cattle, it's often best to stay off the rural roads of Latin America. (Cars hitting cows are a major type of auto accident in Mexico.) In many cases, you'll find flying to be the best way to get from one city to another.

Legal Matters, Safety, and Health: "Legal" raises the issue of bribery, a matter that will touch both the businessperson and the tourist. It is common knowledge that bribery is part of the way of life in much of Latin America. But, what would be considered bribery by others, in Latin America is often thought of as little more than a tip. As we tip the maître d' to get a better table or to be seated sooner, people in some Latin American countries employ the *mordida* to expedite matters. Unless you are using money to persuade a policeman to ignore a traffic offense, you're not trying to get a person to do something illegal; you just want to speed up a legal process. In business, you might want to get a proposal or permit from the bottom of the pile to the top, and the $25 to $50 you pay a bureaucrat may be well worth it.

Bring with you some passport-size photos in case you lose your passport or decide to visit another Latin American country and need a visa. It's also a good idea to make a photocopy of your passport, and keep it—with some extra money—in a location separate from your actual passport and your money supply.

Be aware that, while many drugs available only by prescription in North America are available over-the-counter in many Latin American countries, the name and the dosage may be different.

If you are considering taking fruits and vegetables into a Latin American country, check with its consulate beforehand. Most countries have restrictions on bringing in produce.

To make sure you're not venturing into an unsafe environment, if you're planning a trip from the U.S., call the Citizens' Emergency Center Division of the State Department to find out about any particular trouble spot in Latin America. The phone number is (202) 647–5225, and they're available from 8:15 A.M. to 5:00 P.M., Monday through Friday; and from 9:00 A.M. to 3:00 P.M. on Saturday, Eastern Standard Time. In Great Britain, call the Consular Advice to the Public, a division of the Foreign Office at (01) 270–4129. Canadians should phone the Consular Operations Division of the Department of External Affairs at (613) 992–3705.

You should always, of course, be alert to possible threats to your safety. Wherever you are, ask friends, business colleagues, or hotel porters to advise you which areas of the city should be avoided.

To have a healthy trip, in the U.S., call the Centers for Disease Control in Atlanta, Georgia—(404) 639–3311—to learn about required immunizations and about any special health problems. Or you can call the office of the U.S. Public Health Service Quarantine Station nearest you: Chicago: (312) 686–2150; Honolulu: (808) 541–2552; Los Angeles: (213) 215–2365; Miami: (305) 526–2910; New York: (718) 917–1685; San Francisco: (415) 876–2872; Seattle: (206) 442–4519.

Canadians should write or call for the brochure "Travel and Health," which gives information about health precautions when traveling outside Canada. Address: Health and Welfare Canada, 5th Floor, Brooke Claxton Building, Tunney's Pasture, Ottawa K1A OK9. Phone: (613) 957–2991.

British travelers should ask their travel agents about health conditions, since the agents are updated frequently by the Department of Health and Social Security. Travelers may also telephone the Department at (01) 407–5522 and ask for "Public Inquiries," to learn of any updated health forecasts, and to request a copy of their booklet, "Protect Your Health Abroad."

Keep in mind that you must pay an airport tax when leaving a country, and you must pay it in local currency, not in travelers' checks.

Be sure to bring a more than adequate supply of any prescription drugs you may be taking. Since drugs have different names, and dosages may be different, ask your physician to provide you the generic names of all prescription drugs you are taking, plus prescriptions for them. Pack your medication in your carry-on bag.

If you wear glasses, bring an extra pair as well as a copy of your prescription.

In addition to any medications you may be taking, bring an antidiarrhea medication and a broad-spectrum antibiotic.

Also consider bringing: aspirin or your favorite headache/fever remedy, an antacid, a laxative, a motion-sickness remedy, insect repellant, lotion for insect bites, sunscreen, a cream to relieve sunburn, an antibiotic ointment, Band-Aids, cough medicine, a remedy for muscle pains, salt pills to combat heat exhaustion, and a thermometer. Women may wish to include remedies for menstrual cramps and vaginal yeast infections. Women should also note that supplies of tampons are available in major cities.

Key Phrases: At the end of the book, we've added lists of useful words and phrases in Spanish and Portuguese. Learning the basic courtesies, numbers, and words for common items or places will be a real help.

Some General Advice

Learn before you go. To appreciate the wondrous and mysterious cultures of the Aztec, the Inca, and the Maya, read about the pre-Columbian cultures. Here are some suggestions: Michael D. Coe, *The Maya: Ancient People and Places* and *Mexico* (both New York: Thames & Hudson, $9.95); John Hemming, *The Conquest of the Incas* (San Diego: Harcourt, $9.95); William H. Prescott, *The Conquest of Mexico and Peru* (New York: Irvington, $22.95); George C. Vaillant, *Aztecs of Mexico* (New York: Penguin, $6.95).

Don't judge. Being different is neither better nor worse. Resist the impulse to compare to the way things are done in your country. Your country may be more efficient, but to Latin Americans efficiency is not a god. It is more important to enjoy life than to worry about whether papers have been processed or tickets issued quickly.

Some Special Words for Women

If you're traveling alone—whether for business or pleasure—you might consider wearing a wedding ring. And if someone asks you where your husband is, say that he'll be joining you soon.

In general, as long as you're in the business section of a city, you won't encounter much more harassment from men than you'd encounter in any busy city in the U.S. or Europe. But, especially if you stray from this territory, you might find the sexual signals to be rather overt and annoying.

A good refuge from unwanted advances can be other women, and children. On a bus or train, sit next to an older woman, who will likely be protective of you. Be friendly to women in small villages. They may be helpful if you have trouble. When one woman traveler's bus was canceled in a small village, a woman she had met at the bus stop took her home and put her up. If you're staying with a family, you might invite a child with you on sightseeing excursions.

Also, dress on the conservative side. And, don't forget that it is not customary for a woman to enter street bars. If you want a drink, the best choice is sitting at a table in a hotel bar.

The road for a foreign businesswoman in Latin America will not be an easy one. You must be *extremely* professional, but should never come across as "superwoman." Avoid saying "I," but say instead, "We at our company." Be firm in refusing any personal approach; don't give ambiguous signals merely because a businessman made the approach. Be careful about giving gifts to colleagues and customers, as they may be interpreted as an overture. Stay at a hotel from one of the American chains or at one of the top-of-the-line local hotels. To ensure a good table in a restaurant, if you're dining alone, make a reservation for two. It might be convenient to hire a car and driver for the duration of your stay rather than relying on taxis.

Remember that businesspeople will form an opinion of you in the first ten minutes, judging you on the way that you present yourself.

If a Latin American businessman invites you for a drink, dancing, or a meal in a restaurant and you wish to accept, ask him whether his wife or other members of the firm will come along. This will let him know that you do not consider his invitation to be an approach.

And, finally, there's the issue of time—and the different ways Latin Americans perceive it. Nowhere does the visitor feel more like Twain's round peg trying to stuff itself into a square hole (or the other way around) than in coping with the Latin view of time.

When we were being interviewed on a radio call-in show about our book on European customs and manners, a woman called to say that even though Brazil wasn't in Europe, she had to ask us a question. "I went to visit cousins in Rio," she said. "I was staying at a hotel, but I was spending a good deal of time with them. We would make arrangements for them to pick me up at noon for lunch. I would be in the hotel lobby at noon, and they might arrive at one-thirty—with no apology. The second time this happened, I said perhaps we should adjust our time of meeting. They said there was no need to, that they would come at noon. And they came at two o'clock. What should I have done to make them be on time?"

We gave the only possible answer: Nothing. Frustrating and aggravating though it may feel, a visitor is not going to single-handedly change basic cultural traits (nor should he or she automatically presume that his or her way is better). Remember, you're the visitor.

ARGENTINA

Interested in a country in which Paris and Texas live side by side? Head for Argentina, where Buenos Aires has earned the title "Paris of the Americas." In fact, you'll find that fashion, architecture, cultural life, and manners in Buenos Aires are very close to those in Europe. Argentina's enormous immigrant population, largely from Italy and Spain, explains the Old World flavor.

Some visitors, however, have likened Argentina to Texas—citing the long stretches of grassy pampas, the large ranches (an average of 25,000 acres), and the huge steaks common in Argentina's restaurants.

Visit Argentina, and decide for yourself whether the Old or New World dominates.

GREETINGS

Language: The official language of Argentina is Spanish, with Italian the second language and German the third.

• When introduced, men shake hands with other men. If men and women are introduced by a woman friend, they sometimes kiss, but usually they shake hands. Women usually kiss other women when they're introduced.

• Close male friends hug one another in greeting. Women who are friends shake hands with both hands and kiss one another on both cheeks. Men and women friends usually kiss.

• Use titles. They are important to Argentines. Some common titles: Doctor (for Ph.D. and medical doctor); architect; engineer; lawyer; professor. (See "Key Words and Phrases" at the end of the book for Spanish equivalents.) Use the title with the last name.

• At large parties, introduce yourself. At small parties you will be introduced by the host or hostess. At either type of party, shake hands and say good-bye to each person when you leave.

CONVERSATION

• If possible, bone up on soccer. Men love to discuss sports—especially soccer. Women enjoy discussing the latest trends in fashion.

• Talk about opera (which Argentines love) with members of both sexes.

• Ask people to recommend sights and restaurants to visit.

• With businesspeople, talk about the role of inflation in the economy as well as current government decrees and how they are affecting prices.

• When doing business, don't ask at your first meeting if the other person is married or has children.

• Women should expect personal questions, i.e., "Do you have children?" "If not, why not?" People often make critical comments about physical appearance in front of others, e.g., "Are you going to lose weight?" Don't take it too seriously; it's friendly banter, an Argentine trademark.

• Compliment people about their home and children.

• Never discuss politics or government when first meeting someone. (Especially avoid mentioning the Perón years.) People tend to become very aggressive when discussing politics, since passions run high about Argentina's recent past. After you know people a while, they will ask your opinion of Argentine politics. Read up on the country's most recent history before going to Argentina.

• Keep in mind that Argentines pride themselves on their European heritage (Italian, British, Spanish, German). In general, there is a tendency to look down on Indians. Don't ask anyone if he or she is of Indian descent.

• Steer clear of discussions about religion.

TELEPHONES

• Note that there aren't many public phones. For local calls, you can usually ask for and use, without charge, the phone in restaurants, cafes, and pizzerias. After your call, offer to pay for it.

• Look for orange pay phones in public buildings, offices, bars, restaurants, and on the street. You will need tokens called *cospeles,* which you can obtain at restaurants, bars, newsstands, and kiosks. One *cospel* provides two to six minutes of calling, depending on whether you're calling during prime time (8:00 A.M. to 8:00 P.M.). You can deposit several *cospeles* to extend your time. Those not used will be returned.

• Note that telephones in Buenos Aires do not work very well. You will often hear someone pick up the phone and say, *"Equivocado"* [eh-kee-voh-**kah**-doh], meaning "wrong number."

• Realize that communications

are often better with places outside Argentina than within the country.

• To make a long-distance call in a small town, go to the telephone office, Unión Telefónica.

• Be aware that you may have to arrange to place a long-distance call one or two days in advance.

IN PUBLIC

• Some gestures to note: (1) Shaking the right hand with the index finger hitting the thumb and middle finger means "a lot, a great deal," or "hurry up"; (2) Brushing the top of the hand from under the chin out means "I don't know" or "I don't care"; (3) Extending the fingers of the right hand and twisting it—thumb up, thumb down, thumb up, thumb down—means something is "so-so."

• If you're smoking, always offer cigarettes to the people in your group.

• When you ask Argentines for directions on the street, they will give you very detailed instructions, even if they have no idea where your destination is. It's a matter of pride for Argentines to act as if they know the correct response.

• Note that people love to be photographed but poor people may ask to be paid.

• For a public bathroom, feel free to use the ones in restaurants (even if you're not a patron). Even in remote areas, gas stations (identified by the sign "YPF") usually have decent bathrooms. As a precaution, bring your own tissues.

DRESS

• If you're going to visit Argentina during its winter (June to August), remember that both men and women need warm clothes and topcoats. Central heating is not customary in either public buildings or homes. Homes often have only electric heaters, so you'll need to dress warmly if visiting or staying with a family.

• For business during the summer months (December to March), men should wear lightweight dark suits and women may wear lightweight suits or dresses, and heels.

• Casual wear for men is a sweater, shirt, and pants or just shirt and pants. For women casual wear is a top with very chic pants or a skirt.

• Don't wear shorts on the street. They're acceptable if you're invited to a swimming pool. For swim wear, Argentines prefer conservative bathing suits (unlike the revealing bathing suits worn in Brazil).

• When invited to a meal in a home, men should wear jackets and ties and women a skirt and blouse or dress. To an *asado* (an outdoor barbecue), men and women should wear nice but casual clothes.

• When dining in a formal restaurant, men should wear a jacket with a tie or ascot, and women should wear a dress or skirt.

• Formal wear for men is a tuxedo and for women, mid-calf dresses. Formal wear is for gala functions, such as an opera, a theater or nightclub opening, or a political inauguration.

• Argentines are quite conscious of dress, and are said to evaluate people's attire starting with the shoes.

MEALS

Hours and Foods

Breakfast: Between 7:00 and 8:00 A.M. The food will be a *medialuna* (a sort of croissant) or *pan de leche* (a muffin with cream on top). Beverages: coffee with milk, tea with milk, or *maté* (Argentina's national drink—see "Beverages").

Lunch: Usually served about 1:00 P.M. The meal may begin with *picadas*—appetizers such as sausage, cheese, peanuts, salami, olives—served in the living room with drinks or at the dining table. Next will be soup or a pasta dish (e.g., ravioli or cannelloni) or an antipasto of cold meats and cheeses. Then there'll be a main course such as *milanesa de carne* or *milanesa de pollo* with french fries and a salad. A typical dessert is *flan con dulce de leche*. The meal ends with coffee, espresso style. From 4:00 to 6:00 P.M. is tea time, *la hora del té* (also called *la hora de la leche*—"the milk hour"—for children). Adults have cakes, cookies, tea or coffee with milk, or *maté*. Children have toast with butter, jelly, or honey, and milk or chocolate milk.

Dinner: Served about 10:00 P.M. (later on weekends). Dinner may be a complete meal similar to lunch, e.g., steak and salad or a dish in the *milanesa* style with fruit, dessert, and coffee.

Beverages: Maté, a very popular drink, is a type of tea drunk from a gourd and sipped through a silver straw. It is made from the young leaves of an evergreen tree of the holly family. The dry tea is called *yerba maté.* The drink is usually passed from one person to another. *Maté* is served only in homes, not in restaurants. *Maté* is served in a variety of ways: with sugar, anise seeds, orange peel, or milk. People often drink it instead of coffee; it contains considerable caffeine.

• Common drinks before dinner are vermouth, either plain or with soda, *Gancia* (a type of sweet vermouth), or wine. The most popu- lar after-dinner drink is Scotch.

• The usual drinks with meals are wine and mineral water.

Table Manners

• If you're invited to dinner in a city, expect drinks in the living room before dinner, but in a rural area guests usually go directly to the meal, and no drinks are served before.

• Should you be the guest of honor, expect to sit at the head of the table.

• Note that some families serve family style, while in others a maid serves each person individually.

• If you wish to cut meat as Argentines do, hold it with your fork, and cut the meat through the prongs of the fork.

• To indicate that you have finished eating, cross your knife and fork (prongs down) on the plate.

• Anticipate spending a long time at a meal. Argentines "live to eat."

• After dinner, adjourn with others to the living room for coffee and liqueurs, a custom especially observed in winter.

Eating Out

• Remember that Argentine cuisine is mainly Italian or Spanish. Buenos Aires, however, has a huge immigrant population, so, in addition to creole and Italian restaurants, you'll find many German and French restaurants and Jewish delicatessens. You'll also find Chinese restaurants and North American fast-food restaurants.

• *Picadas* specialize in hundreds of appetizers—seafood, beans, beef dishes, cheese dishes, nuts. Alcoholic and nonalcoholic beverages are available.

• In *churrasquerías*, where you have all the meat you can eat for one price, waiters circulate with skewers, and you tell them when you want what they're serving. With Argentines, innards (kidney, brain, intestines, sweetbreads, etc.) are most popular, but they will understand if you are not used to them.

• *Whiskerías* are informal cocktail lounges that serve all kinds of alcoholic beverages, but sandwiches are the only food.

• To assuage your sweet tooth, try *confiterías*. They offer small sandwiches, pastries, tea, coffee, and sometimes cocktails. Other places for sweets are *heladerías* (ice-cream shops), or *rotiseriás*, which offer very elegant pastries, gourmet-style delicatessen products, and alcoholic beverages.

• There are very few vegetarian restaurants, since Argentines are such great consumers of meat.

• Don't join strangers at their table.

• In Buenos Aires, expect to find steak houses, *confiterías*, and hotel restaurants open all day long. If you want to have an early dinner, go to one of them. Outside Buenos Aires, you won't be able to have dinner until 8:30 or 9:00 P.M., when restaurants open. However, most restaurants stay open until 2:00 A.M.

• Be aware that food such as steak is usually served already salted. If you're on a low-sodium diet, tell the waiter, *"No use sal, por favor"* (Noh ooh-seh sahl, pohr fah-vorr).

• Note that in ordering meat, *cruda* means very rare. To request your meat medium, say *"un poquito cruda."*

• Order only locally made alcoholic beverages, or you'll pay a fortune because of taxes and import fees. Always say *"nacional"* (nah-syoh-nahl) following the generic name, e.g., *"whiskey nacional."*

• Note that Argentina produces many wines. As a rule, the inexpensive red wines are better than the inexpensive white wines.

• Don't summon the waiter by making a "kissing" noise, as you'll hear some people do. It's rude. To call the waiter, say *"mozo"* (moh-soh).

• Remember that who pays depends on the circumstances. When couples are dining together, each couple usually pays for its own meal. An older person may pay for a group of younger people.

Specialties

• Since Argentina is such a meat-loving country, you'll find many meat specialties: *churrasco* is grilled steak; *bife de lomo* is a T-bone steak without the bone; *asado* are small pieces of beef, charcoal grilled and served with French fries; *parrillada* is a mixed grill of short ribs, tripe, sausages, sweetbreads, and blood sausages; *carbonada* is a stew of beef, corn, squash, and peaches, baked in a pumpkin shell; *milanesa de carne* is thinly sliced beef, covered with bread crumbs and eggs and then deep fried.

• For appetizers you may be offered *matambre* (which means "hunger killer")—an hors d'oeuvre of marinated flank steak stuffed with either spinach, hearts of palm, ham, and/or boiled eggs, then baked; or an *empanada,* a turnover, usually oven-baked, filled with ground beef, olives, onions, eggs, and red peppers.

• A special sauce used when barbecuing any kind of meat is *chimichurri,* made of finely chopped onions, tomatoes, garlic, and parsley, and oil and vinegar.

• A few fish specialties: *salmón*—sea salmon; *dorado,* a local freshwater fish; *corvina*—white sea bass; *calamares*—squid.

• A popular chicken dish is *milanesa de pollo,* which is the same thing as *milanesa de carne,* but made with chicken cutlets.

• Four favorite desserts: *dulce de leche*—milk simmered with sugar, vanilla and, sometimes, chocolate, served on *flan,* pastry, toast, or in cakes; *dulce de membrillo*—a thick quince preserve cut into slices and served with a cheese called *queso de Mar de Plata* (similar to Jahrlsberg); *dulce de batata*—sweet potato preserve cut into thick slices; *flan*—crème caramel.

HOTELS

• Be aware that some second-class hotels, many of which have English names, have the same service and comfort as first-class hotels. They may not be as modern inside, but they are very comfortable and less expensive than first-class hotels.

• Note that most hotels in large cities are air-conditioned.

• Be aware that orders for room service often take a long time to arrive.

• Think twice before having your hotel do your laundry. Such service is *very* expensive.

TIPPING

• Give hotel porters the equivalent of 50 cents or $1.00 (U.S.) for all your bags.

• Note that only taxi drivers near hotels expect tips. Tip the driver 15% of the fare.

• Tip gas station attendants only if they wash your windshield. Give them the equivalent of 15 to 20 cents.

• Give porters at the airport the equivalent of 25 cents per bag.

• At a theater, tip the usher 5% of the ticket price. Remember to reserve in advance tickets for plays and movies.

PRIVATE HOMES

• Since phone service is so inadequate, and because many people don't have telephones, feel free to drop in on people you know at tea time (4:00–6:00 P.M.). Check first, however, to see if there is a soccer game on TV. If there is, *everyone* will likely be watching it.

• If you're invited to a home for dinner at 9:00 P.M., arrive at 9:30 or 10:00, unless the host has specified "American time."

• When visiting a family, don't just enter a room and sit down on your own. You may be taking the chair of an important family member. Wait until your hostess asks you to sit down and motions you to a chair.

• Keep in mind that Argentina has a larger middle class than other Latin American countries, so many people don't have live-in maids, although they may have women who come a few times a week to clean and do the laundry. If you're staying with a family, it's best to keep your room neat, make your bed, and do your own laundry.

• Note that most families don't have cooks. Usually the hostess does all the cooking, but she doesn't expect help with it.

• When taking a bath, ask your hostess about heating the water, since it may need to be heated for 30 minutes. Take your shower or run your bath as soon as the water is ready, since the hot water doesn't last very long.

• Insist on paying for all long-distance phone calls you make from a private home.

• If you go out with the family you're visiting, offer to pay for your share of expenses such as restaurant meals and public transportation.

• Remember that families tend to adapt to a guest, rather than hoping the guest will adapt to them. They will be concerned about you and probably won't let you go sightseeing on your own.

Gifts: If you know that a family will be entertaining you, send or bring flowers or imported candy. You may also send flowers after the visit.

• If you're sending flowers, note that Birds of Paradise are considered "classy."

• Consider bringing a bottle of Scotch—Chivas Regal is the most popular brand, with Johnnie Walker second. French champagne is also welcome.

• Don't bring wine. It's too common.

• Avoid bringing personal items, such as ties and shirts.

• If you know a woman very well, bring her (from abroad) makeup or perfume. Bring clothing to children you know. Men enjoy aftershave, AM-FM radios with batteries, cameras, Cross or Parker pens.

BUSINESS

Hours

Businesses: Monday through Friday, 9:00 A.M. to 7:00 P.M.

Government Offices: Some offices are open Monday through Friday, 9:00 A.M. to 1:00 P.M. Others are open Monday through Friday, 1:00 to 5:00 P.M. Call to find out the correct hours for the offices you wish to visit.

Banks: Monday through Friday, 10:00 A.M. to 4:00 P.M.

Shops: Monday through Friday, 9:00 A.M. to 6:00 P.M., and Saturday, 9:00 A.M. to 1:00 P.M.

Currency

• The unit of currency is the *austral*. It was introduced in 1985, with 1 *austral* equaling 100 *centavos*. *Pesos*, the former currency, are still in circulation; they are stamped with the equivalent amount in *australes*. One thousand *pesos* equal one *austral*, 5,000 *pesos* equal 5 *australes*, and so on. Fifty *pesos* equal a 5 *centavos* coin. When using *pesos*, you're dealing with such large figures that it can be confusing; so don't be rushed, until you become conversant with the currency.

• Coins: ½, 5, 10, and 50 *centavos*.

• Bills: 1, 5, and 10, 50, 100, 1,000 *australes*.

• To find the best exchange rate, go to a hotel or a travel agency. It's difficult to cash travelers' checks in small towns.

• Bring your credit cards. Most places accept American Express, Diners Club, Visa, and MasterCard.

• Also bring your checkbook. Some shops in Buenos Aires accept personal checks with an I.D.—and you will get a discount.

Business Practices

• Plan to make several trips to accomplish your goal. If your business style is fast paced, you will have to adjust because there is no way to push people to go faster. At every step you'll find red tape and bureaucracy. Businesspeople have to obtain the consent of many others for approval of a project.

• Realize that it's indispensable to have contacts (e.g., to help arrange appointments) in the government if you're planning to do business with the government (contacts are less important for a nongovernment business deal). If you don't have a contact, get in touch with your embassy in Argentina.

• Be aware that even though you have an appointment, many people don't keep them; the higher the person is in an organization the more likely he is to neglect an appointment or to keep you waiting a long time.

• Bring business cards and documents you'll be using translated into Spanish.

• If you'll be distributing copies of proposals, agreements, and so forth, bring the copies with you, since copying service in Argentina is expensive, time consuming, and not very good.

• To find a good, reliable interpreter, contact the commercial attaché at your embassy. Hotel translation services may not be adequate.

• Be prepared for the work day to extend until 10:00 P.M. Don't be surprised if someone suggests an 8:00 P.M. business meeting.

• Remember that people don't like to do business on the phone, because telephone service is so erratic.

• Be prepared for local businesspeople to arrive five to ten minutes late; foreign businesspeople should be on time.

• Expect executives in most large businesses to speak English. Try to speak a few words of Spanish. It will make a most favorable impression.

• Even if you won't finish your cup, you might accept the offer of coffee, which is always served during business meetings. Coffee is served with sugar on the side, but *not* with milk.

• Remember that meetings always begin gradually with discussions of extraneous topics, and they conclude in the same way. Never grab your briefcase and dash out without making small talk at the end of the meeting. Allow the chief Argentine in the group to decide when the meeting should conclude. Leave only then.

• Realize that Argentines are very efficient businesspeople who use computers and other advanced technology. The only technological problem you'll encounter in doing business is the telephone system.

• Be aware that people are meticulous about details, especially when attorneys are involved in negotiations and contracts. It is difficult for people to sign anything without first dealing with a massive amount of bureaucratic red tape.

• Women should not experience special problems doing business in Argentina, as long as you are professional in manner and dress.

• Be careful not to appear to be threatening or confrontational. Unless you're tactful, you'll be regarded as abrasive and won't accomplish your goals.

Business Entertaining: Keep in mind that business lunches are not popular because people usually return home for lunch.

• Note that Argentines will rarely invite you to their homes, which they regard as places for relatives and extremely close friends. They will entertain you in a restaurant.

• Remember that Argentines don't like to talk business during a meal, whether lunch or dinner. They prefer to socialize. The more cosmopolitan businesspeople will agree to a business lunch, if a foreigner insists on one, but they won't enjoy it.

• If you're being entertained, don't order imported drinks, which are very expensive in comparison to local drinks.

• Whether you are guest or host, expect a dinner in a restaurant to be scheduled for about 10:00 P.M.

• If you're the host, realize that the most popular restaurants among businesspeople are those found in excellent international-style hotels. Businesspeople also enjoy being taken to *parrillada* restaurants to eat beef.

• Don't include an Argentine wife in an invitation to a meal in a restaurant unless you have met her.

HOLIDAYS AND SPECIAL OCCASIONS

The following are national holidays when you will find banks, businesses, and most shops closed.

Check with the tourist office to learn if there are local festivals or holidays which will mean that offices, banks, and stores will be closed in that area.

Holidays: New Year's Day (Jan. 1); Carnival (Saturday before Ash Wednesday through Tuesday); Maundy Thursday (Thursday before Easter—only some offices are closed); Good Friday; Labor Day (May 1); Anniversary of the 1810 Revolution (May 25); Malvinas Day (June 10); Flag Day (June 20); Independence Day (July 9); Anniversary of the Death of José de San Martín (August 17); Columbus Day (Oct. 12); Immaculate Conception (Dec. 8); Christmas (Dec. 25).

• Except in parts of the north, don't expect Carnival to be celebrated in Argentina as extravagantly as it is in Brazil.

• Note that many people traditionally celebrate January 6 (Epiphany) more than Christmas. The Epiphany is the date on which they exchange gifts.

TRANSPORTATION

Public Transportation

• In general, the red-and-black taxis at the airport are not very reliable. Go to the transportation counter and buy a ticket for a taxi; or buy a ticket for the bus, which will take you to a central location at which you can get a taxi.

• To take a bus in Buenos Aires, look for the list of streets on the route at the bus stop. Each bus has its number and its destination marked on the front. Pay when you get on; you don't need exact change. Keep your ticket in case an inspector gets on to check. Local buses are usually uncomfortably crowded.

• Note that *colectivos* are buses found in cities and owned by the driver. Each route has a number and a color. Ask at your hotel for the appropriate *colectivo* for your destination.

• For transportation in Buenos Aires, consider the subway, which is excellent. Entrances are marked

"Subte." Buy tokens at the entrance. The fare is one token (called a *ficha*) for all destinations. Subways are closed between 1:00 and 4:00 A.M. Obtain subway maps at a tourist office.

• Expect many long-distance buses to have reclining seats and elegant appointments.

• Realize that for the most part trains are not in good condition. However, the train from Buenos Aires to Mar de Plata is luxurious. During the 6 to 7-hour ride, you will have heat or air-conditioning. There will also be heat and air-conditioning on a first-class sleeper, but not in ordinary first class; however, it will have comfortable seats. Avoid second class; you'll find it uncomfortable.

• Take taxis, which are inexpensive, rather than renting a car. Parking in cities is a problem.

Driving

• Don't drive unless you're a very confident, aggressive driver. For example, Argentines don't turn their lights on at night. If you turn your lights on, they may try to run you into a ditch.

• Be aware that police sometimes "pick on" the driver of a rented car. Unless you have a diplomatic passport, be prepared to offer the equivalent of $5.00. If you're stopped late at night at a roadblock, you may have to offer $20.00.

• Check which is the *best* road to take to your destination. If you stop at a gas station and ask, "Is this the road to ———?," people may say "Yes," when indeed there may be a better, shorter way.

• Be alert for mountain roads with hairpin curves. Be sure to blow your horn as you're turning at the curves.

LEGAL MATTERS, SAFETY, AND HEALTH

• If your passport, credit cards, and money are stolen, go to your hotel. They will pay your taxi fare and will help you make calls canceling your credit cards.

• The police don't list details of your missing property. Go to them simply to obtain a receipt for your insurance company. Regard your property as permanently lost.

• Usually, unaccompanied women do not go out after dark, especially in small towns. Try to stay in a good hotel in the town's center.

• Women should be prepared for men to stare at them in restaurants. They may send the waiter to your table with a drink or food. If you want no further contact with the person, a gracious but cool response should be sufficient.

• In Buenos Aires, it is fairly safe to drink tap water and eat raw vegetables. Outside the city, observe the usual precautions—drink only bottled water, don't eat raw vegetables or fruit you can't peel. Don't drink anything with ice cubes made from tap water.

• Women should realize that in the interior of Argentina, you must have a woman chaperone until you're in your twenties, and you must have a female companion until you're engaged.

• For information on drugs and hygiene supplies, see "Legal Matters, Safety, and Health" in the Introduction.

BELIZE

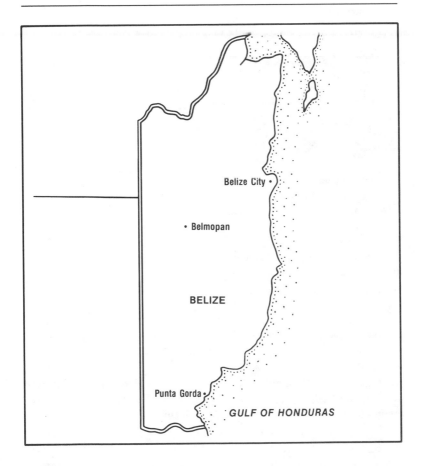

Belize City •

• Belmopan

BELIZE

Punta Gorda •

GULF OF HONDURAS

   Belize's early settlers were pirates who found that its coral reef afforded excellent protection to their ships. Now the great reef (second in size only to Australia's Great Barrier Reef) welcomes scuba divers from all around the world who want to explore the multitude of sea life in the area.

   Belize (formerly British Honduras) offers other opportunities for adventure, with 65% of its land area uninhabited jungle, where some 500 species of wildlife—including jaguars and other great cats—live. In fact, Belize boasts the world's only jaguar preserve.

But that's not all. Belize was once part of the Mayan empire, and it contains ruins of that mysterious civilization, including the great ceremonial center at Xunantunich.

doctor; and "Professor" where appropriate.

• With a group of ten or fewer, expect to be introduced to each person by your host. With more people, you'll probably be presented to the group as a whole.

GREETINGS

Language: The official language of Belize is English. A creole dialect of English is widely spoken, and Spanish is common in the North.

• Note that men shake hands with men when they are introduced. Men and women sometimes shake hands, though women don't usually shake hands with other women.

• Close friends of both sexes hug one another in greeting.

• If you meet women from villages or older women, they will probably give you a one-armed hug and pat on the back.

• Remember that titles are very important (reflecting earlier British influence). Use "Doctor" for a Ph.D., a lawyer, or a medical

CONVERSATION

• Bone up on Belize before you go there. People take great pride in their country, so it's good to compliment the village or town, or the country as a whole. Ask people about the interesting sights of their particular area. They will enjoy telling you about them.

• Avoid discussing politics, race, or religion.

TELEPHONES

• The few pay phones are in Belize City. The fee for a call is 25 cents Belizean.

• For either long-distance or local calls, go to a BTA (Belize Telephone Authority) office. The operator will place the call for you. The BTA office in larger towns is usually next to the post office, except in Belize City.

• If you need a telephone in a small village, go to the police station. It usually has the only telephone in town.

• Make collect or credit card calls overseas from a large hotel, if you wish, but if you stay at a small hotel or want to pay for an overseas call, you must go to the local BTA office.

IN PUBLIC

• To be polite, ask permission before you photograph people. Some may request a fee.

• Don't photograph airports. Army troops often use them for maneuvers.

• Don't expect to find casinos. Gambling is illegal.

• Look for public bathrooms only in hotels and restaurants. In the countryside you won't find any.

• Expect to pay set prices in stores, but feel free to try bargaining with vendors and in markets.

DRESS

MEALS

• For casual wear, jeans are acceptable for both men and women. In fact, you can wear anything comfortable as long as it isn't provocative.

• For business, suits and ties are appropriate for men, and dresses for women.

• For dressy occasions, men should wear a dark suit and women a dress. There's no need to bring a tuxedo.

• Women should avoid shorts or revealing dresses.

Hours and Foods

Breakfast: 6:30 or 7:00 A.M. People eat eggs or beans, tortillas made of corn flour, and thin oatmeal made like a drink. Occasionally there is ham or sausage and sometimes fried jack (like fried dough). In the cities, people often eat bakery bread. Beverages are coffee or tea.

Lunch: 12:00 or 1:00 P.M. A typical meal is rice and beans (cooked together with coconut milk—the national dish) with chicken, meat, or fish. There may also be soup with tortillas. Accompanying the meal may be fried plaintains as well as a salad of shredded cabbage and carrot with vinegar dressing.

Dinner: 6:00, 7:00, or 8:00 P.M. Dinner at home is a lighter meal than lunch. There is usually

rice and beans or soup and a little
meat, with coffee or tea as the beverage. (Dinner is also referred to
as "drinking tea," e.g., "Come to
our house to drink tea.")

• Don't anticipate cocktails and
appetizers before dinner, although
they may be offered in the city.
A popular drink before dinner is
rum and Coke.
• Don't expect dessert or coffee
after a meal.
• Common beverages with meals
are soft drinks, juice, and water.

Table Manners

• If you are a guest, expect to
be seated first. In the countryside
or in a small village, the family
may then eat in shifts, with guests
eating first. In fact, the guest may
be served alone, with the family
eating later. A female guest may
end up eating with men, who are
always served first—even in mid-
dle- and upper-class families.
• Tear up your tortilla and pick
up food with pieces of it.
• Finish everything on your
plate. *Always* accept any food and
drink offered. To refuse such an
offer is impolite, especially in
smaller towns.
• To indicate that you've finished, push your plate forward
with the silverware on it.

Eating Out

• In the north and west, expect
restaurants to serve mainly local
dishes—tortillas, black beans, and
charcoal-grilled beef.
• Expect to find many Chinese
restaurants in Belize.
• Note that it's rare for menus
to be posted in restaurant windows.
• Note that Belizeans don't have
a tradition of dining out, so restaurant meals may not be very cre-
ative.
• In small restaurants, don't expect a wide variety of dishes.
• Don't join strangers at their
table, but at very informal restaurants people do sometimes join one
another.
• Realize that seafood—shrimp
and lobster—and fish are abundant
and inexpensive.
• When ordering beer, remember that imported beer costs twice
as much as beer produced in Belize.
• To call the waiter, say "Miss"
or "Mister," while raising your
hand. Never shout loudly.
• If you suggest a meal in a restaurant, pay for the meal. Women
don't pay for men, however. If a
group informally decides to go out
to lunch, each one pays individually.

Specialties

• Try some of Belize's creole dishes: conch fritters; white rice and kidney beans cooked together or separately—one of Belize's staple dishes; stewed turtle (first fried) with tomatoes, onions, sweet peppers, and seasonings; Johnnycakes—flour, shortening, and coconut cream, first mixed and then baked; dumplings—same ingredients as Johnnycake but boiled and served as a side dish in a "boil up."

• At least twice a month, families have a "boil up": there will be yams, plaintains, cabbage, pickled pig tails, boiled conch, and steamed fish, all served on a single plate and covered with a sauce made of fried onions, tomatoes, and coconut oil.

• Other creole specialties: cowfoot soup with potatoes or yams; conch soup made with okra; creole bread, which is round and made with flour, yeast, and coconut milk; stewed chicken with tomatoes, onions, and sweet peppers; fried fish; iguana—served only in homes, not in restaurants, it tastes like chicken.

• Creole desserts: bread pudding, sweet potato pudding, lemon meringue pie, rice pudding, coconut tarts and pies.

• Belize also offers: *Tamales*—chicken or pork rolled in cornmeal dough and wrapped in banana leaves or aluminum foil. Don't eat the wrapping! *Panades*—ground corn, seasoned, flattened, and filled with fish or refried beans and then shaped into half moons. They're served with a sauce made of boiled chopped onions and vinegar. *Gornachas*—fried tortillas spread with refried beans, onions, and Edam cheese. *Relleno*—a thick soup made of boiled chicken, seasonings, onion, tomatoes, and sweet pepper.

HOTELS

• Expect credit cards and travelers' checks to be accepted at most hotels.

• If you're visiting one of the cays (pronounced keys)—small islands—bring a flashlight. The hotel's generator may not run all night.

• Remember that you can make collect or credit card calls overseas from a large hotel, but if you stay at a small hotel or you want to pay for the call you have to go

to the local office of the Belize Telecommunications Authority.

PRIVATE HOMES

TIPPING

• Note that local people don't
tip for certain services, but in tourist areas, service people expect tips
from foreigners.

• At a hotel restaurant, leave 10
to 15%. At a small, family-owned
restaurant, tipping is optional.

• Give a doorman or porter $1
or $2 Belizean for carrying bags.

• Don't tip a taxi driver unless
he carries your baggage. In that
case, give him $1 or $2 Belizean.

• Give drivers who serve as
guides or fishing guides $2 or $3
Belizean per each member of the
group.

• Feel free to visit friends in the
evening or almost any time on the
weekend. Dropping in isn't regarded as impolite. People don't
usually call in advance, since few
people have phones. If you know
that your friend has a phone, call
before visiting.

• After dinner in a home, leave
about 30 minutes to an hour after
the meal, if conversation is the
only after-dinner activity. If your
hosts expect you to stay longer,
they will suggest games, a video,
or looking at photographs.

• In a home, pay for any long-
distance calls that you make, but
it isn't necessary to pay for local
calls.

• If you're staying with a family,
feel free to take a daily bath or
shower.

• During an extended stay with
a family, offer to help with food
shopping, household chores, and
cooking. Most families will welcome such help, but some upper-

class families won't accept help from guests.

• Expect your host family to want to do everything to please you, including taking you on sightseeing or shopping expeditions.

Gifts: When invited to a meal, bring wine or a dessert. Your hosts won't expect such a gift, but they will welcome it.

• Good gifts from abroad: crystal vases or ashtrays, French perfumes and cosmetics, pocket calculators, blank VCR videocassettes, cassettes of American music, Scotch or a liqueur.

BUSINESS

Hours

Businesses: Monday through Friday, 8:00 or 9:00 A.M. to 5:00 P.M.

Government Offices: Monday through Friday, 8:00 A.M. to 5:00 P.M.

Banks: Monday through Friday, 8:00 A.M. to 1:00 P.M., and Saturday, 8:00 to 11:00 A.M.

Shops: 7:00 A.M. to 9:00 P.M. or 8:00 A.M. to 8:00 P.M.

Currency

• Note that the Belizean dollar is divided into 100 cents. Coins are 1, 5, 10, 25, and 50 cents. Bills are 1, 5, 10, 20, and 100 dollars.
• Note that a 25-cent coin is often referred to as a "shilling."
• Be aware that U.S. currency is accepted in many places. The U.S. quarter, dime, and nickel are often used as coins. Prices are sometimes quoted in U.S. dollars and sometimes in Belizean dollars.
• Keep in mind that hotels and shops that accept your American Express, Visa, or MasterCard may add a surcharge to your bill to cover what they must pay the credit card company.

Business Practices

• To ensure success doing business in Belize, have a contact in the country. If you don't have one, the Belize Chamber of Commerce can be helpful in obtaining one.

• Make appointments from abroad at least one week in advance

• Be sure to be on time. Punctuality is standard in the Belizean business world.

• Realize that time estimates are not usually reliable. People may offer a variety of excuses for not completing work on time.

• Remember that business decisions are made by a few top people in any company.

• Keep in mind that you need include only people with whom you're negotiating when entertaining business associates.

office to learn if local areas will be having celebrations or festivals during your visit. Everything in the area may be closed at such times.

Holidays: New Year's Day (Jan. 1), Baron Bliss Day (March 9—celebrating an Englishman who fell in love with Belize and left an enormous amount of money to the country), Good Friday, Holy Saturday, Easter Monday, the Queen's Birthday (April 21), Labor Day (May 1), Commonwealth Day (May 24), National Day (Sept. 10), Independence Day (Sept. 21), Columbus Day (Oct. 12), Christmas (Dec. 25), Boxing Day (Dec. 26).

HOLIDAYS AND SPECIAL OCCASIONS

Expect businesses, government offices, banks, and many shops to be closed on the following national holidays. Check with the tourist

TRANSPORTATION

Public Transportation

• Check with the Tourist Board for schedules of long-distance buses. You'll probably find such buses crowded and uncomfortable.

• To ensure a seat on a long-distance bus, buy a ticket in advance. You can pay on the bus, but you won't be guaranteed a seat. Fares vary according to your destination. The conductors or drivers will make change, so you don't need to have the exact fare.

• To go from town to town, consider flying as an alternative to buses. Scheduled flights in small planes are the most convenient way to get around. Fares are reasonable—and you'll be able to take in some scenery because the planes fly low.

• Be aware that there are no subways or trains in Belize.

• Keep in mind that taxi fares are fixed by the government. Check with the tourist board for rates, and then make sure the driver agrees to accept the rate before you set off. You can call for a taxi or hail one on the street.

Driving

• Realize that it's difficult to rent a car, and the only place you will find rentals is Belize City. Because of the country's road conditions, try to rent a Land Rover. You may have difficulty finding service stations, so make sure beforehand that it has a spare tire, gas, water, and so forth.

• Expect gasoline to be sold in American gallons.

• In Belize City, always leave your car in a guarded parking area.

• Note that many roads are unpaved and become muddy during the rainy season (from June to mid-November) and are extremely dusty during the dry season (December to May). Many are filled with potholes.

• Be aware that there are no traffic lights in Belize. There are speed-limit signs on the roads, and the police enforce these limits—but not frequently.

• Keep in mind that there are no "on the spot" fines, and Belizean police are not easily bribed.

• Remember that Belizean laws on drinking and driving are not very strict; however, if you're caught there are penalties.

LEGAL MATTERS, SAFETY, AND HEALTH

• When you arrive, declare the amount of currency you're bringing into the country.

• If you get involved with the police, expect a great deal of time to be spent before any decision on the matter of your involvement is reached. The police expend much time on paperwork and procedures.

• Realize that it's illegal to remove or export coral, to take orchids from a forest preserve, to remove archeological artifacts, or to spearfish while scuba diving.

• Beware of accepting the services of those who claim to be guides or who offer to help you find a hotel. For an official guide, ask at the Belize Tourist Office or at better hotels.

• Don't carry valuables around; it's better to keep them in your hotel's safe.

• Don't go out alone after dark in Belize City. Women should not walk in towns or cities late at night.

• Women traveling alone should feel free to take taxis; taxi drivers are reliable.

• Women alone will not usually be harassed.

• Women should not hitchhike; it can be dangerous.

• For advice on medicine and hygiene products, see "Legal Matters, Safety, and Health" in the Introduction.

BOLIVIA

Bolivia has the distinction of having the world's highest capital, La Paz (almost 12,000 feet), and the world's highest navigable body of fresh water, Lake Titicaca (12,500 feet). The country also boasts the world's highest airport, the world's highest golf course, and the world's highest ski slope. In fact, it's nicknamed "the rooftop of the world."

Unfortunately, although rich in natural resources, Bolivia has the lowest per capita income in South America, as well as a high percentage of illiteracy.

The warmth Bolivians feel for North Americans is illustrated in an anecdote recounted by traveler Amy Miller in *The Boston Globe*. She and a companion waited interminably in the countryside for a bus to Cochabamba. They asked two young Bolivian men if they were waiting in the right place. After assuring them that they were, the two young men went into a nearby cafe. Miller recalls, "They came back with two hot dinners wrapped in foil and handed one of them to us. No words, just a simple sign of caring."

GREETINGS

Language: The first official language of Bolivia is Spanish. Second is Quechua, the language of the Indians. Another Indian language, Aymara, is also spoken.

• When first introduced, people shake hands, with members of both sexes.

• Note that women who are good friends kiss on both cheeks in greeting, and close male friends give each other a hug (*un abrazo*) and shake hands. Even if good friends meet several times a day, they greet one another each time.

• Use titles. They are important to Bolivians. Some common titles: *Doctor* (used for Ph.D.'s and lawyers, as well as for medical doctors); *Arquitecto* (architect); *Ingeniero* (engineer); *Abogado* (lawyer).

• At large parties, expect to introduce yourself. At a traditional party hosted by an older person, you may be introduced by your host to each guest.

CONVERSATION

• Learn something about Bolivian culture. People will be im-

pressed if you know about the country and its background.
• Other good topics for conversation are families, soccer, car races, and food.
• Avoid political discussions—international, national, or local.
• Don't praise Chile while in Bolivia. The two countries have been engaged in border disputes since 1880.

TELEPHONES

• Expect to find pay phones in many cities, but expect difficulty in getting tokens to use in them. Buy tokens in candy stores or from newspaper vendors. You have unlimited time on local calls.
• If you can't find a phone, ask to use one at a pharmacy or kiosk and give the owner a tip.
• For long-distance calls, go to any office of ENTEL, the state long-distance telephone company.

IN PUBLIC

• Never whisper to anyone when you're in a group. You would cause suspicion and hurt feelings.
• Expect to see women walking arm-in-arm and teen-age girls holding hands with one another.
• Realize that it's bad manners to eat on the street.
• Note that if someone pats you on the shoulder, it's a sign of friendship.
• Always make eye contact with the person to whom you are talking. Not to do so is insulting.
• Be aware that middle- and upper-class Bolivians identify with their Spanish rather than their Indian heritage. It's very insulting to call someone an Indian. People whose skin is slightly dark but who are not Indian will always volunteer, "I'm not Indian."
• Do not refer to Indians as *indios* but as *campesinos* (peasants).
• If you're with a group and encounter a black, don't be surprised if a friend pinches you and says, *"Negro, negro, buena suerte"* ("A

black person. Good luck!"). There are very few blacks in Bolivia and seeing one is so rare it's considered good luck.

• Be aware that Friday nights in cities are called *viernes de soltera* (bachelor Friday). Men go out drinking with male friends. Women NEVER accompany them.

• Note that holding up the fist with the thumb between the index and the middle finger is an obscene gesture.

• If you're at a market and the vendor holds out his right hand with fingers separated and flips the hand—alternating thumb up and thumb down—he means "there isn't any."

• In dealing with customs officers, policemen, and government employees, the offer of a bribe is fairly standard practice. Since government salaries are very low, accepting bribes is the only way for many of them to live. Ask, "How can I help you?" or "Does this cost something? I don't want you to incur any expenses." If stopped for a traffic violation, ask, "Will $5.00 [equivalent] be sufficient?"

• Don't bargain in grocery stores or stores with fixed prices. In open markets, people love to bargain.

• Remember that Indian women don't like to be photographed, because they think that a camera will capture their souls; they will usu-

ally run away. Indian men usually don't mind, but they will sometimes ask for payment. During a big festival or parade, however, people don't mind your taking their picture.

• Public bathrooms: In cities, you'll find public bathrooms in restaurants and hotels, and city-maintained public bathrooms, called *baños públicos*. In the countryside, the only public bathrooms are in restaurants and hotels.

DRESS

• Be prepared for the different climates in various parts of Bolivia. La Paz is cold year-round because of the altitude. Santa Cruz is warm year-round, Cochabamba is springlike except during the rainy season, from December through February or March.

• For casual wear, both men and women can wear jeans but should not wear shorts. Women may, however, wear shorts while sightseeing in warmer areas such as Santa Cruz, but they may not be allowed into churches and official buildings.

• Men's business dress in La Paz is a three-piece dark suit; in Santa Cruz, a lightweight suit or a *guayabera* (a dressy shirt worn over pants); in Cochabamba, a two-piece dark suit.

• For business, women may wear a suit, a dress, or skirt and blouse, and should be sure to wear stockings.

• Women should wear bras and should not wear miniskirts or revealing dresses.

• When invited to a meal in a home for the first time, men should wear a dark suit and tie and women a dress or a skirt and blouse or sweater.

• Formal wear, suitable for diplomatic functions or lavish private parties, is a dark suit for men and a cocktail dress for women. Tuxedos aren't worn.

• Don't wear Indian clothing, because Indians may think you're making fun of them, and middle- and upper-class people find it very strange.

• Women should not wear men's clothing, e.g., a man's hat or poncho.

• Note that Indian women wear bowler hats. If a foreign man should wear one, he makes himself ridiculous.

MEALS

Hours and Foods

Breakfast: About 8:00 A.M. Bread, butter, and jam are accompanied by hot milk with a little coffee added (Bolivian coffee is very strong).

Lunch: Noon to 2:00 P.M. The day's main meal is usually a hearty one. A typical lunch will offer soup, followed by a main course (e.g., rice topped with fried eggs and a small piece of steak, fried beef served with rice and potatoes), fruit, and then coffee. Water is the usual beverage with meals; on special occasions beer or wine is served. Also popular is a drink similar to "Kool-Aid"— a powdered substance mixed with water.

Tea: Around 4:00 P.M., women invite other women for tea, coffee, soft drinks, cakes, pastries, cookies, and bread with *dulce de leche* (a sweet made with condensed milk). This light meal is usually served in the dining room.

• Note that many families don't have dinner but repeat the 4:00 tea about 9:00 P.M.

Dinner: In La Paz people may start dining as early as 7:30 P.M. or as late as 9:30 P.M. In Cochabamba people begin eating sometime between 6:30 and 8:00 P.M. Formal dinners usually begin around 9:00 P.M.

• A formal dinner will have several courses: *entrada,* an appetizer (e.g., lettuce, ham, hard-boiled eggs, and tuna); soup; a main course of meat, rice, and potatoes; fruit; and cake or pudding on special occasions. People drink water with the meal, except on special occasions, when they will have beer or wine. Coffee (with sugar, but never milk or cream) is served afterward.

Beverages: When invited to a meal, you'll usually be offered wine or beer before dinner. Unless it's a special party, there won't be hors d'oeuvres. Another popular pre-dinner drink is *pisco* (a colorless grape brandy) and orange juice.

• In villages, you'll be offered *chicha,* an alcoholic beverage made from corn. It's less strong than wine, but foreigners often find it difficult to digest. Drink slowly, because your host will refill your glass as soon as it is empty.

• *Chuflle,* another popular drink, is a mixture of soda, *singani* (distilled liquor made from grapes), and lemon juice.

Table Manners

• When invited to dinner, always arrive 15 to 30 minutes late. It's rude to be on time because your host and hostess may not be ready.

• If you are a special guest, expect to be served first. Usually the father of the family is the first served. Food is often placed on individual plates in the kitchen and then brought to the table.

• If there are children in the group, expect them to eat earlier than the adults or separately in the kitchen while the adults are eating.

• Note that the table will be set with fork at the left, knife at the right, and soup and dessert spoons above the dinner plate. There will always be cloth napkins, although if you're staying with a family, your napkin may not be changed every day.

• Never eat with your hands— not even chicken.

• Always use your fruit knife and

fork to eat fruit—even bananas.
• Always keep your hands over
the table. Don't put your hands
in your lap.
• Be careful of red and green
peppers in food. One type, called
locoto, is extremely hot.
• Don't pay a compliment about
a dish unless you really like it,
because then you'll surely be given
a second helping of it.
• Wait until second helpings are
offered. Don't ask for them.
• Never say "Yes" the first time
you're offered more food. Wait until your hostess insists.
• To be polite eat some of each
food, and clean your plate.
• Be aware that it's *very* insulting
to pour wine or any other beverage
with your left hand. And note that
pouring a drink backward into a
glass, rather than forward, indicates that you hate the person
you're serving. Such a gesture
could lead to a fight.
• After a meal in a home, stay
about 30 minutes and then leave.

Eating Out

• *Confiterías* are coffee shops serving light meals, alcoholic beverages, and soft drinks.
• Don't eat in markets. They
may not be very clean.
• Women should not go to bars
unaccompanied.
• Note that most restaurants

serve two meals—lunch from
11:30 A.M. to 2:00 P.M. and dinner
from 6:00 to 9:00 P.M.
• Look for a fixed-price menu
at both lunch and dinner. It is
usually much less expensive than
ordering à la carte.
• Be aware that many of the
dishes in the Altiplano are very
pungent because hot red pepper
is one of the main ingredients.
• Look for two hot sauces, *llajua*
(yah-huah) and *halpahuayca* (ahl-
pah-wy-kah), on restaurant tables.
• Expect steaks to be tougher
and drier than the average.

Specialties

• Try *sopa de maní*—roasted pea-
nut soup. In fact, most soups in
Bolivia are excellent, both filling
and nutritious.
• Some meat dishes to sample:
empanada salteña—meat turnovers;
salteñas—small pies stuffed with
meat or chicken, potatoes, hard-
boiled eggs, and olives—sometimes hot; *pique a lo macho*—bits
of fried beef, French fries, pieces
of hot dogs, raw onions, and tomatoes, all mixed in one dish; *silpan-
cho*—very thin breaded steak
served with rice, French fries, fried
egg, and tomato; *picante de len-
gua*—a spicy tongue dish.
• If you're near Lake Titicaca,
try *trucha,* trout, fried in oil.

• *Picante de pollo* is a spicy chicken dish.

• One variety of potato is *chuño*—freeze-dried potatoes.

• A specialty in the La Paz area is *fricasse*—pork cooked in a hot sauce with potatoes and white corn.

HOTELS

• Expect to find a choice of first-class and deluxe hotels in major cities. They provide central heating, air-conditioning, room service, restaurants, and (often) pools.

• Expect a constant supply of hot water, even in inexpensive hotels. The water is heated as it passes through hot coils. To take a shower, turn on the water; then turn on the electricity by turning the switch outside the shower stall. Be sure you turn the water on first; otherwise the coils could get burned out. Don't touch the switch if you're wet or standing in water. Be sure to dry yourself thoroughly before turning off the water.

TIPPING

• Don't tip taxi drivers (the drivers own their taxis) except for a very long journey. In that case, give them the equivalent of $2.00 (U.S.).

• Give porters at airports the equivalent of 50 cents per bag.

• If you agree to let a boy watch your parked car to prevent the theft of your hubcaps or windshield wipers, tip him 25 to 50 cents.

• Give a gas station attendant who fills the tank and washes the windshield 25 cents.

• It's not necessary to tip at restaurants. Service is included in your bill.

PRIVATE HOMES

• Remember that lunchtime is very important to Bolivian families. If you're staying with a family and plan to lunch with them, be prompt.

• Expect the family's maid to make your bed, but offer to do your own laundry. Ask your hostess where you should do it.

• Use a shower in a home as you would in a hotel. (See "Hotels" for instructions.)

• If you're staying with a family, expect the evening's main entertainment to be watching a soap opera on TV, beginning at 8:00 or 9:00 and lasting for an hour.

Gifts: If invited to a meal, realize that a gift isn't expected. You may bring a bottle of wine or *pisco,* however, or flowers, such as roses. Don't give yellow flowers, which signify contempt, or purple flowers, which are associated with funerals.

• Don't give electronic gadgets. They are now very inexpensive at Bolivian street markets.

• Good gifts are name-brand leather briefcases, leather chess sets, beautiful backgammon sets, and sheets and towels. Women enjoy receiving kitchen gadgets.

• Bolivians appreciate anything—e.g., T-shirts or beach towels—with U.S.A. written on it.

• Don't expect your gift to be opened in your presence.

• Realize that people are most appreciative of any gift. The fact that you've thought to bring them something is much more important than the actual gift.

BUSINESS

Hours

Businesses: Monday through Friday, 9:00 A.M. to noon and 2:00 to 6:00 P.M.; and Saturday, 9:00 A.M. to noon.

Government Offices: Monday through Friday, 9:00 A.M. to noon and 2:00 to 6:30 P.M.; and Saturday, 9:00 A.M. to noon.

Banks: Monday through Friday, 9:00 A.M. to noon and 2:00 to 4:30 P.M. Unlike other businesses, banks are closed Saturday.

Shops: Monday through Friday, 9:00 A.M. to noon and 2:00 to 6:00 P.M. Some shops are open on Saturday morning.

Currency

• In 1986 Bolivia changed its currency from *pesos* to *bolivianos*. Six zeros were eliminated from *pesos* to make them *bolivianos*. Thus one million *pesos* equals one *boliviano*. *Pesos* are still in circulation, but all prices are marked in *bolivianos*.

• Coins are 2, 5, 10, 20, and 50 *centavos* and 1 *boliviano*.

• Bills are 2, 5, 10, 50, 100, and 200 *bolivianos*.

Business Practices

• Make appointments from abroad two to three weeks in advance.

• Realize that several trips may be necessary to accomplish your goal unless your company has a representative in Bolivia.

• Note that the best months for business trips are April, May, September, and October. People usually vacation sometime in the months of January through March. Avoid business trips during Carnival, which begins the Saturday before Ash Wednesday. Also avoid the first week in August, during which the country celebrates its independence.

• To arrange business contacts, use the Chamber of Commerce in major cities, and the commercial section of your embassy. If you speak Spanish reasonably well, go to Bolivia's Ministry of Commerce or its Ministry of Finance.

• Arrive in advance of your appointments, so that you can rest the first day. It often takes a day or two to get used to the altitude. Eat lightly, and don't drink alcoholic beverages or smoke for your first few days in the country.

• If you need an interpreter in La Paz or Cochabamba, call the language school *Centro Boliviano Americano*.

• Bring copies of proposals with you. They can be copied in Bolivia, but it may take as much as a week.

• Realize that Bolivians aren't very strict about punctuality, and delays are tolerated. As a rule, however, foreigners should be on time.

• Since foreign names are often difficult for Bolivians to remember, always present a business card.

Have your card printed in Spanish, a process which takes only two days in Bolivia.

• Have sales literature available in both English and Spanish.

• Distribute copies of your proposals to a few people at the top of the organization.

• Enhance your proposals with charts and visuals. Both will impress.

• Make your sales approach understated and low-key, so that Bolivian businesspeople don't feel any pressure.

• Be aware that Bolivian women are going into business in increasing numbers, so a foreign businesswoman in Bolivia will cause no surprise.

• Expect tea to be served in offices every day at precisely 4:00 P.M.

• You will present an impressive image by staying in the best hotels and eating in the best restaurants.

• Expect business entertaining at lunch or dinner to be in restaurants, rather than in homes. If the meal is strictly business, lunch is the more popular meal. Wives are not usually included in business meals.

• When entertaining, include only those with whom you are negotiating.

• Note that the most popular restaurants for entertaining Bolivians are those where native food is served.

HOLIDAYS AND SPECIAL OCCASIONS

• Following are national holidays on which you can expect to find banks, businesses, and many shops closed. Check with the tourist office to learn about local holidays during which banks, etcetera, may be closed in a specific area.

Holidays: New Year's Day (Jan. 1); Monday before Ash Wednesday, Shrove Tuesday, and Ash Wednesday; Good Friday; Holy Saturday; Corpus Christi (the Thursday after the eighth Sunday after Easter); Independence Day (August 6); Columbus Day (Oct. 12); All Souls' Day (Nov. 2); Christmas (Dec. 25).

• Be alert during Carnival, when people throw water-filled balloons at everyone in sight.

• An important local holiday is

the January 24–31 Alasitas Fair in La Paz. It's held in honor of Ekeko, the pre-Columbian god of prosperity and good fortune. Traditionally, Ekekos made of gold, silver, tin, clay, or rock are kept in Indian homes. Miniature objects are sold at the fair; whatever you purchase in miniature, you'll obtain in real life.

TRANSPORTATION

Public Transportation

• When taking a bus in a city, pay the fare when you get on. Be careful of your wallet, since there are pickpockets who slash bags.

• Consider taking a *colectivo* or microbus. *Colectivos* are like taxis and run along certain routes. The fare is based on the distance traveled. They accept as many people as can be seated. The microbuses, small versions of regular buses, go on different routes. There's one fare, whatever the distance, and they're often as packed as a New York subway car. Again, beware of pickpockets in crowded situations.

• For inter-city buses, buy tickets in advance, and bring food and drink along if the trip is a long one.

• Avoid buses called *Transportación Interurbana*. They are pick-up trucks packed with people standing in the rear.

• Note that trains, improved in the last several years, run only between large cities. The best and fastest service is the *ferrobus*—two comfortable first-class carriages. Regular trains have Pullman class and second class. Pullman has compartments with two beds for night and comfortable upholstered seats for daytime travel. It also has dining cars and cafeterias. Seats in second class are not so comfortable. Some trains don't offer both Pullman and second class. Be prepared for trains to be cold at night.

• If you wish, reserve your train accommodations in advance at the train station. Advance booking is necessary only during the Christmas season, since there isn't much demand for train service during other times of the year.

• Prepare for long train delays due to heavy rains during the rainy season (December through February/March).

• Consider planes for transportation between cities. They aren't expensive and they are much more comfortable than a long train ride.

• Be aware that taxis don't have meters. Find out from your hotel or from an acquaintance what the approximate fare to your destination should be, and arrange the fare with the driver before you start the trip.

• Note that many taxis take several passengers to different destinations. If you want to have a taxi to yourself, arrange it through the hotel concierge.

Driving

• Don't drive between cities; roads are not usually paved outside major cities. Driving within cities isn't a big problem. There are no parking meters, but children will volunteer to "watch your car." Give them the equivalent of 25 to 50 cents when you return to the car.

• Keep in mind that, though there are no laws regarding drinking and driving, if you're involved in an accident and are drunk, you can easily be sent to jail. An arrest may cost a great deal in bribes, but bribing may not work with a judge.

LEGAL MATTERS, SAFETY, AND HEALTH

• Remember that chewing and making tea of coca leaves is legal, but cocaine is not. Drug laws in Bolivia are very harsh. Before trial, there's a long waiting time in prison, and then, if you're found guilty, there could be a long prison sentence.

• Women should not walk alone at night or take taxis after dark.

• Don't drink the tap water. Use mineral water instead.

• Don't eat raw vegetables or fruits that cannot be peeled.

• If you visit La Paz, take precautions because of the 12,000-foot altitude. Rest for a few days, avoid alcoholic beverages, and eat lightly.

• Bring suntan lotion if you visit La Paz; even in the winter (June-Sept.), you can get sunburned.

• For information about medicines and hygiene products, see "Legal Matters, Safety, and Health" in the Introduction.

BRAZIL

In movies, people seem to go to Rio the way the rest of us go to the corner drugstore. Fred Astaire and Ginger Rogers went *Flying Down to Rio*. Jane Powell led Ann Sothern, Scotty Beckett, and many others on a merry chase in *Nancy Goes to Rio*. And when his love affair went sour, Michael Caine had to *Blame It on Rio*.

One taste of Rio—the bronzed bodies on Copacabana Beach or the colorful frenzy of Carnival—and you'll understand the reasons for all the fascination.

Brazil itself is conscious of its place in film. One of Rio's tourist attractions is the Carmen Miranda Museum, a tribute to the film star of the forties, who introduced the fruit-salad headdress to the world. Of course, there is more in Brazil than just Rio. There's the economic boomtown of São Paulo, the rain forest of the Amazon, and the amazing Iguaçu Falls, where the water falls over 2½ miles.

If you venture into the wild and unspoiled center of the country, you may identify with naturalist Alfred Wallace's 1848 experience: "We received a fresh inmate into our verandah in the person of a fine young boa constrictor." Its breath, he wrote, sounded "like high-pressure steam escaping from a Great Western locomotive." Wallace's reaction? He bought the boa.

GREETINGS

Language: The official language of Brazil is Portuguese, *not* Spanish.

• Note that when first introduced to a person of either sex, men and women shake hands. When two men are introduced, they shake hands for quite a long time. When two men know each other well, they shake hands and slap each other on the back, shoulder, or stomach. When women who are good friends meet, they kiss by putting cheeks together and kissing the air. Married women kiss twice—on alternate cheeks. If one or both women is single, they kiss a third time to wish marriage for the single.

• Prepare for first names to be used in introductions. Doctors, professors, and priests usually go by their title plus their first name (e.g., *Doutor Antonio*). (In fact, if you're looking for someone's name in a list or file, remember that they are usually alphabetized by first name.) Remember that people with university degrees as well as lawyers and M.D.'s are addressed as *Doutor.*

• In business, address men as *Senhor* plus his family name and a woman as *Senhora* plus her family name.

• At a party—in fact, any time you meet a group of people—shake hands hello and good-bye with each person. If you don't, people will be insulted.

CONVERSATION

• Good topics of conversation: with men, soccer, politics, and places to visit; with women, family and children.

• Don't be surprised if Brazilians are *extremely* candid about personal characteristics, even negative ones—e.g., "You're really fat." Try not to interpret such comments as personal insults; they aren't intended to be.

• Don't ask about a couple's marital status, unless a Brazilian mentions it first.

• Don't refer to Brazilians as Hispanics. They're not. Although they certainly identify with the rest of Latin America, they're proud of their unique place as Portuguese-speakers, and of their culture. They are generally more informal, fun loving, and less reserved. It sounds like a stereotype, but sometimes it seems as if Brazilians are always ready to have a party.

• Expect people to stand very close to you when they talk to you.

Try not to back away, because such action may be interpreted as aloofness. Keep constant eye contact during a conversation. Brazilians also touch frequently while conversing—a sign of friendship.

• Don't be surprised (or offended) at constant interruptions during casual conversation. Brazilians regard them as a sign of enthusiasm.

• Delicate subjects are the political situations in Brazil and Argentina, and AIDS.

TELEPHONES

• Note that public phones are called *orelhãos* (big ears). The yellow-with-blue phones are for local calls. The all-blue phones are for inter-city calls. Buy tokens—called *fichas*—for the phone at newspaper stands. *Fichas* for local calls cost 30 *centavos;* those for inter-city calls cost three *cruzados.*

• In an emergency, ask someone on the street for a *ficha*. Most people carry a supply.

• To make a local call from a public phone, pick up the receiver and listen for a dial tone. (Be aware that many public telephones don't work. If one doesn't, try another.) Drop a *ficha* into the slot, wait for another dial tone, and then dial. To prevent being cut off during a long call, deposit several *fichas;* those you don't use will be returned. If you don't deposit several *fichas,* you'll hear a beep after three minutes. You must deposit more *fichas* or you'll be cut off.

• To make a long-distance call outside your hotel, go to an office of EMBRATEL—the name of Brazil's telephone company. You may also hear people refer to the *cia telefónica,* a popular nickname for the telephone company. The cashier in the telephone office will give you a key. Go into the phone booth, and insert the key into a slot underneath the phone. Make your call. Return the key, and pay the cashier when you're finished.

• When you place a call to Brazilians, expect them to answer by asking, *"Quem fala"*? (keym fah-lah), which means "Who is speaking?" Respond with your name.

IN PUBLIC

• Don't be surprised when people bump into you in crowded places and don't apologize.

• In lines at banks or stores, be prepared for people to stand much closer to you than people do in the U.S. or northern Europe.

• If you see someone you know across the street, don't shout at her or him.

• Don't eat while walking on the street.

• Don't chew gum on the street. Brazilians regard it as impolite. They don't, however, disapprove of littering—throwing paper cups, napkins, or cigarette butts on the ground. Fortunately, city streets are cleaned daily.

• Note that Brazilians do not usually send greeting cards or flowers. They regard such gestures as too impersonal, a way of avoiding personal contact.

• Some gestures to recognize: (1) To add emphasis to a statement, Brazilians snap the fingers while whipping the hand. (2) The ends of the fingers brushed under the chin means "I don't know." (3) Taking the earlobe between the thumb and the forefinger expresses appreciation. (4) Patting people on the shoulder, either men or women, is a sign of friendship. (5) Shaking the hands with the index finger hitting the thumb and middle finger means "a lot, a great deal." (6) Clenching one fist with the thumb between the index and middle fingers says "Good luck." You'll see Brazilians wearing amulets showing this gesture. (7) The American "O.K." gesture (thumb and finger forming a circle) is an obscene gesture in Brazil.

• If you go to an outdoor market, anticipate a crowd of teenage boys at the entrance who will pester you to let them carry your parcels or perform other services. If you let one of them perform some chores, give him the equivalent of a dime. If you don't want their services, be very firm in refusing.

• Try bargaining in markets, but be aware that you get the best bargains only if you speak Portuguese. In stores where prices are marked, you can ask for a discount if you buy in quantity, e.g., four tapes instead of one.

• Don't expect to encounter begging, but people may try to sell you pencils, emery boards, or other small items. If you simply refuse, they won't bother you.

• Keep any photographic equip-ment in a simple bag so as not to invite theft.

• You have to leave your camera at the entrance to churches or museums. There will be someone to watch over it.

• Ask people before you take their photograph. Most people will be friendly and receptive.

• Don't photograph in religious ceremonies. Be especially careful of *macumba* (known in different regions also as *candomblé* or *xangô*), a kind of voodoo practiced in Brazil. It's best to avoid these ceremonies altogether, since participants don't like observers, and they often drink heavily.

• To find a public bathroom— a scarce commodity—go to a hotel or a restaurant. You can't flush used toilet paper, since there isn't enough water pressure. You'll find a basket for the used paper.

DRESS

• Try not to dress so that you will easily be identified as a foreigner—and thus invite robbery.

Avoid shorts, sneakers, sandals with socks—and a large camera. For casual wear, men should wear shoes (not sneakers) and slacks or clean, pressed jeans. Women can wear pants or skirts.

• Note that usually only young people wear jeans (always clean and ironed) on the street.

• Never wear an outfit of green and yellow—the colors of the Brazilian flag. People will laugh at you.

• Women should dress modestly unless they want to attract attention. They should not wear shorts, except along the beach. Never wear them to go shopping. Neither men nor women should wear shorts in cities.

• In Rio, men must wear trousers in cinemas and restaurants. In São Paulo, men should wear trousers and a jacket or sweater.

• When invited to a home to a meal, men should wear suits and women should wear dresses or skirts and dressy blouses.

• Restaurants rarely require jackets and ties. However, men should wear a jacket, and women a wrap—because air-conditioning may make one necessary.

• Note that executive men wear three-piece suits, while office workers wear regular suits. Men should always wear long-sleeved shirts.

• Businesswomen from abroad should dress elegantly in suits, dresses, or skirts and blouses. Short-sleeved blouses and jackets are acceptable. Be sure that your nails are manicured.

• If an event requires formal wear—tuxedos for men, cocktail dresses for women—the invitation will tell you.

• Both sexes should wear clothing of natural—not synthetic—fabrics because natural fabrics are much cooler.

MEALS

Hours and Foods

• First, a caution. Don't drink tap water or fruit juices to which unboiled tap water has been added. Don't use ice cubes made from tap water. Don't eat any raw vegetables or unpeeled fruit. Don't eat raw shellfish. And don't eat food bought from street vendors.

Breakfast: Between 7:00 and 9:00 A.M. The usual meal is juice (sometimes drinks made in a blender with fruits, milk, and ice—called *vitamina*), bread and butter, sometimes fruit, and coffee with milk, called *café com leite*.

Lunch: Noon until about 2:00. Usually the day's main meal, it frequently features soup as a first course, followed by a main course of meat (steak or chicken) or fish with rice and beans—possibly with a plate of salad on the side, then fruit or fruit salad, and finally coffee.

• At 4:00 or 5:00 P.M., Brazilians pause for an afternoon snack (*lanche*) of cookies, cake, and a beverage.

• Also at 4:00 or 5:00 P.M., many women give parties to which other women come for about an hour and a half before going home to dinner with their husbands. These teas play a very important role in the social lives of middle- and upper-class women.

Dinner: From about 7:00 until 9:00 P.M. Usually, it's a light meal. Dinner parties, however, don't begin until 10:00 P.M. with drinks and hors d'oeuvres before dinner. The meal itself may appear about midnight. People may stay until 2:00 A.M., even on a week-night; sometimes people stay up talking until 6:00 or 7:00 A.M. Never rush to leave right after the meal.

• Expect Brazilian food to be spicy. It shows both Portuguese and African influences. The African influence dominates in Bahia, in the east of Brazil.

• In Bahia, you'll find a hot sauce, called *pimenta malagueta* (pee-mehn-tah mah lah goh tah), on the table along with salt and pepper. Be careful. It's *very* hot. The sauce is made from the *malagueta* pepper, which is not a chile pepper, but rather resembles black pepper. It's also common in the north and northeast.

• Throughout Brazil, look for another shaker on the table, with toasted *mandioca* (cassava) meal, which Brazilians sprinkle over many dishes. It tastes somewhat like cream of wheat. Because they use so much *mandioca,* most Brazilians don't eat bread as much as North Americans and Europeans do. The most common bread is *pão francês,* similar to French bread.

• Brazilians usually serve fruit as a separate course after all lunches and dinners. It's usually peeled and sliced, and eaten with a knife and fork.

• Cheese may be served with the dessert course, e.g., guava paste and cheese or coconut pudding with a wedge of cheese.

Beverages: Beer is usually considered a man's drink; women drink wine, liqueurs, or hard liquor. To order draft beer, ask for *chope* (shaw-pih).

• With meals, people drink water, carbonated beverages, fruit punches, or beer.

• A very popular drink is *cachaça*, sugarcane brandy. Mixed with lime and sugar, it's called *caipirinha* and is similar to a margarita.

• After-dinner coffee—the very strong *cafezinho*—is always served in a demitasse, with lots of sugar. It's quite strong, and most Brazilians drink only one cup, but feel free to drink more.

Table Manners

• Realize that it's far more common for Brazilians to entertain you in a restaurant rather than at home.

• If you're the guest of honor, expect to be seated at the head of the table. The host and hostess usually sit at one side of the table.

• At the table, expect to see forks to the left of the plate and the knife to the right. Spoons will either be on the left nearest to the plate or above the plate.

• Remember that formal meals are always served in sequence, course following course. Informal meals are usually—but not always—served that way.

• When not using your knife, place the tip of it on your plate with the handle resting on the table.

• Don't use the side of the fork

to cut—even the softest foods. Always cut with your knife.

• Don't use your hands to eat anything. It's considered both bad manners and unhygienic. Any food eaten with the hands is wrapped in a napkin so that the fingers don't touch it.

• Should you be dining with a wealthy family, expect a servant to prepare the meal; he or she will then proceed around the table, serving each person in turn. After dinner, coffee will be served in the living room.

• Help yourself as the platters of food are passed around. At a formal party, men usually serve the women next to them.

• If sandwiches are served on a plate, eat them with a knife and fork. Brazilians usually serve sandwiches as appetizers or at teas.

• To indicate that you have finished eating, place your utensils horizontally across your plate. Don't overlap the knife and fork.

• Don't expect much conversation during meals. Brazilians wait until after the meal for talk.

• Don't smoke during a meal. Many Brazilians smoke (you'll see very few *"Proibido Fumar"*—"No Smoking"—signs in the country), but they usually don't light up until coffee is served at the end of the meal.

• Cover your mouth with your

hand or a napkin when using toothpicks. You'll find a supply on tables in homes and in restaurants.
They are usually in little holders
which look like pepper shakers.
If you plan to add a dash of pepper
to your food, check to be sure
you're not about to sprinkle it with
toothpicks.

• Never drink directly out of a
bottle or can. Even in the most
humble establishments, Brazilians
drink from glasses.

• Be aware that any time people
are eating and a friend or visitor
arrives, they feel obligated to share
their food. If you are the visitor,
always decline, since there may not
be enough food.

Eating Out

• *Rodizios* are restaurants where
you eat all the meat you want for
a set price. Waiters bring around
spits of barbecued meat and carve
it onto your plate. They will also
bring a selection of side dishes
throughout the meal.

• In the southeast, for meats
grilled on charcoal, look for *churrasquerías*.

• *Barzinhos* are street-corner bars
that offer food and alcoholic
drinks. Some have tables, but others are just stands. The quality
of food varies greatly, but you can
usually judge the place by the appearance of its exterior. Women

should never go into one of these
bars unescorted.

• *Vitaminas* serve fresh fruit
drinks made in blenders.

• Check to see if the menu is
posted in the window or outside
the restaurant. Some places follow
this European practice.

• Be aware that many restaurants don't open until 8:00 or 9:00
P.M. for dinner. They often stay
open all night, however.

• In a casual restaurant, seat
yourself. In elegant restaurants,
wait to be seated.

• To summon the waiter, say
"Garçom" or *"O moço"* (oh-**moh**-
soh). You can also glance at him
and beckon with your index finger.
You will hear people calling
"Psst," but don't do it—it's rude.
Never snap your fingers to get the
waiter's attention. That's the way
Brazilians call a dog or cat.

• Expect the waiter to serve you
from platters.

• In fast-food places, pay when
you order or as soon as your food
is served. In more formal restaurants, ask for your check. The
waiter won't bring it until you
ask for it.

• Don't ask for separate checks,
and remember that your check
won't be itemized.

• If the service charge is not included, don't leave the tip on the
table. Hand it to the waiter, or
give a large bill to pay for the

check and leave before receiving the change.

• Note that there's no age limit for buying alcohol, but you must be 18 years old to drink it.

Specialties

• *Feijoada* is a typical Brazilian dish: black beans, rice, dried beef, smoked bacon, *mandioca* meal, and slices of pork sausage and orange. Most restaurants offer it on Wednesdays and Saturdays.

• Try *frango com arroz*—chicken and rice with peas, olives, and hard-boiled eggs; and *churrasco gaucho*—barbecued pork, steak, and sausages served with peppers, onions, and *mandioca* meal.

• Observe the yellow-orange color of much Brazilian food. It's the result of *dendê* oil, a palm oil which is used a great deal in Brazilian cooking. You'll also find the *malagueta* pepper, a very hot type of ginger, used frequently in Bahia.

• Fish and seafood lovers, sample *bacalhau*—dried, salted cod, served grilled or in a sauce; *moqueca*—shellfish fried with onions, tomatoes, and coconut milk; *acarajé*—a dumpling appetizer made of dried shrimp, onions, and mashed beans dropped by spoonful into hot oil; *vatapá*—a stew with fish and dried shrimp in a sauce made of onions, tomatoes, coconut milk, peanuts, cashew nuts, coriander, ginger, and *dendê* oil. Popular in Bahia are *peixe em moqueca*—fish cooked in banana leaves; and *carurú*—shrimp, okra, and coconut cooked with hot pepper and ginger.

• A popular side dish is *farofa,* made with *mandioca* meal with eggs and seasoning, and fried in butter. Sometimes it contains cheese, bacon, vegetables, and olives. *Farofa* can also be used as stuffing for poultry.

• A popular meat dish is *picadinho com quiabo*—chopped meat with okra.

• Note that Brazilians don't care much for vegetables. Japanese immigrants, however, have increased vegetable and fruit production, especially in the region of São Paulo. A favorite way of eating vegetables is to make them into croquettes, adding meat or shrimp, e.g., *chuchu com camarão*—chayote (a green, pear-shaped, squash-like vegetable) with shrimp.

• In the north, expect *cuscuz* to be a dessert made of tapioca, fresh grated coconut, coconut milk, water, sugar, and salt. In São Paulo in the south, *cuscuz* is made with cornmeal to which vegetables, meat, or fish are added.

• Be prepared for Brazilian desserts to be very sweet. *Doce de leite,* which looks like fudge or caramel, is made of slowly simmered milk and sugar. *Goiaba* is guava paste.

HOTELS

• To reserve a room in one of the best hotels during Carnival, book a year in advance.

• Be aware that motels are reputedly for lovers and often are rented for just a few hours at a time.

• Ask whether the price of your room includes a buffet breakfast. Many hotels offer this bonus.

• To see how people in the country live, plan a stay on a farm, or *fazenda* (your travel agent can make the arrangements). The family will probably have one or two rooms for paying guests; you'll share the bathroom with the family.

TIPPING

• Note that restaurants add a 10% service charge. Give the waiter an extra 5%.

• Give a taxi driver 10% of the fare.

• At the airport, tip the last porter who handles your bags. All the porters will share the tip.

• For small services, give doormen, ushers, and washroom attendants the equivalent of ten cents.

• Tip chambermaids the equivalent of $1.00 per week.

PRIVATE HOMES

• Respect the strong Brazilian sense of privacy about the home and the family. Don't expect to be invited to someone's home, even if you know them very well. They aren't being unfriendly or cold. They, however, find the North American notion of needing time alone to be bizarre. To them, being alone indicates sadness. In Brazil, extended families usually share one roof, and all branches of a family gather to spend Sunday afternoon and evening together.

• Never drop in without calling first. People will feel obliged to entertain you, even if they have something important to do.

• Remember that most people take a siesta between 1:00 and 3:00 P.M. Don't phone or drop in on people during those hours.

• Realize that you're more likely to be invited to a party at a private club than to one in a home. Should you be invited to a home, always arrive between 15 and 30 minutes late.

• If you're invited to a small party and must leave early, inform your host or hostess when you arrive.

• Be aware that Brazilians almost always accept when invited to do something. People often make promises—to avoid offending by refusal—and then forget them. For example, don't be too surprised if you invite people to dinner and they don't show up.

• In a country area where the door of a house is hidden behind a wall, clap your hands to get your host's attention. Don't shout or scream. If no one appears, go to the door and knock on it.

• If you pay an afternoon visit, leave by 5:00 P.M. so that the family can prepare dinner.

• Expect to find servants in most middle-class homes. Never offer to help servants. If there aren't any, however, offer to help clear the table.

• If you stay with a family a few days, ask if you may tip the servants and, if so, how much you should give each one.

• Expect hot water only in the homes of the rich and of many middle-class families in the south. The water tends to be tepid rather than cold. Most families take four or five showers a day because of the heat and find it strange if foreigners don't do the same.

• Keep in mind that *Q* on the water faucet stands for hot and *F* for cold. Shower heads have button indicators for hot and cold. Adjust the buttons before you turn on the water or you'll get quite a shock.

• A woman staying with a family that has male servants should be careful to be formal with them, or her behavior might be misinterpreted.

Gifts: When invited to dinner, bring a basket of strawberries, candy, or a bottle of champagne.

• Don't give purple flowers; they're associated with death.

• Good gifts from abroad: small electronic gadgets (they're extremely expensive in Brazil); music tapes from the U.S. (imported tapes are also very expensive); calculators, the more modern the better, for men; perfume for women; watches for children and servants.

BUSINESS

Hours

Businesses: Monday through Friday, 8:00 A.M. to 12:00 noon, and 2:00 to 6:00 P.M.

Government Offices: Monday through Friday, 9:00 A.M. to 5:00 P.M.

Banks: Monday through Friday, 10:00 A.M. to 4:30 P.M.

Shops: Times vary from city to city. In Rio, Monday through Friday, 9:00 A.M. to 6:30 P.M.; and Saturday, 9:00 A.M. to 1:00 P.M. Shopping malls are open 10:00 A.M. to 10:00 P.M. during the week, and until 6:00 P.M. on Saturday.

Currency

• Remember that 1 *cruzado* is made of 100 *centavos*. Coins are 1, 2, 5, 10, 20, and 50 *centavos*, and 1 *cruzado*.

• Look for notes in denominations of 1, 5, 10, 50, 100, 500, and 1,000 *cruzados*.

Business Practices

• Plan to do business in Brazil only if you're interested in a long-term commitment to working in the country. Those are the terms on which Brazil welcomes foreign investment.

• Write to the Brazilian Trade Bureau in your country. They offer free publications on doing business in Brazil, including opportunities in and restrictions on foreign investment.

• Investigate Brazil's import controls; they are dedicated to making it easy to export from Brazil and difficult to import into the country.

• Be aware that there is often great distrust of a foreigner who wants to buy a share of a company.

• If you are planning to set up a new enterprise in Brazil, realize that while unskilled labor is plentiful, skilled labor may be difficult to find.

• Keep in mind that you'll have to deal with at least one of Brazil's regulatory agencies, and that these agencies have broad discretionary powers to control manufacturers' selling prices.

• Cultivate patience. Brazilians find some North American attitudes to business offensive, e.g., getting straight to the point and aggressive confrontations. You may feel frustrated with the inefficiency and the bureaucracy, but don't let it show.

• Be prepared for several trips to Brazil, especially if you're involved in negotiations. (Brazilians love to bargain, so the negotiating process can be drawn out.) If you're involved in a project that involves building, expect a protracted period while you're getting permits from many different agencies or authorities.

• Realize that it's *very* important to have a contact in the country. The Chamber of Commerce and the Brazilian Trade Department can help. If possible, bring the business card of a mutual acquaintance with a note from her or him introducing you.

• Hire a *despachante,* an expediter

who will help you deal with the various bureaucracies.

• Enlist the help of secretaries at firms you'll be visiting to help you find an interpreter.

• Stay in the best hotels to enhance your image. It's not, however, necessary to eat at the best restaurants, except when you're entertaining Brazilian colleagues; then you should be sure to go to the best places.

• From abroad, make appointments two weeks in advance.

• Try to schedule one morning and one afternoon appointment, so you won't be running frantically from place to place—especially since the Brazilians have a very flexible sense of time. The best times for appointments are between 10:00 and 11:30 A.M. and 3:00 and 5:00 P.M. Don't suggest an appointment during the hours between noon and 3:00 P.M., since that is lunch time.

• Always schedule appointments at offices. Never suggest meeting in a restaurant or bar.

• Expect Brazilians to use first names very quickly. Wait until they use your first name before addressing them by theirs.

• Before getting down to business, engage in preliminary conversation about interests or hobbies. Don't discuss family or salary unless a Brazilian brings them up.

• Be sure to bring business cards

to exchange at your first meeting. Have them printed in Portuguese and English, which can be done in a stationery shop in Brazil in about 24 hours.

• Don't lower your estimate of someone who's sharing an office. Only the most senior businesspeople have private offices.

• Expect to be offered coffee when visiting businesses. You should probably accept, even if you don't finish it. It will be served black and in small cups. Brazilians add a large amount of sugar.

• Have materials you plan to present translated into Portuguese. *Never* use materials in Spanish. Bring enough copies so that they can be distributed to the top people in management.

• Be prepared for Brazilians to be anywhere from 30 minutes to an hour and 15 minutes late for an appointment. If the meeting is very important, they may be only 15 minutes late. People tend to be more punctual in business centers such as Rio, São Paulo, Belo Horizonte, and Pôrto Alegre.

• Don't be surprised if people you're meeting with are often interrupted. Public officials especially deal with many issues and people simultaneously. One way to get around this is to invite your colleague to lunch.

• Expect Brazilian businesspeople to talk constantly; there's no such thing as a moment of thoughtful silence at a Brazilian business meeting.

• Anticipate a great deal of physical contact during a meeting pushing, tugging, and so on.

• Note that, unlike businesspeople in some countries, Brazilians say "No" frequently. Business researcher John Graham called them "the world's top naysayers."

• Don't telephone a business associate at home unless he suggests that you do so.

• Foreign businesswomen can have successful dealings with Brazilian businesspeople as long as they act in a professional manner and don't appear aggressive or confrontational.

• If you plan to entertain a client, ask the secretary of a top-level manager to recommend a restaurant. Secretaries will know the type of luxurious restaurant at which Brazilian businesspeople appreciate being entertained.

HOLIDAYS AND SPECIAL OCCASIONS

Expect businesses, banks, and many shops to be closed on the following holidays and on election days, which are considered holidays. Remember that there are many regional holidays; check with the Brazilian tourist office to find out about holidays celebrated only in certain regions. Remember that some shops and businesses close early the day before a holiday and that some holidays are celebrated on the nearest Monday so that people can have a long weekend.

Holidays: New Year's Day (Jan. 1), Epiphany (Jan. 6), Feast of Saint Sebastian (Jan. 20), Carnival (from the Saturday before Lent through Ash Wednesday), Easter, Labor Day (May 1), Ascension Day (40 days after Easter), June Festival (June 24–29), Feast of the Assumption (Aug. 15), Indepen-

dence Day (Sept. 7), Columbus Day (Oct. 12), All Saints' Day (Nov. 1), All Souls' Day (Nov. 2), Declaration of the Republic (Nov. 15), Flag Day (Nov. 19), Christmas (Dec. 25), New Year's Eve (Dec. 31).

• Carnival (*carnaval*) begins on the weekend preceding Ash Wednesday. Though you must book hotel rooms a year in advance, expect only minimal services during the festivities—rooms not cleaned, late breakfasts, and so on. Carnival has three main aspects: costume balls, the street carnival (the parade of *samba* groups along Avenida Presidente Vargas), and *blocos* (street parades held by residents of city blocks).

• Carnival is especially famous for the balls, most of them given by semi-private organizations such as athletic and social clubs. The ultra-posh ball is the Municipal Ball, held on the final night of Carnival. The most spectacular event is probably the parade of the *samba* groups, *escolas de samba,* also on the final night. *Escolas de samba* (literally, "*samba* schools") are clubs or groups of dancers and musicians, usually organized by neighborhoods. Each year each *escola* has a special theme for the parade, and its members compose a special song and prepare elaborate costumes to go with the theme. The parade route is lined with judges, police, press, TV and movie crews and ordinary spectators. Each *escola* takes its place in the parade—playing music, chanting, dancing, and marching in a rapture of rhythm and melody. It may take an hour for a single *escola de samba* to pass in front of the judges. The *blocos* are local celebrations and usually not of interest to travelers.

• Try to go to Carnival with a group of people you know. It's not wise to go alone. In 1986, newspapers reported that it had been a good year—*only* 80 people had been murdered during Carnival.

• More cautions for Carnival: Don't walk on dark streets or on the beach at night. Don't wear any jewelry, not even costume jewelry. Keep money in your underwear, or wear a money belt. Be wary of thieves and pickpockets.

• Don't attempt to drive in cities during Carnival. There are impromptu parades everywhere, and streets can be blocked for hours.

• On New Year's Eve, expect to see people dressed in white. It's a ritual to touch water at the stroke of midnight. The beaches are filled with people carrying lit candles. At midnight, they launch little rafts with offerings for the goddess of the sea.

TRANSPORTATION

Public Transportation

• At whichever airport you arrive, go to the taxi stand, state your destination, and buy a voucher. The voucher covers your fare, so you have no additional cost but the tip.

• Try to avoid buses in cities. If you don't speak Portuguese, you may not know when to get off. Other problems are the incredible overcrowding and the ever-present pickpockets and chain-snatchers.

• If you decide to take a bus, bring a supply of small change because conductors usually don't have change. Enter at the rear of the bus, pay the conductor, and get off at the front. You must signal before your stop by pulling a cord.

• If you're seated on a bus, don't be surprised if standing passengers ask you to hold their bundles— or even their child.

• One bus line to try is Rio's new *jardineira* line. It has plain-

clothesmen on board to foil pickpockets. The line's route runs past
the main beaches.

• Ask if the city you're in has
buses called *frescões*. They are more
expensive, but they're air-conditioned. Brazil's economic problems have caused a cutback in the
number of *frescões*.

• In Rio or São Paulo, consider
taking the subway. Both systems
are modern, safe, and fast, although they go only to limited
parts of the cities.

• Note that buses that run between cities are air-conditioned
and have bathrooms. They have
attendants who serve coffee, and
they make stops for food.

• Ask your travel agent about
the inexpensive travel pass valid
for a few weeks' flying between
cities within Brazil. You must buy
this pass outside Brazil.

• Note that the trains between
Rio and São Paulo are inexpensive
and comfortable, and provide dining cars and food service in your
compartment.

• Remember that taxis in Rio
are more expensive between 10:00
P.M. and 7:00 A.M. Drivers also
charge night rates for traveling up
steep hills.

• Be sure that the taxi driver
turns the meter on. Recently the
government has been changing
fares. If your charge is more than
that shown on the meter, the

driver must show you the latest
charts indicating the increases.

• Note that you can save money
by sharing a taxi with several
friends. Drivers don't mind.

• If you leave the airport at Manaus to fly to another Brazilian
city, remember that you'll have
to go through customs. Manaus
is a duty-free city.

Driving

• The best advice about driving
in Brazil: don't. Take taxis in cities
and planes for long-distance trips.
Travelers have likened driving in
Brazil to "jungle warfare." There
are potholes everywhere and there
is general disregard of traffic laws.

• Don't drive unless you have
a knowledge of Portuguese. It's
difficult to find your way, and
you'll almost surely have to ask
directions.

• Be aware that people ignore
stoplights and stop signs—especially at night, when they're afraid
of robbery.

• Remember that drivers—not
pedestrians—have the right-of-
way.

• Note that only parking lights
are used at night in cities. Drivers
honk when they see other drivers
with their headlights on at night.

• Realize that roads between cities are narrow, in bad condition,
and filled with truck traffic.

• Remember that there are no laws regarding passing other cars.

• Expect to see children on every street corner serving as "parking attendants." They will guard your car while you're parked. Give them the equivalent of 25 cents. If they wash your car, give them the equivalent of $1.00 (total).

LEGAL MATTERS, SAFETY, AND HEALTH

• If the police stop you, and you speak English, you will usually be allowed to go. Police do, however, expect formality and deference. If, for any reason, you need to go to the police station, don't wear shorts or grubby clothes.

• Note that Brazil has no liquor laws. The only time liquor isn't sold is when the polls are open for an election.

• Never bring valuables to the beaches. There are signs at the beaches telling you never to leave your car unattended. You'll see little boys asking to guard your car for a small fee. Always hire one.

• In the cities—even if you're just out for a walk—leave jewelry, watches, and money in the hotel safe.

• Women walking alone can expect to hear remarks about them and to be the subject of obvious stares. At Carnival, whether you're alone or in a group, expect to be pinched and grabbed. If such behavior bothers you, the only way to avoid it is not to go out.

• Drink only bottled water. Milk sold in plastic bags must be boiled. Milk sold in cardboard cartons does not require refrigeration and is safe without boiling.

• For advice about medicine and hygiene products, see the "Legal Matters, Health, and Safety" section of the Introduction.

CHILE

Stretching between the Andes and the Pacific Ocean, and with islands well into the Pacific, Chile offers the visitor destinations as varied as Santiago, with its laid-back urban scene, and Easter Island, one of the world's most mysterious places.

In Santiago, join Chileans in favorite pastimes—eating shellfish and enjoying the excellent wine the country produces.

Even though science, technology, and exploration have solved many of the mysteries of outer and inner space, no one has definitively cracked the riddle of Easter Island, some 2,300 miles off Chile's coast and the most isolated inhabited island on earth. It was "christened" by Jakob Roggeven, the Dutch admiral who discovered it on Easter Sunday, 1722. Visiting the volcanoes, the great stone statues, and the "factory" in which the statues were made, you will realize why Easter Island's enigmas provoke pilgrimages by anthropologists, archeologists, and adventurous travelers.

GREETINGS

Language: The official language of Chile is Spanish.

• Expect men to shake hands with other men when they are introduced. After they know each other well, they shake hands and pat one another on the back.

• When introduced and when they know each other well, women kiss one another on one cheek.

Women don't usually shake hands with either sex.

• At a small party, greet each person individually. At a large party, simply say "Hello" to the group as a whole.

• Note that the only title regularly used is *Doctor*—for a medical doctor.

CONVERSATION

• As a conversation opener, ask about families, children, and the like. However, don't ask people their occupation. Wait for them to volunteer that information.

• Ask advice about what to see and do, where to eat, and so forth. Chileans enjoy helping others enjoy their country.

• Before visiting Chile, learn about the country's background. Chileans really appreciate foreigners having some knowledge of the country. Businesspeople should make a special point of learning about Chile's economy. Chileans enjoy discussing their exports, of which they're very proud.

• Keep in mind that many Chilean businesspeople have traveled abroad. If you have traveled, bring up the places you've visited. It's a good way to establish rapport.

• Avoid any references to politics, especially issues relating to human rights.

TELEPHONES

• Look for telephone booths on main streets in cities. Deposit five *pesos* for three minutes. When the time is up, you'll hear a buzzing. Deposit more money or the call will be cut off.

• If you can't find a phone booth and you're making a local call, ask to use the telephone in a bar. If you don't want to do that (or the bartender says "no"), go to the Compañía de Teléfonos, where you can make local calls.

• To make a long-distance call, go to the other telephone office, ENTEL.

• Note that most long-distance operators are bilingual.

IN PUBLIC

• Be careful to avoid any behavior that could be interpreted as aggressive. Chileans, who emphasize respecting people and never hurting anyone, regard aggressive actions as very rude.

• Some gestures to note: (1) Palm up with fingers separated means stupid. (2) Clenched right first slapping the open palm of the left hand is obscene. (3) A driver sticking his hand out the window and holding it as though he's holding an apple is also making an obscene gesture. (4) Right fist raised to the level of the head is a Communist sign (*not* recommended).

• Don't be surprised if there's a long wait to change money in banks. People pay their bills there.

• To mail a package to an address outside Chile, bring string and wrapping paper to the post office. Don't wrap the package first, since the clerk must check to see what's in it. After the clerk has checked the contents, you wrap the package and the clerk puts sealing wax on it. To avoid the long wait that this process entails, ask for a courier at your hotel and pay for him to take care of the mailing.

• Never photograph strikes or street demonstrations. The most likely dates for such events are May 1 and September 11.

• Don't try to bargain, even at markets or with street vendors. If you buy a great deal in one store, you may ask for a discount—but expect it to be minimal. Every time you buy something, ask for a receipt. The shop owner may say, "I'll give you a discount and *no* receipt." He then won't have to report the sale for taxes; however, both the shop owner and the customer would be fined for such a transaction. You have to choose whether or not to break the law.

DRESS

• When planning your wardrobe, remember that Chile has extremes of heat and cold, depending on the altitude.

• For business and social occasions men should wear a conservative suit of good quality. Never wear a sports jacket. Don't wear anything in the lapel. Women should wear a suit and heels for business.

• On weekends, expect to see Chilean men and women wearing good jeans for shopping, errands, and the like; they don't, however, wear shorts.

• If invited to dinner, men should wear a suit and tie and women a dress.

• For elegant restaurants, men must wear a tie, and women should wear a dress.

• Note that formal dress is rarely worn, even for weddings. If an occasion is formal, the invitation will so state. Men should wear a dark suit and women a cocktail dress.

MEALS

Hours and Food

Breakfast: Between 7:00 and 9:00 A.M. It's usually a light meal—instant coffee or tea with milk, and toast. Some people have larger breakfasts, e.g., ham and eggs. Cereal is never served. When tea is served, it's usually half tea and half hot milk. If you want your tea made differently, tell the person preparing it, or the waiter.

Lunch: 1:00 or 1:30 P.M. until about 3:00 P.M. Expect several courses: the meal opens with soup or an avocado half or *empanadas* (turnovers filled with meat, cheese, or seafood); the main course may be steak, seafood (clams, mussels, oysters, or abalone), or a meat dish such as *cazuela* (chicken, corn, and squash cooked together); lentils and mashed potatoes are popular side dishes; fruit or ice cream for dessert.

• At 5:00 or 6:00 P.M. comes a snack called *onces,* featuring cheese, toast, cookies, and tea or coffee.

Dinner: Between 8:00 and 9:00 P.M.—usually 8:30 P.M. in homes on weekdays and 9:00 on weekends. The meal will be similar to lunch. After dinner, you'll be offered a demitasse of instant coffee and a selection of herbed teas (mint, anise, chamomile).

Beverages: Typical drinks before dinner: *vaina* (a sweet wine beaten up with eggs, sugar, and cinnamon); *pisco* sour (*pisco* is a liquor made from grapes); *pisco* and Coke; *pinchuncho* (*pisco* and vermouth); gin and tonic. Men usually drink whiskey and expect foreign businessmen to do the same because Chileans regard whiskey drinking as a sign of sophistication. With meals, men usually drink wine—sometimes beer—while women have soft drinks. It's acceptable for foreign women to have one glass of wine, but no more.

• Expect to find Coke, Fanta, and Sprite available in Chile.

• Remember that *café con leche* is made by pouring hot milk into a cup that has a single spoonful of coffee in it. *Té con leche* is a small amount of tea with hot milk.

Table Manners

• At a dinner party, expect little snacks such as olives, pickles, and chips with pre-dinner drinks. It's also likely that bread will be served both before and during dinner.

• Anticipate receiving your plate with the food already on it or for service to be buffet style.

• If the dinner is a formal one, never eat anything with your hands. "Finger food" is never served on formal occasions.

• Try to force yourself to eat at least a bit of what is served even if you don't care for it. Many Chileans don't understand health food fanatics, vegetarians, and the like. They will be understanding if a medical problem or allergy prevents you from trying something.

• If you're serving another person wine, don't do it with your left hand.

• Don't offer to help clear the table or do the dishes, since most middle-class families have a maid.

• When leaving a party or dinner, spend about ten minutes talking and saying good-bye. Don't just dash out the door.

Eating Out

• Note that Santiago has many foreign restaurants: Chinese, Italian, Mexican, Indian, and Brazilian. You'll also find fast-food spots and vegetarian restaurants.

• Be aware that *fuentes de soda* (soda fountains) serve juices, soda, and sometimes beer. The lower the class of the soda fountain the more alcoholic beverages they offer.

• Avoid small, sleazy bars. In better neighborhoods you'll find pubs (that's what they're called). Most sell only drinks but some offer *empanadas* or small sandwiches. Often they feature a singer or a play.

• For the best food in small cities and towns, go to a hotel restaurant.

• Be aware that downtown Santiago has good restaurants for lunch, but after 6:00 or 7:00 P.M., when businesspeople go home and the streets are somewhat deserted, you won't want to be out looking for one. Either have dinner in your hotel or go to a restaurant in the residential areas.

• Don't join people you don't know at their table, except in fast-food restaurants.

• To attract the waiter's attention, say "Garçon." You may see people clapping to summon the waiter, but Chileans regard that action as rude.

• In ordering wine, remember that *vino blanco* (**blahn**-coh) is white wine, *vino tinto* (**teen**-toh) is red, *seco* (**seh**-coh) is dry, and *dulce* (**duhl**-seh) is sweet.

• If you're on business and invited to a meal by a Chilean businessperson, realize that he or she pays. If you issue the invitation, you pay.

• Remember that one person

pays for the group even at a friendly dinner. Those who are treated should reciprocate later, since it's unlikely that the person who paid will allow you to pay him your part of the bill. Splitting the check is very unusual and is called "American treat."

Specialties

• Try some of Chile's most popular foods: *caldillo de congrio,* the country's national dish—a soup with conger eel, potatoes, and onions; *humitas*—ground corn, wrapped in corn husks and boiled; *pastel de choclo*—ground corn, meat or chicken, onion, boiled eggs, and raisins baked in the oven; *cazuela de ave*—a casserole of chicken, corn, rice, green beans, pumpkin, carrots and herbs; *bife a lo pobre*—grilled steak with fried potatoes and sautéed onions, served with fried eggs on top; *sopaipillas*—fried pumpkin fritters.

• Sample some of Chile's many famous seafood and fish treats: *albacora*—swordfish; *camarones*—shrimp; *centolla*—king crab; *cholgas*—mussels; *choritos*—small mussels; *congrio*—conger eel, grilled, baked, fried, or stewed; *corvina*—sea bass, considered the best quality fish; *erizos*—sea urchins, which are about the size of tennis balls, served raw with chopped onion, parsley, ground

pepper, salt, and oil (each urchin has a miniature crab attached to it; Chileans like to pop these into their mouths—live; if you would like to eat *erizos* this way, ask that the crab be left on); *gambas*—large deep-water shrimp; *langostas*—large spiny lobsters served broiled or boiled with butter and lemon; *langostinos*—small rock lobsters, usually broiled; *locos*—a type of abalone, resembling fat clams and served cold in salads with mayonnaise, baked, or in a stew called *chupe de locos; machas*—razor clams, eaten raw with lemon or baked with grated Parmesan cheese; *curanto*—mixed grilled seafood.

HOTELS

• Note that you'll find hotels in the top international class only in Santiago and Valparaíso/Viña del Mar. In smaller towns, there are fewer hotels and fewer amenities, but the warmth and hospitality of the smaller hotels may compensate for the absence of luxuries. For example, don't be surprised if the manager has dinner with the guests.

• For the least expensive accommodations, stay at a *hospedaje* (ohs-peh-**dah**-heh), a family house with a few rooms for rent, always with hot water and often including breakfast in the room price. Family and guests share a sitting room. *Hospedajes* vary greatly in comfort.

• A *residencial* is a small hotel, often including breakfast in the price. Amenities are basic: a bed, sheets and blankets, a table, a chair. Some have heat; some don't. Many have hot water, but in the south you'll have to pay for it.

• *Pensiones* offer better amenities and higher standards than *hospedajes* or *residenciales*. Often there's a restaurant, and you'll usually have a private shower and toilet.

• In the Lake District, look for chalets, generally run by people of German descent. They have pools, hot water, and restaurants.

• If you plan to stay in a youth hostel, *hostería,* note that for some you need only an International Youth Hostel card, but in others you'll need a Chilean Youth Hostel card. Hostels are usually open only in January and February and sometimes in March.

• Make reservations well in advance for the peak season (Dec. through March) in the coastal resort areas. If you visit the resorts between mid-March and mid-November, ask for off-season rates.

• Don't leave valuables in hotel rooms. Many have locks which don't function; in the south, many don't have locks at all.

• Feel free to ask for extra blankets, even in budget accommodations.

TIPPING

• Remember that service is usually included at restaurants, but to be polite, leave 100 to 200 *pesos* on the table in an elegant restaurant or if several people are dining together. For two people, leave 30 to 50 *pesos*.

• Don't tip taxi drivers; the driver usually owns the taxi.

• Tip gas station attendants 10 to 20 *pesos*.

• Because of high unemployment, people will offer to wash your windshield, show you where to pull over when you're parking, or guard your car. Tip these people 10 to 20 *pesos*.

• At a movie theater, where you choose your seat when you buy the ticket, tip the usher 10 to

20 *pesos*. At other movie theaters, where seating is unreserved, there's no need to tip.

PRIVATE HOMES

• Don't drop in on people you don't know well. If possible, telephone in advance.

• If you're invited to dinner at someone's home, always arrive 10 to 15 minutes late. If you're invited to a party, come 30 minutes late.

• Don't make dinner plans if you're invited to drinks at a home. Usually you'll be expected to stay to dinner.

• When invited to a meal, send flowers to the hostess in advance or bring a box of chocolates. People don't often bring wine, since it's so inexpensive in Chile. If you're invited to a large party, bring a bottle of whiskey.

• If someone has had you to dinner, call and say "Thank you" before leaving the country. Written thank-you notes are not common.

• When staying with a family, adapt to their schedule (getting up when they do, adhering to their meal schedules) and try to participate in activities they invite you to join. If your visit is a long one, bring some token of appreciation—e.g., flowers, a cake—every three days or so.

• If there is no maid and you're staying with a family for a few days, offer to help with setting and clearing the table and doing the dishes.

• Feel free to take a daily shower. Most people shower in the morning; some also shower and change before dinner. Many homes have constant hot water, but some don't. Ask your hostess if the water needs to be heated before showering. There may also be a bidet in the bathroom.

• If you make long-distance calls, be sure to pay for them. When you place the call, tell the operator that you want to know the cost at the end of the call, and she'll call back and let you know.

• Should you be home alone when the postman arrives, be aware that he expects a tip of two or three *pesos* per letter. (If no one is home, he will leave the mail but will expect to be tipped the next day.)

• Realize that it's appropriate to buy a gift for the maid (an article of clothing such as a skirt or sweater is a good choice) after a visit of a few days or more.

• If you're invited to stay on a farm, be prepared for facilities to be primitive, i.e., no hot water, outdoor toilets. Some farms, however, have very modern facilities.

Gifts: Good gifts are leather appointment books and photo albums, calculators (especially those that store messages), good quality pens, cigarette lighters, or whiskey.

• Don't give yellow roses. They signify scorn or contempt.

• For a girl's fifteenth birthday, give gold jewelry. Don't give costume jewelry—Chileans wear only the real thing.

BUSINESS

Hours

Businesses: 9:00 A.M. to 5:00 P.M., Monday through Friday.

Government Offices: 9:00 A.M. to 4:30 P.M., Monday through Friday.

Banks: 9:00 A.M. to 2:00 P.M., Monday through Friday.

Shops: 10:00 A.M. to 7:00 P.M., Monday through Friday; and 10:00 A.M. to 2:00 P.M. on Saturday.

• Note that everything is closed on Sunday.

Currency

• The unit of currency is the *peso,* whose sign is $.

• Coins: 1, 5, 50, and 100 *pesos.*

• Bills: 100, 500, 1,000, and 5,000 *pesos.*

• Remember that you can change travelers' checks at a bank only up to 12:00 noon. Hotels and *cambios,* which give better rates than banks, will change such checks later.

• If you're going to a small town, bring a supply of currency with you, since you won't be able to change travelers' checks.

Business Practices

• Realize that Chileans take summer holidays in January and February; avoid making business trips during that time.

• For excellent (and free) information about doing business in Chile, write to the Economic Department of the Chilean Embassy in your country.

• Note that if you're dealing with a franchise of an international company you will need to plan fewer trips to Chile than if you are dealing with a Chilean firm.

• Make appointments with businesses or government offices at least two weeks in advance.

• Create a good impression by staying in one of the best hotels.

• Using business cards in English is acceptable; however, be sure to put the telephone number of your hotel on the card, so that business colleagues can reach you.

• Keep in mind that in most cases people in top management speak English; Chilean businesspeople are sophisticated and are usually of English, German, Italian, or Spanish descent. If you should need an interpreter, ask at your country's embassy in Santiago. Embassy staff will also be helpful in finding legal advisors for you. Your need for an interpreter will depend on whether you're dealing with a multinational or a Chilean firm.

• Schedule business appointments during the hours 10:00 A.M. to 12:30 P.M. and 2:30 to 5:00 P.M.

• In general, be punctual for business appointments, though it's acceptable to be 15 minutes late.

• Don't be surprised to find businesspeople working long hours—until 7:00 or 8:00 P.M.

• Remember that the first meeting is an introduction to discuss your company and your position. Most of the time will be spent in nonbusiness conversation. Since most businesspeople ski or fish (the south of Chile is world famous for its trout and salmon), bring up these sports if you know about them. Another good subject at a business meeting is Chilean wines, which are well known in many countries.

• Never use "hard sell" techniques. Chileans are conservative and won't react well to them.

• Expect Chilean businesspeople to value truth and honesty. For example, if a product is inferior they want to know why.

• Note that business decisions are usually made by the few people at the top of an organization.

• Don't forget that the *worst* offense to a Chilean is the offer of a bribe.

• Women should realize that they can be successful doing business in Chile, since women there are very advanced professionally. Women will be taken seriously without having to be aggressive to prove that they're professional.

• Note that Chileans are very open about inviting visiting foreigners to their homes for a meal.

• If you've been to a family's home and return to Chile two or three times, bring toys for the children. The family will appreciate your remembering the sexes and ages of the children.

• Don't expect spouses to be included in a business lunch. For business dinners that are primarily social, it's okay to include foreign and Chilean spouses. (If you've been invited and aren't sure the occasion is social, ask your host.)

• If you want to invite Chileans to a business lunch, ask them to suggest a restaurant. For a dinner, entertain at your hotel's restaurant. The top hotels in Santiago have outstanding restaurants.

HOLIDAYS AND SPECIAL OCCASIONS

Expect banks, businesses, government offices, many stores, and many restaurants to be closed on the following national holidays. Check with the tourist office to learn about the regional holidays in areas you'll be visiting.

Holidays: New Year's Day (Jan. 1); Holy Thursday, Good Friday, and Easter Sunday; Battle of Iquique, honoring Chilean hero Arturo Pratt (May 21); Feast of the Assumption (August 15); Independence Day (Sept. 18); Armed Forces Day (Sept. 19); Columbus Day (Oct. 12); All Saints' Day (Nov. 1); Feast of the Immaculate Conception (Dec. 8); Christmas (Dec. 25).

• Watch out for riots and protests on September 11, the anniversary of the 1973 coup.

• Join the Independence Day celebrations on September 18. *Fondas,* stands decorated with leaves, are installed in public parks, where crowds congregate to celebrate and eat *empanadas* (meat turnovers), drink *chicha* (a drink made of fermented grapes), and dance the *cueca* (the national folk dance) to the accompaniment of guitars.

• Two religious celebrations to remember: on November 1, people visit the graves of relatives. On Friday and Saturday in Holy Week, people eat only fish and shellfish—no meat.

TRANSPORTATION

Public Transportation

• On buses, enter from the front, and pay the driver. You don't need the exact fare, but don't expect the driver to change a large bill. Keep your ticket for the inspector who will get on. He will rip your ticket in half and return half to you. Should the bus be in an accident, you'll need your ticket to prove you were on the bus and thus get reimbursed for medical costs.

• Consider taking the subway in Santiago. It's clean, quiet, and the least expensive way to travel. Buy a ticket (a single fare, whatever the distance) from a seller in a booth. The subway runs every four minutes from 6:30 A.M. to 10:30 P.M., Monday through Saturday; and 8:00 A.M. to 10:30 P.M. on Sundays and holidays.

• Note that taxis use meters. There's a 50% surcharge for rides after 9:00 P.M. and on Sunday.

• Be aware that there is train service only from Santiago south, none to the north. There are four classes: super salon, the most expensive, has carpets, blankets, pillows, reclining seats, and meal service at your seat; salon provides reserved seats and reclining chairs, but you must go to the dining car to eat; first class offers reserved seats; second class has no reserved seats and is very crowded, usually with people standing in the aisles.

• Think about taking a bus for long-distance travel. Buses usually have numbered seats, toilets, and (sometimes) attendants who serve tea and coffee. Special sleeper buses, *bus cama* (boos **cah**-mah), also have reclining seats and foot rests. These buses, available only for long journeys, cost twice as much as ordinary buses, but the comforts may be worth the price.

• Note that on short trips you may have to stand in the aisle. In January and February (the vacation period) and on weekends and holidays, buses are packed.

Driving

• If your stay is only in Santiago, use taxis. You might want to rent a car for traveling around the country, however. Chile is an easy country to drive in.

• Be aware that seat belts are required for every passenger for whom a seat belt is available. If the passengers aren't wearing seat belts, the *driver* will be fined.

• Be especially careful not to drink and drive on weekends. Police sometimes stop cars to give breathalyzer tests to the driver. If you're drunk, you'll have to leave your car, you'll be detained by the police, and you'll have to pay a fine.

LEGAL MATTERS, SAFETY, AND HEALTH

• Realize that you aren't allowed to bring *any* fruit into Chile (a precaution to prevent the spread of insects) nor to transport fruit from the north of Chile to the south.

• Stay away from street demonstrations. Don't let curiosity move you to see what is happening. All such demonstrations have political motives, and police are known to arrest everyone on the scene.

• Note that the risk of theft is minor. Nevertheless, don't be careless with money or possessions.

• Women should travel accompanied if possible, although in general women should not expect unwarranted, persistent advances. As a precaution, women should not wear jewelry when traveling.

• Remember that major cities have chlorinated water, which is safe to drink.

• If you are going to any of the high-altitude locales (e.g., the ski resort Portillo, which is at 9,300 feet), take precautions against altitude sickness. Eat very lightly for your first few days in the area, avoid alcoholic beverages, and don't smoke.

• For advice on medicine and hygiene products, see "Legal Matters, Safety, and Health" in the Introduction.

COLOMBIA

In no other country in Latin America will behaving correctly be so important as in Colombia, where you'll find courtly and traditional behavior. You will also notice a kind of reserve. Don't interpret this formality as aloofness toward a foreigner—Colombians are very reserved with one another.

Besides tasting hand-picked Colombian coffee, you can browse through jewelry shops and possibly pick up one of the country's famous emeralds. Or you can visit Bogota's stunning Gold Museum, with the world's largest collections of pre-Columbian gold, where you most definitely *can't* pick up one of the artifacts.

GREETINGS

Language: The official language of Colombia is Spanish.

• Expect men to shake hands with other men and with women. Women clasp one another's forearms; they don't shake hands.

• Among good friends, both men and men and women and women kiss on one cheek. Sometimes good men friends embrace and pat one another on the back.

• Remember that titles are extremely important to Colombians, as they are very conscious of social class. Anyone who has a university degree should be addressed as *Doctor.*

• At parties, expect the hostess to introduce you to others individ-

ually. When you leave, say goodbye to each person.

Conversation

• Before you visit Colombia, learn something about Colombian history, art, and literature—and also about soccer.

• Don't make negative remarks about bullfighting; Colombians regard it as an art.

• Avoid discussing politics, a delicate subject. Businesspeople should be especially wary of political topics.

Telephones

• Note that Colombia's phone system is very modern.

• To make a call from a public phone, deposit one *peso,* which allows you three minutes. A tone will sound when it's time to deposit more.

• Remember that it's much less expensive to call Colombia from abroad than vice versa. If possible arrange to have people from home call you rather than your calling them. Businesspeople may want to have their offices call them at regular intervals.

• If you have to make a long-distance call, go to a TELECOM office. Go to the counter where you'll be assigned a cabin. Pay after the call. You can make long-distance calls from most hotels, but, before you do, inquire whether there's a surcharge and if so, how much.

• When making a business call, never plunge right into business discussions. First, ask how the other person is, and make small talk.

IN PUBLIC

• Don't expect people to wait politely in line—for example, for a bus. You'll have to join the pushing match if you want a place.

• If you're smoking, always offer others in your group a cigarette.

• Some gestures to know about: (1) Tapping the elbow with your hand says that the person you're talking to or about is "stingy."

(2) Holding one hand palm down while the other hand makes a sawing motion across it suggests making a deal with the intention of sharing the profits. (3) The American "O.K." sign placed over the nose means that the person you're discussing is homosexual.

• Keep in mind that people will hardly ever respond negatively to a request for a favor or to an invitation, whether or not they have any thought of doing the favor or coming to the party. You can often pick up cues from the Colombians. (For example, if you invite people to dinner, they may say, "We'll try to come," meaning that they don't intend to.) Only experience will teach you what people mean. Never pressure anyone for a firm commitment, however. Colombians regard directness by foreigners toward them as insensitive.

• When visiting churches, don't photograph using a flash.

• Feel free to bargain in open markets but not in stores.

• In a shop, if you're paying with cash, rather than a credit card, ask for a 5 to 10% discount.

• Note that public toilets are scarce. You'll find them in hotels, restaurants, and shopping malls. In small towns, the bathrooms are not clean and often lack toilet paper. Bring tissues with you. At airports, women stand outside the public toilets selling toilet paper for ten *pesos*.

DRESS

• Remember that Colombians judge people by how they look and how well they are dressed.

• For business, men should wear a dark suit and tie, and women should wear a suit or a dress. Men should arrive for a business meeting wearing a jacket, no matter how hot it is. They will probably be invited to remove it immediately.

• Don't wear shorts on the street or when visiting churches. If you wear jeans, be sure that they are stylish and clean. Never wear grubby jeans.

• In small towns and villages women should not wear pants— only dresses or skirts.

• When invited to a meal in someone's home, men should wear a suit and tie and women a skirt or dress.

• The major occasions for formal wear are weddings and graduation parties. The invitation will specify formal dress.

• Don't be surprised to see people in business clothes wearing a woolen poncho (called a *ruana*) over their business attire.

MEALS

Hours and Foods

Breakfast: Not usually a family meal in Colombian homes. Each person eats according to her or his personal schedule. If there is a maid, she prepares breakfast, and will probably offer juice, fruit, eggs, butter, jam, pastry, and coffee. Soup is sometimes served at breakfast. Try *arepas,* which are like thin English muffins; they are made with ground corn mixed with salt, water, cheese, eggs, milk, and butter, then shaped into small round cakes and pan fried or deep fried.

Lunch: 12:30 or 1:00 P.M. until 2:00 or 2:30 P.M. It's the most important family meal; husbands return from work for it. There will be several courses: soup, a main course of meat with vegetables, rice (a staple served every day), dessert (a home-made sweet), and finally black coffee in a demitasse. Fruit juices and milk are the usual beverages with meals.

Dinner: About 7:00 P.M. In some homes dinner is much the same as lunch but without soup. In other homes, it's a very light meal—soup, toast, fruit, and coffee. While wine is often served at dinners for guests, it's not typically served at a family meal.

Beverages: Local liquors include rum and *aguardiente* (both made from sugar cane). *Aguardiente* is served straight in small glasses. It tastes like "fire water," which is roughly what its name means.

• Colombian coffee is mild. The small cup of black coffee, the national drink, is called *tinto* (teen-toh); coffee with milk is called *café perico* (kah-**feh** peh-ree-koh); a cup of milk with a little coffee added is called *café con leche* (kah-**feh** kon leh-cheh).

Table Manners

• When you're invited to a meal in a home, expect several drinks to be offered—mainly Scotch, vodka, gin, port, or sherry. Wine is rarely served before meals. If you don't drink, ask for soda water. At the meal itself, there will probably be wine since a meal for guests is a special occasion (Colom-

bians don't usually drink alcoholic beverages with meals). If you don't want to drink the wine, take one small sip and leave it. If you drink the wine, it's polite to compliment your host on it after the first sip.

• Note that little snacks (e.g., olives, ham, and cheese) will be served with before-dinner drinks.

• Anticipate receiving a plate with food already on it, though in some homes service is family style.

• Don't worry about highly spiced food; Colombian food isn't. If hot sauce is used, it's served separately.

• To be polite, leave a small amount of food on your plate to show that there has been an abundance of food.

• To indicate that you've finished, place your eating utensils horizontally across your plate.

• After dinner at a home during the week, stay until 10:00 P.M. If the dinner is on the weekend, stay until 11:00 or 11:30. If you're invited to a dancing party in a home, expect it to last from about 11:00 P.M. to 5:00 A.M.

Eating Out

• A *café concierto* is a cafe with music (e.g., guitar). You can have drinks, coffee, and light snacks.

• Don't expect to find menus posted in restaurant windows.

• Realize that in a good restaurant, there will be three to four waiters per table. To attract their attention, just raise your hand or make eye contact.

• Remember that wine can be very expensive, since Colombia doesn't produce wine, and it must be imported. Local beer is, however, good.

• When you go to a nightclub not in your hotel, take only as much money as you need, be careful not to drink too much, and pay as soon as you're served.

Specialties

• Some main-course specialties: *hallacas*—a meat mixture stuffed into ground corn dough, wrapped in banana leaves and boiled; *pabellón criollo*—shredded beef with rice, black beans, and plaintains; *sancocho*—chicken, meat, or fish and vegetable stew; *sobrebarriga*—rolled flank steak, stuffed and breaded; *lechona*—suckling pig; *tamales*—corn dough, meat, and vegetables, wrapped in a banana leaf; *puchero bogotano*—boiled beef, vegetables, and potatoes; *ajiaco*—chicken, white and yellow potatoes, cream, capers, and avocados.

• Also try: *mogollas*—whole wheat rolls; *almojábanas*—corn muffins; *cuajada con melado*—fresh farmer's cheese covered with molasses.

• Good choices for dessert: guava paste with milk; *manjar blanco*—soft toffee made with milk, sugar, and spices.

HOTELS

• Remember that on the Caribbean coast, high season is from December 15 to April 30 and June 15 to August 31.

• Note that the top hotels are equivalent to those in Europe in the excellence of the accommodations and service. Reserve at them well in advance because hotels in Bogota and on the Caribbean coast are often fully booked.

• Be aware that the downtown section of Bogota is not safe. Even though there are top hotels there, it is better to stay in hotels in the more residential area where many embassies are located. The district is about 15 minutes by taxi from downtown.

• Realize that only deluxe hotels have central heating; however, it's usually not cold enough so that you'll need it.

• In many hotels in small towns, prepare to pay for a room plus meals. There won't be a refund if you miss any meals. However, food is so inexpensive that the additional cost shouldn't be a problem.

• Expect private bathrooms in most hotels except the least expensive. Only more expensive hotels and hotels in colder areas of the country will have hot water.

• Consider bringing a plug for the sinks, since most hotels won't have them.

• If you're going into the Amazon area, bring a small flashlight, as electricity frequently goes off.

• Remember that there is a tourist tax of 5% on all hotel rooms.

TIPPING

• Don't tip in regular taxis; however, if you rent a private taxi for the day, give the driver the equivalent of one hour's charge.

• Expect 10% service charge to be added to your restaurant bill. If it isn't, leave 10%.

• Give porters 50 *pesos* for each piece of luggage. At a luxury hotel, give a bit more.

PRIVATE HOMES

• Feel free to drop in on friends without telephoning in advance.

• Don't be surprised to find the woman of the house spending a great deal of time in her bedroom or in the upstairs hall. Women visitors are often brought to the bedroom to socialize and watch TV with family and friends. The living room is used much less than it is in North American or European homes.

• If you stay with a family for a few days, ask your hostess what would be an appropriate tip for the maid. Hand the maid the money in an envelope.

• Note that water for a bathroom must be heated in most homes (though some homes have constant hot water). Ask when it's convenient for you to bathe so you won't interfere with the schedule of the family's working members. The hot water heater is not usually lit at night.

• Be aware that most homes have showers rather than bathtubs. Many bathrooms also have a bidet.

• Wear a robe, pajamas, and slippers when you go to the bathroom. Colombians don't like to see people going barefoot and are shocked by foreigners who do.

• Bring your own facecloth, if you use one, and your own soap. Colombians consider soap a very personal item.

Gifts: If you're invited to dinner, send roses in advance, or bring an imported liqueur—e.g., Grand Marnier or cognac—a bottle of imported wine, or chocolates.

• Don't give personal gifts such as neckties or perfume unless you know the man or woman very well. Colombians are very conservative.

• Good gifts are T-shirts and sweatshirts with logos, cosmetics, and French perfumes.

• If you want to bring a video cassette as a gift, be aware that Betamax is more common than VHS.

• Don't expect your gift to be opened in your presence; in fact, the recipient may never mention the gift.

BUSINESS

Hours

Businesses: Monday through Friday, 9:00 A.M. to 5:00 P.M.

Government Offices: Monday through Friday, 9:00 A.M. to noon and 1:00 to 4:00 P.M.

Banks: Monday through Thursday, 9:00 A.M. to 3:00 P.M.; Friday, 9:00 A.M. to 3:30 P.M.

Shops: Monday through Saturday, 9:00 A.M. to 12:30 P.M. and 2:00 to 7:00 P.M.

Currency

• The unit of currency is the *peso.*
• Coins: 1, 5, 10, 20, and 50 *centavos.*
• Bills: 1, 5, 10, 20, 50, 100, 200, 500, and 1,000 *pesos.*
• Expect major credit cards to be accepted in first-class hotels, restaurants, and shops.

Business Practices

• Plan business travel for some time between March and November. Businesspeople usually vacation in December and January and in Barranquilla during June and July as well. Avoid the five days before Ash Wednesday in Barranquilla; it's Carnival time. Also avoid the two weeks before and after Christmas and the week before and after Easter.

• Realize that it's very important to have a contact in Colombia. If you don't have one, seek assistance from your national Chamber of Commerce or your embassy in Bogotá.

• Note that Colombian contacts will make hotel reservations, usually in a hotel near their home. They will also arrange for you to be picked up at the airport, picked up for business appointments, and so forth.

• Make business appointments at least a week in advance if you're making them in the country or by phone or telex from outside the country. Allow extra time if you're making arrangements by mail.

• Prepare to spend much more time in Colombia than you think you'll need. What you can accomplish at home in two days will probably take at least a week. Expect to wait several days before you even *begin* to discuss business. Colombian businesspeople will want to know about you, your spouse, your family, your city or town, sports you play, and so on. Don't begin discussing business until Colombians do.

• Arrive at least a day—preferably two—before you begin your appointments, since you may have a reaction to the altitude in Bogotá. To minimize the altitude's effects, don't drink alcohol, smoke, or eat heavily for a day or two after arriving.

• Men should be sure to wear their hair fairly short.

• If you have several appointments in one day, hire a private taxi, for which you will be charged by the hour. Your hotel will know of trustworthy drivers. If you make several trips to Colombia, it can be advantageous to build up a relationship with a single driver. Be sure to give the driver lunch money if you've hired him for the day.

• Be punctual for business appointments, but don't expect Colombians to be on time.

• Expect to be offered coffee when you arrive for a meeting. Be sure to accept.

• Always start by dealing with people at top levels in companies. A large number of these executives speak English and may resent your bringing an interpreter. If you know that the Colombian doesn't speak English, you should of course bring an interpreter.

• Don't feel that you need to have your business card printed in Spanish. Be sure, however, that your title is included on your card. Present your business card with the printed side facing the person receiving it. Hold one end of the card between your index and middle fingers so that no words are covered up.

• Be aware that it's very easy to have materials photocopied in Bogotá.

• Remember that Colombians don't always meet deadlines. They will come through eventually, but you will have to wait patiently without complaining.

• To ensure that people meet your deadlines, tell them why it's important, and keep checking on progress in a friendly, personal manner.

• If you meet workers in factories, shake hands with those near you when you are introduced and again when you leave. Never participate in any manual labor, however, because you will demean yourself in the eyes of Colombians. Status is very important.

• Women should remember that they won't accomplish their goals if they seem aggressive or bossy. When something hasn't been done correctly, be pleasant and patient, and you will usually get what you want.

• Don't try to bribe anyone. Some people will regard it as an insult, while others may try to obtain more money from you when they realize that you're willing to offer a bribe. Example: If you're trying to bring a computer through customs, let your Colombian contact deal with the issue; don't try to bribe the customs officer.

• Note that people appreciate it very much if you say, "You must come visit me in ————." Say it only if you really mean it because people may take you up on your offer.

• Expect to be entertained in business associates' homes; they like you to meet their spouses and families. Don't, however, discuss business when having a meal at someone's home.

• Reciprocate hospitality by hosting a meal in a restaurant that serves continental cuisine.

• Good business gifts are Cross pens with the recipient's name engraved on them, pocket calculators (especially solar-powered ones), or a bottle of Scotch.

HOLIDAYS AND SPECIAL OCCASIONS

Prepare for banks, offices, and many stores to be closed on the holidays listed below. Check with the tourist office to find out if any of the country's many regional religious festivals will be celebrated during your stay. As a traveler, you may wish to include such festivals in your itinerary, but you might want to avoid them on a business trip.

Holidays: New Year's Day (Jan. 1); Epiphany (Jan. 6); Saint Joseph's Day (March 19); Holy Thursday, Good Friday, Holy Saturday, and Easter; Labor Day (May 1); Ascension Day (40 days after Easter); Feast of Sts. Peter and Paul (June 29); Independence Day (July 20); Battle of Boyacá (August 7); Feast of the Assumption (August 15); Columbus Day (Oct. 12); All Saints' Day (Nov. 1); Independence Day—Cartagena (Nov. 11); Feast of the Immaculate Conception (Dec. 8); Christmas (Dec. 25).

• Don't plan "fun" activities on November 1. It's a somber day on which Colombians go to cemeteries and decorate graves with flowers.

TRANSPORTATION

Public Transportation

• To get a taxi after you arrive at the Bogotá airport, go to the dispatch booth, where you'll be told the fare and given a piece of paper with the license plate number of your assigned taxi on it. Keep the piece of paper; if you have any trouble, call the taxi company and report the driver. Another way to find a taxi at an airport is to look for a Tourist Police officer, who will tell you how to find one.

• When possible, use one of the green-and-white taxis assigned to the major hotels. They are registered with the Tourist Police and are trustworthy. They are, however, more expensive than other taxis.

• Realize that Colombia's taxis are the least expensive of any major country. Between 7:00 and 9:00 A.M., noon and 2:00 P.M., and 5:00 and 7:30 P.M., you should telephone for a taxi because they are difficult to find on the streets at those times.

• Be aware that there are two classes of buses in Bogotá, Medellín, and Cali: *buses* (boo-sehs) and *busetas* (boo-seh-tahs). The *buses*, which look like school buses, are often driven by the owners, who pack in as many people as possible to make the maximum profit. If you decide to take one of these buses, enter from the front and exit from the rear. You don't need exact change for your fare, but remember that drivers usually can't change large bills.

• Consider taking *busetas* (minibuses). They are much more costly than the larger buses but also *much* less crowded. Enter from the front, pay your fare (you don't need exact change), and exit from the rear.

• Whatever type of bus you decide to take, avoid traveling during the rush hour; buses are very crowded, and there is a danger of pickpockets.

• Note that for inter-city travel, there are large buses, called Pullmans, with air-conditioning, videos, and bathrooms. Despite the comfort of these buses, you might want to fly between cities if time is of any importance. For example, the bus trip from Bogotá to Medellín takes 11 hours, while a plane takes only 20 minutes.

Driving

• Avoid driving at night; you may find animals on the road, potholes, and—sometimes—robbers.

• Prepare to stop at police checkpoints, which are located at intervals along most highways.

LEGAL MATTERS, SAFETY, AND HEALTH

• Be sure to carry your passport with you at all times.

• If you walk or take a bus in Bogotá, wear a money belt. If you take a taxi or are driving yourself, lock doors and close windows. Thieves are known to attack when people are stopped at red lights.

• Be on the lookout for gangs of small children, between 5 and 12 years old. They look innocent but can be dangerous.

• Never leave luggage or packages even for a moment. On a bus, don't put your bags in the luggage compartment; keep them with you. In restaurants, keep packages between your legs.

• Be aware of the following trick: someone with lottery tickets runs by and drops lots of tickets on the ground. If you stop to help him pick them up, a crowd may gather, thus helping someone to pick your pocket.

• Never accept food, drink, or cigarettes from strangers on buses. It's happened that people have been drugged with these items and then robbed.

• Women should expect harassment from all men, including the police and the military. Colombia is a country in which you'll encounter some of the worst displays of *machismo*.

• Women should *not* go out unaccompanied at night—even in a taxi. Eat at the restaurant in your hotel.

• When you arrive in Bogotá, take precautions to prevent *soroche*—altitude sickness, whose principal effect is severe headaches. For your first few days, eat lightly (on your first night, have just a bowl of consommé), don't drink alcoholic beverages, and don't smoke.

• During your entire stay in Colombia, don't drink tap water or eat unpeeled fruits and vegetables or raw shellfish. Never buy cooked food from street vendors.

• Be careful when buying imported liquor. Some bottles have been opened and refilled with other liquids; the bottles could then be dangerous. Stick to rum and beer.

• For advice on medicine and hygiene products, see "Legal Matters, Safety, and Health" in the Introduction.

COSTA RICA

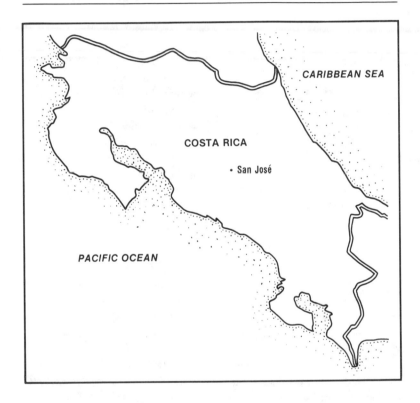

It wasn't until his fourth (and last) voyage to the New World that Columbus discovered "the rich coast" (Costa Rica), where he was convinced he had found a major source of gold for Spain.

In the 20th century, the "gold" is flowing into, rather than out of, Costa Rica. Its stable political climate has attracted large amounts of foreign investment, and not a few fugitive financiers have arrived with their fortunes.

Its geography makes Costa Rica a delight for lovers of flora and fauna.

Animals and plants that thrive in countries to the north and south find happy homes in Costa Rica.

In reporting on Costa Rica and its amiable lifestyle for *60 Minutes,* CBS correspondent Morley Safer said that the national motto should be "No sweat."

• At large parties, introduce yourself. At small parties you will be introduced by the host or hostess. At either type of party, shake hands and say good-bye to each person when you leave.

GREETINGS

Language: The official language of Costa Rica is Spanish.

• Remember that men always shake hands with both new acquaintances and old friends.

• Note that when women are introduced to one another they don't shake hands. They pat one another on the left arm. Women who are good friends kiss each other on the cheek.

• Use titles. They are important to Costa Ricans. Some common titles: Doctor (for Ph.D. and medical doctor); architect; engineer; lawyer; professor. (See "Key Words and Phrases" at the end of the book for Spanish equivalents.) Use the title with the last name.

CONVERSATION

• Ask about people's children. Both men and women adore children.

• Feel free to discuss politics. Costa Rica is very stable, with a long democratic tradition.

• Ask advice about what to do and see in Costa Rica, especially the nature reserves. Costa Rica has the largest number of wildlife preserves in the world.

• Be aware that people have a strong sense of personal honor; never say anything that could be

construed as personal criticism.
• Don't use the word *rica* when referring to a person. It has bad connotations. Costa Ricans refer to themselves as *ticos* (**tee-kohs**).
• Don't ask a woman about her job unless you know that she works outside her home. Most women don't.

TELEPHONES

• Expect to find telephone booths in cities as well as all along highways.
• Deposit two *colones* for a local call and five or ten *colones* for long-distance calls within the country. When you hear a series of beeps, deposit more money or you'll be cut off. If you want to have a long conversation, give the other party the number of the pay phone (it's on a yellow sign above the phone), and he or she can call you back.
• For long-distance calls outside the country, go to the telephone office, Radiográfica Costarricense.

IN PUBLIC

• Note that Costa Ricans don't make distinctions among people based on social rank. All people receive equal respect.
• A gesture to avoid: making a fist with the thumb sticking out between the index and middle fingers.
• When asking directions, expect to be told how far your destination is from a landmark. If you're giving directions to someone who's picking you up, tell them how many meters you are from some recognizable place. Most Costa Ricans ignore street numbers. (Street numbers are attached to the sides of buildings near intersections.)
• Expect to find public bathrooms everywhere—even in small snack bars in the countryside. Some are kept locked, and you must ask for the key at the counter. Bring tissues, because there is usually no toilet paper, but public bathrooms are usually very clean.

Shopping: Note that there's no bargaining in Costa Rica. If you're buying something in quantity, you can ask for a discount, e.g., "One pineapple costs XXX. How much do you want for three pineapples?"

• To buy anything from canned goods to toilet paper to rope in the countryside, look for a *pulpería*. In the cities you'll find *supermercados*.

skirts and blouses, with stockings and high heels.

• There are only two major restaurants in San José at which men must wear ties. Most restaurants are very casual.

• Wear shorts only on the beach or for sports.

• Remember that nude swimming and sunbathing are *extremely* offensive to Costa Ricans. A beach may look deserted, but homes may be right behind it.

DRESS

• Note that the climate varies a great deal, depending on the altitude. In the cities at higher altitudes, nights are cool, and you'll need a sweater or jacket.

• For casual dress, anything except shorts will be acceptable. Women shouldn't wear anything revealing.

• For business, in San José, men should wear a conservative dark suit. A jacket isn't necessary in coastal cities. Women should wear silk or cotton dresses or dressy

MEALS

Hours and Foods

Breakfast: Between 6:00 and 7:00 A.M. In the city, the usual meal is orange juice, bread, and coffee, sometimes with eggs. In the countryside, people eat *gallo pinto* (mixed rice and beans) with sour cream and tortillas, and they drink coffee.

Lunch: 11:30 A.M. to 1:00 P.M. A typical lunch might be *casado* (rice, black beans, salad, meat or egg), *picadillo* (fried vegetables), fried plaintains, fruit, and coffee.

• People stop for the *hora del café* (coffee hour) from 4:30 to 5:30 P.M.

Dinner: About 7:00 P.M. A lighter meal than lunch, it might consist of *olla de carne* (a stew with beef, potatoes, corn, onions, beans, and tomatoes) with rice and beans.

Beverages: Common drinks before dinner at a home are rum and Coke, whiskey and soda, or vodka. Don't have more than one or two drinks. With cocktails there may be appetizers such as cheese sticks, chips, and ground bean dip.

• With meals the usual beverages are soft drinks or fresh fruit juices: *fresco de mora* (blackberry juice), *fresco de tamarindo* (tamarind juice), *fresco de carambola* (starfruit juice).

• Avoid one of the country's most popular beverages: *horchata,* a crude "aquavit" made from corn. Since you don't know where or how it's been made, don't try it.

• Note that it's safe to drink the water in San José but *not* elsewhere. You won't find mineral water; substitute soda water, which is called *soda blanca.*

Table Manners

• Expect the table to be set with forks to the left of the plate, knives to the right, and the coffee spoon above the plate.

• Don't feel obliged to finish everything on your plate, even though people will probably push you to eat more.

Eating Out

• *Sodas* are places offering light meals, sandwiches, coffee, tea, and alcoholic drinks.

• In San José, expect to find a wide variety of restaurants— French, Swiss, Italian, Chinese, and vegetarian.

• A note for vegetarians: The word *carne* in Spanish means "meat"; however, in Costa Rica it usually means "beef." If you see on a menu or are told *"No tiene carne,"* which means "There's no meat in it," it really means that the dish contains no beef—but it may contain other types of meat.

Specialties

• The national breakfast dish is *gallo pinto:* rice and beans cooked together.

• For fish lovers, Costa Rica offers *ceviche* (fresh white sea bass marinated in lemon juice, coriander, and onions) as an appetizer, and *corvina* (white sea bass served grilled, baked, or steamed).

• Two stews to try: *casados* (rice, black beans, cabbage and tomato salad, meat or egg, and fried plaintain) and *guiso de maíz* (corn stew).

• *Palmito* are hearts of palm; they are used in salads or as an elegant vegetable dish.

• *Tamales* in Costa Rica are a filling of pork or chicken, raisins, rice, and olives, stuffed in white cornmeal, all wrapped in banana leaves. To eat them, you unwrap the *tamal*, and discard the leaves.

• *Tortas* are sandwiches of meat or cheese on rolls.

HOTELS

• Note that Costa Rican hotels range from the basic to the luxurious. Luxury hotels usually have excellent food, room service, swimming pools, and flowering tropical plants and bushes. You may also find small hotels that are clean and have helpful management.

• Expect the high-season rates to be in effect from December through March.

• Some alternatives to traditional hotels: (1) *apartoteles*—rooms with kitchen facilities, offering weekly and monthly rates; (2) *cabinas*—motel-like rooms; (3) *pensiones*—inexpensive basic hotels with no meal service; (4) rooms in a home (usually with meals and laundry service)—find one by calling language schools or checking at the University of San José.

• Be aware that most hotels in San José and the surrounding area don't have air-conditioning because, with the altitude, the nights are always cool.

• If you're staying on the coast, make sure that there is a fan in your room.

• Realize that the small, inexpensive hotels on the coast often don't have hot water—just tepid tap water.

• Expect to find at least one person who speaks English at most hotels.

• Be aware that some hotels on the coast include meals in the room rate, and you must pay for them, whether you eat them or not.

• Keep in mind that most hotels change travelers' checks, but you can obtain a better rate at a bank. Most hotels also accept major credit cards.

clear the table, do the dishes, and make your bed.

• Realize that people often take two or three showers or baths a day because of the heat. Your hosts will be offended if you don't take at least one bath or shower a day.

TIPPING

• Recall that restaurants add 10% service charge.
• Don't tip taxi drivers.
• Give porters 30 *colones* (about 50 cents U.S.) per piece of luggage.
• Give gas station attendants 5 to 10 *colones*.

Gifts: When invited to a meal, bring flowers or a good wine. Roses and carnations are popular, but don't give calla lilies—they're for funerals.

• Bring women makeup, perfume, or silk scarves. Bring men shaving cream and aftershave.
• Both men and women enjoy delicacies, e.g., baskets of fancy jams, smoked fish, fancy chocolates, unusual crackers, mustards.
• Scotch and wine are also welcome gifts.
• Because many Americans live in Costa Rica and because there aren't many import restrictions, American-made products are easily obtainable and aren't considered special.

PRIVATE HOMES

• When invited to dinner at someone's home, leave soon after the meal. People begin work very early because of the heat, and children start school at 7:00 A.M.
• Note that few families have maids. If you're staying with a family with no maid, offer to help

BUSINESS

Hours

Businesses: Monday through Friday, 8:00 A.M. to 5:00 P.M., closing for lunch from 11:00 or 11:30 A.M. to 1:00 P.M.

Government Offices: Monday through Friday, 8:00 A.M. to 4:00 P.M.

Banks: Monday through Friday, 9:00 A.M. to 3:00 P.M.

Shops: Monday through Friday, 8:00 A.M. to noon, and 2:00 to 6:00 P.M. Saturday: 8:00 A.M. to noon.

Currency

• The currency is the *colón* (plural, *colones*). One *colón* consists of 100 *céntimos*.
• Old coins (5, 10, 25, and 50 *cénatimos*, and 1 and 2 *colones*) are being phased out.
• New coins are 25 and 50 *céntimos* and 1, 2, 5, 10, and 20 *colones*.

Bills: 5, 10, 20, 50, 100, 500, and 1,000 *colones*.

• Remember that it's illegal to change money anywhere other than at banks and some hotels. If you change money on the street, both you and the seller may be prosecuted.
• Change money in San José, since some towns in the country don't have bank branches.
• Remember that it's often difficult to change *colones* into dollars when you leave Costa Rica. Spend them.

Business Practices

• Note that the best months for business travel to Costa Rica are February and March, and September to November. Avoid the two weeks before and after Christmas and the week before and after Easter. December and January are popular times for vacations.
• Be sure to have a contact before you make a business trip to Costa Rica. Look for one through the Costa Rican Chamber of Commerce.
• Stay in the best hotels to make a good impression.
• Make appointments about two weeks in advance with businesspeople and government officials.
• Be punctual. Costa Ricans honor appointment times much more than businesspeople in other Latin American countries.

• Remember that Costa Ricans are very serious, formal, and European in style. Don't expect the *abrazo*—the bear hug with which men greet one another. One visiting businessman observed, "Meeting some Costa Rican businessmen is the equivalent of meeting an English lord."

• Men should *always* keep their jackets on at meetings.

• Never put your feet up on furniture.

• Have your business cards printed in Spanish and English.

• Don't worry about getting proposals or other materials copied in Costa Rica. It's very easy.

• To make a good first impression, offer a compliment on the beauty of the country, especially the nature reserves. Don't discuss the politics of Central America during your initial meeting because people are likely to remain on the subject and you'll have a very difficult time returning to a business discussion.

• If you will be offering sales literature, have it printed in Spanish as well as English, though most younger businesspeople speak English. Should you need an interpreter, consult the ads in the *Tico Times,* the English-language newspaper.

• Be sure to have a lawyer to get government approval for starting a business. (Costa Rica has one of the highest percentages of lawyers per capita in the world, and many of them are fluent in English.)

• Remember that time estimates for deadlines are not reliable; however, you should never complain about Costa Rica or Costa Ricans because people will be *very* offended.

• Note that foreign investors can own 100% of any business or property. In most Latin American countries, foreigners are limited to less than 50% of any business.

• Inviting as it is to be able to own 100% of an investment, don't buy large amounts of land unless you plan to live on it or actively farm it. You could have problems with squatters. Once they've stayed on a property for more than a year, they have certain rights of possession, which makes it difficult to evict them.

• Keep in mind that decisions are usually made by the consensus of a group, not just by the top people, as in other Latin American countries. Head officials defer until a consensus is reached.

• Realize that Costa Ricans are notoriously late in paying their bills. Be sure you know in advance the method of payment. It's best to have a contract backed up by a letter of contract or a performance bond from a bank in *your* country.

• Consider the explanation of one Costa Rican government official for the delays in payment (an explanation that says much about attitudes in the country): "We in

Costa Rica are all individual farmers. Farms operate on credit. A gentleman would never ask another to pay off a debt during a year with a bad harvest. We in Costa Rica have had bad harvests for the past eight years."

• Women should note that they will have a better chance to succeed in business in Costa Rica than in other Latin American countries.

• Expect business entertaining to be in the evening, since most businesspeople return home for lunch.

• Entertain only the people with whom you are negotiating.

• Invite spouses—both foreign and Costa Rican—to business dinners.

HOLIDAYS AND SPECIAL OCCASIONS

Below are national holidays on which you should expect to find government offices, banks, businesses, and many shops closed.

Check with the tourist office to learn if there are any local festivals during your stay. Such festivals may cause everything to be closed in that area.

Holidays: New Year's Day (January 1); Feast of St. Joseph, patron saint of the city of San José (March 19); Holy Thursday through Easter Sunday; Labor Day (May 1); Feast of Corpus Christi (the Thursday after the eighth Sunday after Easter); Feast of Sts. Peter and Paul (June 29); Annexation of the Guanacaste Province (July 25); Feast of Our Lady of the Angels (August 2); Feast of the Assumption, Mothers' Day (August 15); Independence Day (Sept. 15); Columbus Day (Oct. 12); Feast of the Immaculate Conception (Dec. 8); Christmas Eve and Christmas Day (Dec. 24 and 25).

• Be aware that Good Friday is kept as a day of mourning throughout the country.

• Expect to hear fireworks when a local saint's day is being celebrated. If you hear loud explosions, such a festival probably explains them. Sirens, on the other hand, may mean that an important person has arrived in town.

TRANSPORTATION

Public Transportation

• Note that within cities there are different bus companies with different fares. The more modern buses are slightly more expensive. People queue for buses very politely and quietly. Pay on the bus. You don't need exact change.

• Be aware that buses are not air-conditioned and can be very hot for long trips.

• Remember that there is no smoking on either city or inter-city buses, no matter how long the ride.

• For long-distance buses, buy tickets in advance at the terminal or on the bus.

• Consider taxis for short distances in cities. They are readily available, clean, and well maintained. Drivers are careful. There are meters, but check in advance and find out what the fare should be.

• Realize that there is no public transportation on Holy Thursday or Good Friday.

• Note that trains run between San José and Puntarenas (on the Pacific coast) and San José and Limón (on the Caribbean coast). They are old-fashioned, narrow-guage trains and go very slowly, make many stops, and take a great deal of time. Seats are padded; floors are wooden. There is only one class and no reserved seats. At some stops, vendors climb on and sell food, fruits, drinks, potato chips, and ice cream.

• Think about taking a plane for travel between cities. Airfare is reasonable, and people often travel by plane because of the mountainous terrain. The domestic airline is called SANSA. Make reservations in advance, and pay for your ticket by the day before the flight. Be prepared for the plane to land at tiny airports with cattle on the runways.

Driving

• If you plan to rent a car, shop around for the best price. There are many car rental agencies.

• Expect little traffic on highways outside the city. There are some excellent highways, but road signs are poor. At some places—when you least expect it—a paved road may become a dirt road covered with rocks. Determine exactly where you're going and what the road conditions are; you may want to rent a jeep.

• Note that Costa Ricans drive relatively slowly outside San José, but in the city, be sure to drive defensively.

LEGAL MATTERS, SAFETY, AND HEALTH

• Be aware that it's illegal to change dollars anywhere except at banks and hotels (and only registered guests can change money at hotels). In an illegal transaction, both buyer and seller are liable.

• When crossing the street in San José, remember that pedestrians *don't* have the right of way.

Check cars coming from behind you, since drivers tend to shoot around corners.

• Some precautions: Don't wear backpacks in cities as they can be opened easily by thieves. Don't carry wallets in back pockets. Don't wear expensive jewelry.

• Don't worry about dining alone in restaurants if you're a woman alone, but don't go into local bars.

• If you camp out or stay in a primitive place and must hang your clothes outside, shake out your clothes and shoes before putting them on—to get rid of insects and snakes.

• Realize that riptides occur at several beaches. Don't swim alone, even if you are an experienced swimmer. Ask local people which beaches are safe.

• Don't eat raw vegetables and fruit that can't be peeled. Avoid raw shellfish.

• For advice on medicine and hygiene products, see "Legal Matters, Safety, and Health" in the Introduction.

ECUADOR

While Ponce de León searched for the fountain of youth, many modern travelers look for a climate that's eternal spring. They'll find it in Quito, whose warm days and cool nights give the city as close to ideal weather as you're likely to find. Venture just a few miles outside Quito and you can straddle the equator, with one foot in the Northern and one in the Southern Hemisphere.

For many travelers, Ecuador is the gateway to one of the world's great adventures—a trip to the Galápagos Islands, the remote archipelago (mostly still uninhabited) where Charles Darwin gathered a great deal of the evidence that led to his theory of evolution, and where you can still see giant tortoises who may have been members of Darwin's welcoming committee.

GREETINGS

Language: Ecuador's official language is Spanish, though Indians speak Quechua.

• Note that when introduced, when greeting, and when departing, Ecuadorans shake hands, with people of both sexes.
• Be aware that greetings are often more affectionate between good friends. Women and women as well as men and women kiss on one cheek when greeting and departing. Men shake hands with other men.
• Be sure to use titles in greeting others. They are very important, as they confer status. The major titles are: *Abogado* (lawyer), *Arquitecto* (architect); *Ingeniero* (engineer), and *Doctor* (lawyer or medical doctor).

• At a party, expect to be introduced to everyone individually by your host. Depending on the formality of the occasion and whether people are elderly, they either shake hands or kiss on one cheek. At an informal party with young people, everyone will kiss on one cheek.

CONVERSATION

• Good topics for conversation are family and jobs.
• Avoid bringing up politics, your personal problems, your (or anyone else's) sex life, or any subject implying your country's superiority.
• Don't compliment Peru. Relations between Ecuador and Peru are strained, due partly to dispute about the border between the two countries.

the green pages of the telephone directory. Some sections are in English.

• Note that there is no telephone service to the Galápagos Islands, only radio communication.

TELEPHONES

• Expect to find a limited number of public telephones—mostly in hotels and at the airports—in Ecuador's main cities. Deposit one *sucre* for three minutes. If you want to talk longer, deposit more money. If you can't find a public telephone, ask to use one in a shop.

• From a private home, make long-distance calls through the operator; expect to wait at least 30 minutes for the call to go through. Some private offices have direct dialing, but service is limited.

• Look for IETEL offices to make international calls as well as long-distance calls within Ecuador. The company has an office—open from 6:00 A.M. to 10:00 P.M.—in every town. In small towns, IETEL offers only telephone service, but in large towns you can also send telexes and telegrams.

• Realize that collect calls are available only to countries with which Ecuador has an agreement.

• For tourist information, check

IN PUBLIC

• Realize that English is understood only in first-class hotels, travel agencies, and airline offices. Most Indians are bilingual in Quechua and Spanish, but some speak only Quechua.

• Expect to find two very different cultures in the country's two major cities. Quito, in the mountains and with a large Indian population, is traditional, conservative, and Catholic, while Guayaquil, on the coast, is a bustling city and the center of Ecuador's economic life.

• If you're planning to travel outside the major cities, remember that rainstorms sometimes cause landslides, closing roads and businesses, and interrupting telephone service.

• Should you be invited to a girl's fifteenth birthday party, expect to be one of hundreds of guests. The party is often held in a club, but sometimes in a home. If the invitation specifies formal wear, men should wear tuxedos or suits, and women long dresses. Bring the invitation with you, as it may be checked at the door. Good gifts are jewelry or clothing.

• Bargain in markets, but not in stores or supermarkets. First check in shops to find out what they charge for the items you would like to buy. That will give you an idea as to how much you can probably lower the price by bargaining at a market.

• Be prepared for some people, especially Indians, to become angry if you try to photograph them (they consider it a severe intrusion). On the other hand, they *may* let you take their picture—for a fee.

• In a city, expect Indians to ask if they can guard your car or carry your bags. If you want their services, tip them the equivalent of a quarter. If you don't, be firm in rejecting the offer.

• Look for public bathrooms in hotels and restaurants. You can also try asking in a shop if you can use the facilities. When traveling through the countryside, however, prepare to use the woods.

DRESS

• In the coastal areas (Guayaquil, Manta), which tend to be hot, stick to natural fibers such as cotton, linen, and silk. Synthetic fabrics can be very, very hot.

• Feel free to wear jeans on the streets. Women can wear pants in the cities. Shorts are appropriate for the coastal cities but not downtown or at public or private offices.

• Business dress in the highlands (Quito, Cuenca) is more formal. Men should wear dark suits, and women, suits, dresses, or skirts, and stockings. On the coast men wear *guayaberas* (shirts worn over the trousers) and women wear sleeveless dresses, because of the heat.

• When invited to someone's home to a meal, men should wear suits and women dresses.

• Note that formal dress for men is a dark suit and for women a cocktail dress. Long dresses and tuxedos are worn only on very special occasions.

• At beaches, wear a one-piece bathing suit; bikinis are not acceptable.

MEALS

Hours and Foods

• A caution: Don't drink tap water or eat unpeeled fruits and vegetables. Never eat cooked food bought from street vendors.

Breakfast: Usually served between 7:00 and 8:30 A.M. (though it may be earlier in families with children in school). The meal is light—juice, bread, coffee, and milk.

Lunch: From 1:00 to 2:00 P.M. It's a substantial meal: soup, chicken or fish (in a restaurant, the main dish is often meat), served with rice and salad or potatoes, fruit or ice cream, and coffee.

Dinner: About 8:00 P.M. Usually a light meal of soup and coffee. Office workers who have only 30 minutes for lunch will have a large dinner at home.

• Note that on Saturdays, Sundays, and during vacations, lunch and dinner are usually served later.

Beverages: Common beverages are natural fruit juices, mineral water, and beer. The most common drinks with meals are fresh fruit juices, served unchilled. To order juice, ask for *jugo puro* (hoo-goh poo-roh), *sin agua* (seen ah-gwah) without water.

• Try to stick to soft drinks, natural fruit juice, or beer. People may not boil the water in their homes, so there's a risk with any drink that has cold water.

• Note that many Ecuadorans make coffee by boiling it for hours and then pouring the syrup into a pitcher to which they add milk or water. Espresso is available only in finer restaurants. Tea or *té* (teh) is always served with lemon and sugar. If you ask for tea with milk, you'll get hot milk with a tea bag in it.

Table Manners

• Realize that an invitation to a dinner party is unusual. People are more inclined to have parties that start late at night and go on until 4:00 or 5:00 A.M. Snacks such as canapés and *empanadas* will appear during the party, and the night often ends with guests staying for breakfast. If you leave as early as 1:00 A.M., your hosts will think you're not having a good time.

• In upper-class homes, expect to be offered whiskey before dinner. Appetizers—shrimp, cold cuts, and cheese—will be offered. Don't pass them up, thinking you'll spoil your dinner, because it will be served very late; it may start at 11:00 P.M. or midnight and last until 2:00 A.M.

• In middle-class homes, before dinner expect a local alcoholic drink made from sugarcane. There probably won't be any appetizers, but there will be a hearty meal.

• Women should note that it's not considered polite for them to drink hard liquor, though it's acceptable for them to drink wine.

• Expect to sit at the head of the table if you are the guest of honor.

• In the countryside, note that peasants use spoons instead of knives and forks.

• In a middle- or upper-class home, anticipate being served individually by a maid or your hostess.

• Don't worry if you're not fond of spicy foods. Ecuadoran food is

not spicy. If you would like to add some zest to it, note that you'll find a little dish of homemade hot sauce (*salsa picante*) on the table.

• Expect rice as a staple in the coastal area, while potatoes are the staple in the mountains.

• If you eat with the lower middle class, the poor, or peasants, finish everything on your plate. Despite the fact that they serve huge portions, they feel that leaving food on your plate means you haven't enjoyed the food, which they interpret as an insult. The upper classes, who (ironically) serve much smaller portions, understand if you leave something on your plate.

• If you're dining in a home for the first time, leave about an hour after the meal is over. Good friends may stay longer.

Eating Out

• Anticipate a variety of international restaurants only in large cities. Quito has the best selection of Italian, French, and Chinese restaurants. Only in Quito and Guayaquil will you find many snack bars and fast-food places for pizza, fried chicken, and hamburgers.

• In Quito, you'll find pastry shops as well as sidewalk cafes where tourists and young people congregate.

• To find a Chinese restaurant, ask for a *chifa* (**chee**-fah).

• A *pollo a la brasa* specializes in fried chicken.

• *Parrilladas* are steak houses or grills. Chicken, liver, pork chops, steaks, and tripe are served on a grill, which is placed on the table. If you don't want the whole mixed grill, ask for just the item or items you do want—e.g., *sólo pollo* (**soh**-loh **poh**-yoh), just chicken.

• Don't plan to read the menu before entering a restaurant. Menus aren't posted outside.

• Enter the restaurant and choose your own table, but don't join others whom you don't know. Only in very expensive French and Italian restaurants are guests seated by a maître d'.

• Anticipate finding restaurants open seven days a week, with dinner served until 11:00 P.M.—sometimes later. People don't usually go out to dinner until 8:30 P.M.

• If eggs are your breakfast staple, note that while they are available, boiled and poached eggs are usually presented barely cooked. Ask for them *bien cocidos* (byen koh-**see**-dohs), well cooked.

• Call the waiter *señor* (seh-**nyohr**), *mesero* (meh-**seh**-roh), or *mozo* (**moh**-soh). The latter two both mean "waiter." Though you will see some people clap their hands over their head to summon the waiter, realize that it's considered rude.

• Be aware that imported liquor is extremely expensive. Drink Ecuadoran beer, which is very good, or imported Chilean wines, which aren't as expensive as those from Europe. *Pisco* is akin to rum. *Aguardiente* (a drink like schnapps or *eau-de-vie*), anise-flavored and mixed with lemon, is called *paico* (**py**-koh). Sangria is another common beverage in restaurants.

• For mineral water, look for *Guitig* (**wee**-teek). It's good and it's fairly inexpensive. If no shops are available, you'll have to ask for it in a restaurant. You can't remove bottled water from restaurants (i.e., to take on a bus or train trip). Bring a canteen, a thermos, or a plastic bottle if you want to take water with you from a restaurant.

• Don't suggest separate checks or splitting the check. Ecuadorans consider it insulting to pay individually. One person pays for everyone.

• If you eat at a lower-class restaurant, don't be surprised to see children hang around to eat your leftovers. It's a common (and accepted) practice.

Specialties

• Note that the most commonly used herb is fresh coriander leaf;

in Spanish, it's known as *cilantro* (see-**lahn**-troh).

• Soups are called *caldos, sopas,* or *locro. Caldo de gallina* is chicken soup. Somewhat heartier is a *seco,* a stew. *Seco de gallina* is chicken stew, while *seco de cordero* is lamb stew.

• Three fish dishes: *ceviche,* raw fish marinated in lime, onion, and coriander; *corvina,* white sea bass; *trucha,* trout, which is widely available.

• Other specialties: *yaguarlocro,* potato soup with blood sausage; *lechón,* suckling pig; *tostadas de maíz,* fried corn pancakes; *humitas,* corn *tamales,* especially popular at breakfast; *patacones,* fried plaintains with cheese.

HOTELS

• Don't be surprised if you're charged extra in Quito hotels during the festival celebrating the foundation of the city (the week ending Dec. 5) and the New Year fiesta (Dec. 28 to Jan. 6). During those two periods, hotels are allowed to raise their rates.

• If you're staying in a smaller hotel in the highlands (Quito, for example), check to make sure that there is central heating. If not, make sure your room has a large supply of blankets.

• Expect parking problems if you arrive in Quito by car. To avoid them, choose a hᵣ cel outside the center of the city.

• Plan on a 10% service charge and a 5% tax being added to your bill in first- and second-class hotels.

TIPPING

• Be aware that in restaurants 15% is added to your bill for taxes and service, but you should add another 10 to 15% for the waiter.

• Give porters the equivalent of 50 cents.

• Don't tip taxi drivers, ushers, or gas station attendants.

PRIVATE HOMES

• Don't drop in on anyone during the siesta hour, 1:00 to 3:00 P.M.

• Realize that street numbers often don't go in sequence because houses are numbered according to the original building plot. If you're visiting a house, make sure that the host knows when you're coming so he can leave the entrance gate open. Gates are usually kept locked, and often bells don't work.

• Expect to see Indians standing on every street corner guarding the homes. The residents of the neighborhood pay them to stand watch.

• If you're staying with a family in which everyone works, arrange to sightsee on your own.

• Anticipate waiting for a supply of boiled water if you're a very early riser. Maids get up early to boil the day's supply of water for drinking and cooking. Never drink unboiled tap water.

• Should you stay with a family for several days, tip the maid the equivalent of $5.00 (U.S.). The maid will make your bed and do your laundry, which she will usually have ready for you the day after you give it to her.

• Don't put used toilet paper in the toilet. Put it in the basket next to the toilet.

• Be aware that there is no water or electricity after midnight in some areas.

• If the family you are staying with isn't wealthy, offer to help by buying groceries. Upper-class families appreciate a token gift.

Gifts: As thanks for an invitation to a meal, bring pastries, chocolates, or flowers. Don't give lilies or marigolds because they are associated with funerals.

• From outside the country, bring women clothing, perfume, nail polish, or hair ornaments. Men like high-tech gadgets, calculators, and after-shave lotion. To teenagers, give T-shirts or sweatshirts with English writing on them, popular music cassettes or records, or mousse or gel for the hair (it's very expensive in Ecuador).

• Exchange money in major cities because it's difficult to change money in smaller towns, and the rate there is lower. You can also change money at good restaurants and hotels.

BUSINESS

Hours

Businesses: 9:00 A.M. to 1:00 P.M. and 3:00 to 6:00 P.M., Monday through Friday.

Government Offices: 8:30 A.M. to 12:30 P.M. and 1:30 to 4:00 P.M., Monday through Friday.

Banks: 9:00 A.M. to 1:30 P.M., Monday through Friday.

Shops: 9:00 A.M. to 12:30 or 1:00 P.M. and 3:00 to 7:00 P.M., Monday through Friday; and 9:00 to noon, Saturday.

Currency

• The unit of currency is the *sucre* (written as S/), which consists of 100 *centavos*.
• Coins: 10, 20, and 50 *centavos*, and 1 *sucre*.
• Bills: 5, 10, 20, 50, 100, 500, and 1,000 *sucres*.

Business Practices

• Expect to make several trips to Ecuador to accomplish your business goals.
• Realize that it's important to have a lawyer or consultant as a contact in Ecuador.
• Avoid business travel during school vacations; they occur from mid-January through April in Guayaquil and mid-July through October in Quito.
• Arrange appointments two weeks in advance.
• Arrive one or two days before your business appointments begin to allow your body to adjust to the altitude. To minimize problems, avoid eating heavily or drinking alcohol.
• Schedule business appointments after 10:00 A.M.
• Be punctual, but be prepared to wait at least 20 minutes for your business meeting to begin.
• Have your business cards printed in Spanish. Bring a supply with you as it will take a week to have them printed in Ecuador.
• Have business proposals and other materials translated into

Spanish beforehand, since few people are really proficient in English.

• Note that there are photocopy machines and secretarial services easily available in Quito and Guayaquil, and most good hotels have telex machines.

• Be relaxed and easygoing when doing business. Ecuadorans are not formal and reserved as businesspeople.

• Realize that time estimates aren't very reliable. It's important to allow a certain margin for delays.

• Women should never be aggressive or argumentative. Be subtle and polite. Speak softly. Dress conservatively.

• Women will find it difficult to pay for a businessman's meal in a restaurant.

• A woman who is entertained by a business colleague should never have more than one alcoholic drink.

• Don't expect to be invited for a social drink after working hours.

• Realize that lunch is the most common meal for business discussions. Dinners are more formal, usually social occasions.

• Don't include spouses in invitations to business dinners. Ecuadorans consider business a man's affair.

• When you host a meal, take businesspeople to well-known restaurants that specialize in French or international cuisine.

HOLIDAYS AND SPECIAL OCCASIONS

Expect banks, businesses, and many stores to be closed on the following national holidays. Check with the tourist offices to learn about local holidays in regions you plan to visit.

Holidays: New Year's Day (Jan. 1); Epiphany (Jan. 6); Tuesday and Wednesday before Ash Wednesday, Holy Thursday; Good Friday; Labor Day (May 1); Pichincha Day, the anniversary of the Battle of Pichincha (May 24); Bolivar's Birthday (July 24); Independence Day (August 10); Columbus Day (Oct. 12); All Saints' Day (Nov. 1); All Souls' Day (Nov. 2); Christmas Eve and Christmas Day (Dec. 24 and 25).

• Note these holidays, since they take place in important areas: Guayaquil Day (Oct. 9); Cuenca Day (Nov. 3); Quito Day (Dec. 6).

• Enjoy dancing in the street in

Quito on the night of Dec. 5 (the night before Quito Day).

• If you're walking around during Carnival, wear waterproof clothing. People throw water balloons or pails of water at each other—and sometimes at tourists.

TRANSPORTATION

Public Transportation

• Note that there are no subways, even in the large cities.

• Be aware that buses are very crowded. Pay the fixed fare (no matter how far you're traveling) as you board. You don't receive a ticket. Buses, which always have a name and number, usually have a fixed route but may detour because of road repairs. One alternative to the crowded buses is a minibus. It costs slightly more.

• Negotiate the fare in advance with a taxi driver, since only some taxis have meters. You can hail taxis on the street, but at night it's better to telephone for one.

• Don't plan to travel by train.

There are no trains except for a small tourist service offered by a local travel agency.

• Should you plan to travel by train in the country, check when you arrive to see what is operating. The severe floods of 1983 and the earthquake of 1987 damaged much of the railway system.

• Note that long-distance buses don't have different classes of seating. Tickets are available at the bus terminal sometime between a few days and a few hours before departure. If you buy a ticket, you're assured a seat. Along the way, the driver may pick up people who are going a short distance and who will be packed in—standing. Some companies are better and safer than others; Occidental and Tranesmeraldas are usually reliable.

• Consider traveling by plane within Ecuador. Domestic air service is very inexpensive. The small difference in price between planes and buses is well worth the expense. Planes may take a few minutes to make a journey which will take hours by bus.

• Don't expect planes or buses to adhere to (or even to have) schedules. They leave only when they are full.

Driving

• Drive *very* defensively. Ecuadoran drivers are aggressive and pay little attention to driving rules.

• Though seat belts are not required, wear them for safety—especially in the countryside.

• Be aware that people honk their horns constantly.

• As a foreigner, do *not* try to bribe a policeman if you are stopped for a traffic violation.

• Note that there are laws regarding drinking and driving, but they are not strict and are only sometimes enforced when an accident has occurred.

LEGAL MATTERS, SAFETY, AND HEALTH

• If you have something stolen, report it to the police, obtain a copy of the report (to use with your insurance company back home), and put the incident out of your mind. You'll get nowhere pursuing the matter in Ecuador.

• Prepare to bribe the postmaster if you expect to receive packages from abroad. He will not inform you that a package is waiting; you will have to estimate its date of arrival. After you've filled out many, many forms and been passed from one person to another and find that you aren't getting anywhere—offer some money.

• Keep in mind that coca leaves, which are legal in Peru and Bolivia, are illegal in Ecuador.

• Women shouldn't travel alone in Ecuador unless they can speak Spanish. It's best not to travel alone outside cities. If you're traveling in a small group in the countryside, be sure that at least one of the group speaks Spanish fairly well.

• In Quito and in certain sections of Guayaquil, a woman can safely take a taxi alone at night. Ask at your hotel what areas of the city are safe. Guayaquil is more dangerous at night than Quito. There's a very active "night life" in Guayaquil, whereas Quito is more conservative, and people don't go out so much at night.

• Women should *never* go to beach areas alone at night.

• Few Ecuadoran women go to restaurants alone. Most businesswomen prefer to have meals in their hotel.

• Note that Ecuadoran women never speak to strange men. If, as a foreigner, you speak to men— even casually—it will be interpreted as a signal that you are interested and available.

• Indians (40% of the population) present no threat to women traveling alone. They remain detached from travelers, from *meztizos,* and the coastal black population as well.

• For advice on medicine and hygiene products, see "Legal Matters, Safety, and Health" in the Introduction.

GUATEMALA

What happened to the Maya, one of the most mathematically sophisticated civilizations ever? We can date the fall of Rome and the conquest of the Aztecs, but the Maya seem to have slipped away into the mists of time. Guatemala holds some of the most intriguing clues they left behind, especially in the greatest of the Mayan cities, Tikal, which the dense jungle made inaccessible until recently.

Though the Spanish arrived there in 1523, Guatemala (in contrast with the other countries of Central America) is still largely Indian in culture and language.

GREETINGS

Language: In addition to Spanish, the official language of Guatemala, many Indian languages and dialects are spoken.

• Expect a handshake when you are introduced to a member of either sex.

• If you are a woman being introduced to another woman, don't be surprised if she pats your right forearm or shoulder rather than shaking hands. Return the gesture by patting her shoulder with your left hand.

• Don't expect—or give—a firm handshake. Such handshakes are for those from urban areas or those who are Americanized. Men and women usually offer a limp handshake.

• Note that men and women who are good friends and women who are good friends often kiss on one cheek in greeting.

• Men who are good friends embrace and pat one another on the back.

• Remember that titles are very important. *Licenciado* (lee-sehn-syah-doh) is anyone with a college degree (e.g., B.A.). Use this title without the name, unless you're asking a question such as "Are you *Licenciado* Rodríguez?" Other titles: *Arquitecto* (architect); *Ingeniero* (engineer); *Doctor* (lawyer or medical doctor); *Profesor* (professor).

• Realize that at parties, people are always introduced individually. Shake hands with everyone.

• Note that in the highlands, it's courteous to say *"Buenos días"* ("Hello" or "Good morning"), *"Buenas tardes"* ("Good afternoon"), or *"Buenas noches"* ("Good evening") to anyone you pass on a street or road. In the cities, don't say anything to passersby.

CONVERSATION

• Learn about Guatemala before you visit the country, so that you can show an interest in the country's people, history, and culture.

• A good subject for conversation is travel—within Guatemala and abroad.

• Talk about children, your hobbies, and your job.

• Don't be surprised if people ask about your job and marital status on very short acquaintance.

• Avoid discussing politics or "the violence" (of which Guatemala has suffered a great deal since 1978).

• If you are talking to a man and a woman and ask a question, expect the man to answer it. You'll find this attitude especially prevalent in the indigenous population. If you want to talk seriously to a woman, wait until she is alone.

• Never discuss anything relating to sexuality with a woman when a man is present.

TELEPHONES

• Keep in mind that you'll find public telephones only in a few large cities (i.e., Guatemala City, Antigua, Quetzaltenango). In those cities, look for phones in pharmacies and hotel lobbies. Deposit several coins (5, 10, or 25 centavos) if you wish to speak longer than three minutes, since you'll be cut off if you haven't deposited enough. If you deposit more than you need for your call, money will be returned.

• To make long-distance calls, go to an office of GUATEL, the telephone company.

IN PUBLIC

• Speak softly; otherwise people will consider you very rude.

• Carry small change to give to beggars, who are usually physically handicapped people. Guatemalans themselves often give to beggars.

• To gesture "Come here," stretch your arm out, palm down, and wave your fingers.

• To wave good-bye, raise your arm with the palm facing you, and wave your fingers together back and forth.

• Don't photograph religious ceremonies (unless they are public fiestas) without asking the permission of the people involved.

• Never photograph any private home or property or business without asking permission from the owner—even if you see others taking pictures.

• In certain villages, especially in the lake district, anticipate a request for payment if you wish to take someone's picture. The person will ask for the equivalent of five or ten cents. Don't begrudge the money, since the economic situation—especially for Indians—is extremely difficult.

• Expect to bargain in markets, antique shops, and other small shops. Ask the price. Offer half. Wait for a counter offer, and keep going up a bit. If the vendor's final offer is too much, walk away. You may be called back and offered the vendor's lowest price, or he or she may not call you back. If you really want the object, go back and agree to the lowest price the vendor offered.

• Note that the most popular items for tourists are those which are handwoven by Indians. When bargaining for them, remember the months of work that have gone into the pieces and the extremely poor economic situations of the people.

• To find a public bathroom in a city, go to the town hall, restaurants, or hotels. In the country-side, go to a service station if you're near one (they often have clean bathrooms).

DRESS

• For casual occasions, don't wear shorts in the cities or the highlands. Don't wear jeans in cities. Men should wear pants and shirts (and sweaters in the highlands). Women should wear a skirt and blouse. Indians may be offended by seeing women wearing pants. If you must wear pants, wear a skirt over them.

• Women should avoid wearing revealing dresses.

• For business, men should wear a lightweight suit, in either a light or dark color. Women should wear a dress or skirt and blouse—never pants.

• When invited to a meal in a home, men should wear a jacket and trousers but no tie (ties are considered very formal) and women should wear a dress or skirt and dressy blouse.

• Formal wear—i.e., tuxedos for men—is worn only for certain weddings and diplomatic receptions.

• Note that each village has its own hand-loomed clothing for men and women. If you decide to wear native dress, be sure you're wearing the costume for the correct sex. Otherwise you'll make a fool of yourself. Embroidered pants are for men only, and the blouses called *huipiles* are for women.

MEALS

Hours and Foods

Breakfast: 7:00 to 8:00 A.M. The meal usually consists of eggs, black beans, bread, orange juice, and coffee.

Lunch: 12:30 or 1:00 P.M. Many homes will have soup, meat with vegetables (usually boiled) or salad, followed by fruit and coffee. Lunch in a traditional home consists of black beans, tortillas, and fried plaintains.

Dinner: 7:00 P.M., 8:00 P.M., or later. The meal will be much the same as lunch, but lighter. There might be black beans, rice, and fried plaintains;

or corn *tortillas,* tamales, and salad; or eggs with *tortillas* and beans.

Beverages: The most popular liquors are *ron* (rum) and *aguardiente* made from distilled sugarcane. Note that imported liquors are very expensive, while Guatemalan beer is excellent.

• Common drinks before dinner are *Cuba libre* (rum and Coke) and Scotch.
• With meals people drink soda, fruit juices, or beer. Wine is only for elegant meals. After dinner the drink is always coffee.
• Popular drinks in homes are two hot drinks—*atole de maíz,* made with corn, and *atole de arroz,* made with rice. Both are boiled, so tourists will have no problems with them.

Table Manners

• Women should never have more than one drink before dinner.
• With drinks before dinner, expect appetizers called *boquitas*—crackers, olives, peanuts.
• Note that female guests sit to the right of the host and male guests to his left.
• Note that in some families a maid will serve each person individually while in others you will help yourself from platters on the table.

• Realize that you're expected to finish everything on your plate. If food is served "family style," take small portions the first time. People will appreciate it if you take seconds.

• After every meal expect everyone to say—either individually or together—*"Muchas gracias"* ("Thank you") or *"Buen provecho"* (bwehn proh-**veh**-choh), which is often said before a meal, much like "Good appetite," but actually means, roughly, "May it do you good."

• On week nights, stay until about 11:00 P.M. On weekends feel free to stay until midnight.

Eating Out

• In Guatemala, a *restaurante* is a high-class restaurant. A *comedor* is a small eating place serving typical Guatemalan food. A *bar/cantina* offers alcoholic beverages. For pastries to take out, visit a *pastelería;* a *café* offers sandwiches, coffee, tea, and hot chocolate in addition to pastries. For bread and rolls to take out, look for a *panadería.*

• Anticipate a large choice of restaurants in Guatemala City, where there are many German, French, Italian, Oriental, Mexican, and Spanish restaurants.

• Expect to find menus posted outside only at lower-class restaurants.

• Men should note that many better restaurants require them to wear a jacket and tie.

• To attract the waiter's attention, raise your hand. At informal restaurants, people summon the waiter or waitress by saying "Tch, tch." Never do it in an elegant restaurant.

• At an inexpensive restaurant, don't expect good coffee. It's usually very weak because it's made with inferior beans; at better restaurants, the coffee is excellent. Note that if you order coffee with milk, half the cup will be filled with hot milk. At some restaurants you'll be served a pot of coffee and a pot of hot milk to mix yourself.

• Call the waiter to request the check. It won't be brought automatically.

• Note that there are no set rules or customs about whether one person pays for a group or whether each person pays individually. Offer to pay your share. If one person absolutely insists on paying, let her or him do it, and then reciprocate. If a group goes out for drinks and not a meal, then each person usually buys a "round."

Specialties

• Try some of the following special dishes: *plátanos fritos*—fried plaintains; *guacamole*—mashed avocado with onions and tomatoes; *chiles rellenos*—stuffed peppers;

carne guisada—stewed beef in a sauce; *chuchitos*—corn dough stuffed with meat and sauce and then wrapped in a corn husk; *chirmol*—a sauce of onions, tomatoes, and spices served with grilled steak.

HOTELS

• For the peak seasons—January, Easter, August, and December—be sure to make reservations well in advance.

• Realize that deluxe and first-class hotels have different prices for Guatemalans and foreigners. Moderately priced hotels, which are often clean and well run, don't raise their prices for foreigners.

• Check a guidebook for names of inns in various towns. Some have fireplaces in rooms, antiques, room service, and swimming pools. They are small and are much more interesting than the large, anonymous hotels.

• Expect international cuisine in the restaurants of deluxe and first-class hotels.

TIPPING

• Note that a service charge is *not* included in a restaurant bill. Leave 10 to 15%.

• Give porters the equivalent of $1.00 per bag.

• Tip gas station attendants who perform extra service 25 or 50 cents.

• Don't tip ushers.

• Give boys who carry parcels out of the markets 25 cents.

PRIVATE HOMES

• Call before visiting unless you know people extremely well. The usual time for visiting is after dinner and on weekends.

• If you're staying with a family,

be aware that meal times are extremely important, and people will be upset if you are late, especially for the midday meal when fathers usually come home from work and children from school.

• Be sure to pay for international calls made from a private home. It isn't necessary to pay for local calls.

• Since there are different types of heaters for showers, be sure to ask your hosts how to use the one in their house. Don't try to use one without asking; you could get an electric shock.

• If you stay with a family for a week or more, and there is a maid, tip her the equivalent of $5.00 for each week of your stay at the end of your visit. Just hand her the money.

• If you want to go hiking in the mountains, whether you're a man or woman, your hosts will probably object strongly, fearing that the guerrillas may harm you. You should probably abide by your hosts' wishes.

Gifts: When invited to a meal, bring a bottle of imported wine or flowers. Don't bring white flowers, as they are associated with funerals.

• From the U.S. or Europe, bring the latest gadgets (e.g., watches, small tape recorders), the latest best-sellers (for people you know read English), or liquor.

• For business, bring a bottle of cognac or wine—but not on your first visit. (See advice in "Business" section.)

BUSINESS

Hours

Businesses: Monday to Friday, 8:00 A.M. to noon, and 2:00 to 6:00 P.M.

Government Offices: Monday to Friday, 8:00 A.M. to 4:30 P.M., or 9:00 A.M. to 3:30 P.M. No closing for lunch.

Banks: Monday to Friday, 9:00 A.M. to 3:00 P.M.

Shops: Monday to Saturday, 9:00 A.M. to 1:00 P.M., and 3:00 to 7:00 P.M.

Currency

• Note that the unit of currency is the *quetzal.* One *quetzal* contains 100 *centavos.*

• Coins: 1, 5, 10, and 25 *centavos*.

• Bills: 50 *centavos* and 1, 5, 10, 20, 50, and 100 *quetzales*.

• Change money in Guatemala City, where banks give a better exchange rate than do those in other parts of the country.

• Note that major credit cards are accepted by large hotels, restaurants, retail stores, airlines, and car rental agencies.

• Don't be surprised if there is a shortage of small change. If you need change for a tip or a phone call you may not be able to get it, or someone to whom you hand a bill may say, "I don't have any change."

• Don't accept a torn bill if someone tries to give you one, because many places will not accept one from you.

• Be aware that you cannot change *quetzales* into dollars when you leave Guatemala. Don't change more dollars into *quetzales* than you'll be able to use during your visit.

Business Practices

• Realize that contacts are important. Obtain them through your embassy, A.I.D. (U.S.'s Agency for International Development), or shippers. Sometimes you can make personal contacts at conferences for people in your business.

• Prepare to make several trips to Guatemala to achieve your goal.

• Avoid business trips in January, April, August, November, and December. Many businesspeople vacation in August, and during the two weeks before and after Christmas and the week before and after Easter. Also avoid the two-to-three-day celebration around Independence Day (Sept. 15).

• From abroad, make appointments at least two weeks in advance. If you're in the country, a few days will be enough.

• Be punctual, as businesspeople usually are in Guatemala.

• Don't feel obliged to have business cards translated into Spanish; however, materials for use outside the office (e.g., manuals on how to operate machinery) should be translated into Spanish.

• Remember that you must establish a personal relationship with a Guatemalan businessperson before discussing business. He or she will want to know about you and your background.

• Ask questions quietly, and be patient. Never raise your voice or insult anyone.

• Expect delays. They may be caused by the country's frequent power shortages.

• Note that although there are women involved in business in Guatemala, it's still unusual to find them in a company's upper echelons.

• Don't bring gifts on your first business trip, but for subsequent trips ask people what they would like from abroad. (One businessman requested American cereal for his children, another asked for unsalted peanuts, and a third wanted razor blades.)

• If a colleague invites you home to a meal, don't discuss business there.

• Note that business lunches and even breakfasts are more popular than dinners.

• If your spouse is accompanying you on business, invite your Guatemalan counterpart and his or her spouse to a social dinner in a restaurant.

HOLIDAYS AND SPECIAL OCCASIONS

• On the following holidays, banks, businesses, government offices, most stores, and many restaurants will be closed. Before visiting an area, check with the tourist office to learn if there are local holidays or religious festivals that will result in closings.

Holidays: New Year's Day (Jan. 1), Easter week (Weds., Thurs., and Fri. before Easter), Labor Day (May 1), Army Day (June 30), Assumption Day (August 15), Independence Day (Sept. 15), Revolution Day (Oct. 20), All Saints' Day (Nov. 1), Christmas Eve and Christmas Day (Dec. 24 and 25), Last Year's Day (Dec. 31).

• Expect a strange mixture of moods on November 1. People go to cemeteries to pay respects to the dead. It's a serious day, but in the evening people go out to cinemas or some other entertainment.

TRANSPORTATION

Public Transportation

• Enter local buses from the front. Pay on the bus. You don't need exact change. Keep your ticket because there are sometimes inspectors who check them.

• Note that during Holy Week bus fares may be doubled. Avoid travel on Good Friday, when everyone goes home to their family for Easter.

• Don't expect to find subways in Guatemala.

• After buses have stopped running, look for a *ruletero;* they run along fixed routes and charge a fare based on distance. Stand on a street corner and wait for one to come by. If a driver stops, ask *"¿Taxi o ruletero?"* since the two look exactly alike.

• Be aware that taxis have no meters. Negotiate the fare in advance.

• Note that for long-distance travel, there are first- and second-class buses. For first-class buses, you can go to a bus station, buy your ticket, and reserve a seat in advance. First-class buses are usually old U.S. Greyhound buses. They have bathrooms, which usually don't work. Second-class buses, which are like old school buses, don't have reserved seats, and people squeeze on. Buses make bathroom stops and will stop if necessary. If you need to go to the bathroom between stops, however, you probably won't have toilet facilities—just the space behind the bus.

• Unless you're a train buff,

avoid the country's one train—a banana train that runs from Guatemala City to Puerto Barrios on the Atlantic coast. The trip takes up to 21 hours while the bus takes only 6 hours. No food is served. Soft drinks, beer, and sandwiches are available.

Driving

• Note that traffic lights are turned off after 8:00 P.M. When they are off, traffic on *avenidas* (avenues) has the right of way over traffic on *calles* (streets).

• If you want to see the countryside, consider driving, during the day. Roads are good, and there are adequate signs.

• Don't drive after dark. There aren't any street lights. There are drunken drivers. People drive without headlights.

• Stay off the roads on Sundays and market days, when you're more likely to encounter drunk drivers.

• Always carry your passport. There are army checkpoints on main roads. You must stop at them. Look for signs that say "ALTO" (stop).

• If you're driving near military vehicles, stay 200 meters in front of or behind them.

LEGAL MATTERS, SAFETY, AND HEALTH

• As mentioned above, carry your passport at all times.

• Don't carry pocket knives. They're illegal weapons.

• Note that it's illegal to wear military-style clothing or to bring such clothing into the country.

• If you make several trips to Guatemala and see the same customs official every time, be polite and courteous, but *never* offer him money to expedite matters.

• Beware of pickpockets; men and women should wear a money belt, or men should carry their wallets in their front pants pocket. A woman should be aware that thieves are known to slash purses.

• Be aware that earthquakes are frequent, but they are usually minor. If there is a major earthquake, go outside, or stand in a doorway.

• Remember to drink only bottled water. Milk and cheese in inexpensive restaurants are usually not pasteurized, but milk in better restaurants may be. Be sure that any meat you eat is well done. Don't eat fruits or vegetables that can't be peeled, or any uncooked vegetables.

• For advice on medicines and hygiene products, see "Legal Matters, Safety, and Health" in the Introduction.

MEXICO

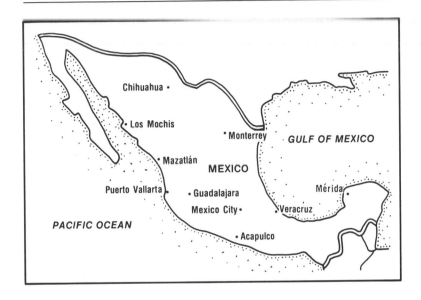

We visit Mexico for many reasons. Some want to worship the sun in Acapulco, Puerto Vallarta, or Cancún. Some go to explore the great Indian civilizations—Maya, Aztec, Toltec—at one of the world's outstanding museums, the Museum of Anthropology in Mexico City's Chapultepec Park, or in the great ruins of Yucatán. Others want the exquisite silver of Taxco and San Miguel de Allende.

Whatever your reason for visiting, it's hard to be disappointed, except by the dreadful pollution in Mexico City. As one visitor commented about the city's air, "It was like vacationing in a tunnel."

Sometimes one can fully forget the air pollution, as at Christmastime when the Paseo de la Reforma is festooned with garlands and decorated with statues of children, or on Sundays when Chapultepec Park explodes with festive people, or when the gardens at Xochimilco are a mass of blooms.

GREETINGS

Language: Mexico's official language is Spanish.

• Note that both men and women shake hands when being introduced to someone of the same sex. A man being introduced to a woman will bow slightly; he will shake hands only if the woman initiates the gesture.

• Be aware that among good friends, women kiss on the cheek, and men and women who are good friends often kiss.

• Note that Mexican males who are good friends often embrace when they meet. Don't be the first to make this gesture. Allow your Mexican friend to begin.

• Don't use first names even after two or three meetings.

• At a party, bow slightly when you enter the room. Then go to each person and shake hands. Usually your host will come with you to make introductions. When you leave, shake hands with each person, addressing her or him as *Señor, Señora,* or *Señorita.*

• In business, use the title and last name with senior managers, e.g., *Doctor, Director,* and *Ingeniero* (engineer). After you have worked with the person a while, use just the title without the last name. *Licenciado* (lee-sehn-**syah**-doh) is used very commonly, to refer to any person who has received any degree of higher education.

CONVERSATION

• To make a good impression, learn something about Mexican art and literature.

• Note that Mexicans are impressed by university degrees, so mention yours if you have one.

• Good conversation openers are your home area, your school, your job. Try to find points in common, such as a mutual interest in travel or film.

• Be aware that Mexicans are rather open in discussing personal feelings. They often regard North American reluctance to do so as insensitive or unfriendly.

• Men should not withdraw

from a Mexican male's expressions of warmth and friendliness, such as touching you on the shoulder, holding your arm, or touching your lapel. To shrink from such gestures is insulting.

• Don't criticize the Mexican government or suggest possible improvements in it. Be sure to avoid mentioning illegal aliens or the U.S.'s Mexican War. Be aware that the present-day states of Texas, California, Nevada, Utah, Colorado, New Mexico, and Arizona were part of Mexico until the late 1840s.

• If you're from the U.S., refer to yourself as a North American (*norteamericano,* masculine; *norteamericana,* feminine), or as from the United States (*de los Estados Unidos* [deh lohs ehs-**tah**-dohs oo-nee-dohs]). Don't forget that Mexico is just as much a part of the American continent as the United States.

• Be careful of behavior or remarks that could be construed as insults to a person's dignity—e.g., not saying good-bye to a person, expressing distaste for the food, implying to a man in some way that his sister's morals aren't all that they should be. Mexicans consider such remarks serious provocations and would end either a personal or business relationship because of one.

• Steer away from subjects related to money, e.g., salary, prices. Don't ask what someone paid for something.

• Never make denigratory remarks about Indians. Mexicans play down racial differences, and Mexican Indians exert a strong influence on political and social life. (Only 10% of Mexicans are pure Caucasian.) An oddity: While Mexicans will go out of their way to show you the achievements of the Maya and the Aztecs, many don't want you to think that there is any Indian blood in their personal background. Don't say, "You look Indian" or "Are you part Indian?"

• Be sure that you *never* tell an off-color joke in the presence of a woman.

TELEPHONES

• Remember that public telephones in Mexico City have been free since the earthquake of 1984. Not all phones work, however. You can ask to use the phone in a shop—especially if you buy something.

• If you will be making long-distance calls, ask at your hotel if there is a surcharge. If there is, and you don't want to pay it, go to a public telephone office, Teléfonos de México.

• To use a public telephone, put a 20-*centavo*, 50-*centavo*, or 1-*peso* coin in the slot. Dial. The coin will drop when the phone is answered. To continue the call after three minutes (when you will hear a tone), deposit another coin. There's no refund if you overpay, but public phone calls are so cheap that it doesn't really matter.

• Be prepared for erratic telephone service in small towns. Heavy rains or other abnormal weather conditions often cause disruptions.

IN PUBLIC

• Don't be surprised if someone hisses "psst-psst" to you. It's the common way to get attention and isn't considered impolite.

• In giving someone an item such as money or keys, always hand it to the person. It's very rude to throw or toss it. When paying, always place the money in the cashier's hand rather than on the counter.

• Men should not put their hands in their pockets in public.

• Note that putting your hands on your hips signifies a challenge or threat.

• Be aware that "first come" doesn't always mean "first served." Great deference may be shown to someone because of age, position, or social status. Don't express annoyance at another being served first.

• Remember that asking Mexicans for information will always produce an answer designed to please you by telling you what they think you want to hear, though it may be far from the truth. For example, don't say "Is the train station that way?" because a Mexican will most certainly say "Yes," whether it is or not. Ask "Where is the train station?" and then continue to ask people along the way.

• Be cautious in expressing admiration for objects. The owner may feel obliged to give it to you.

• Note two important expressions about time: To give the time and add *a la gringa* means to be strictly punctual. Time *a la mexicana* implies a less precise punctuality.

• Be aware that anyone who has decision-making power could take a bribe. Be discreet, and protect the person to whom you're giving the bribe. For example, if you're stopped for speeding, slip the money into the policeman's pocket and say, "This is for your beer." YOU must offer the bribe; don't expect someone to ask for it. Be very polite.

• Always ask permission before photographing anyone—even vendors, beggars, and children. Be especially sure to ask Indians before photographing them, because they often resent being regarded as anthropological objects. After taking the picture, give your subject a few *pesos*.

• Don't photograph the subway in Mexico City, or military installations.

• Note that there are no public bathrooms. If you need one, go to a department store, museum, hotel, or restaurant (even if you're not a customer there). In the countryside bring tissues, because there probably won't be any toilet paper.

Shopping: Remember that you can bargain virtually everywhere. Someone who doesn't bargain and pays the first asking price is considered very foolish. Mexicans regard such people as ignorant and even unfriendly.

• Never become angry when bargaining; it's supposed to be a game.

• If you and the seller agree on a price, and you buy the item, you may conclude the deal by shaking hands.

DRESS

• When choosing your wardrobe for a visit to Mexico, keep in mind that clothing is more conservative than in the U.S. and is strongly influenced by European fashion.

• For business, men should wear dark suits, ties, and black shoes. Women should wear nice dresses or suits accented with jewelry and should be sure to wear makeup and heels. Men shouldn't remove jackets or loosen ties unless their host suggests it.

• Casual wear for men is shirt and pants; for women, it's a skirt and blouse. Don't wear shorts except in resort areas such as Cancún and Acapulco.

• Note that jeans are one step below casual wear. Always well-tailored, clean, and pressed, they are worn mainly when city people go to the country.

• If you're invited to a home for dinner, wear business clothes on a first visit.

• Never wear shorts or halter tops when visiting a church. Some churches have signs indicating that you won't be admitted in such an outfit.

• Note that Mexicans appreciate foreign men wearing a *guayabera*— a shirt worn over trousers, used during the hot summer months. Especially outside of Mexico City, they are acceptable for social occasions, including dinner in a restaurant and even as business wear. There are simple ones for everyday wear and others with lace and heavy embroidery, which are worn for formal occasions.

• Traditional formal wear for men is tuxedos and, for women, long dresses. The major occasions for such costumes are evening and night weddings and diplomatic functions. Invitations don't specify formal dress, so it's wise to ask the person who issued the invitation what the appropriate dress is.

MEALS

Hours and Foods

• First, a few words on food safety. Don't drink tap water. (Many hotels leave sealed bottled water in your room, but be sure that the seal is intact.) If you're not confident of the water quality in the hotel, buy a brand of bottled water with which you're familiar (e.g., Tehuacán) at a supermarket or liquor store. It's safe to drink fruit juices if no water or ice has been added. Don't eat vegetables or fruit that you can't peel. Avoid lettuce and green salads. Avoid all raw shellfish. Don't eat custards or mayonnaise unless you're sure that they have been refrigerated. Never buy cooked food from street vendors.

Breakfast: Between 7:30 and 9:00 A.M., it consists of bread or tortillas, fried beans, eggs, and coffee; or "continental-style" biscuits, fruits, and coffee.

Lunch: Usually the day's largest meal, from 1:30 to 3:30 P.M.

The first course is often soup; followed by a course of meat, rice, vegetables, and beans; followed by a dessert of fruit or *flan* (custard), and coffee. Tortillas are usually served with the meal. Usual beverages are beer, wine, fruit juices (e.g., tamarind juice, watermelon juice), and lemonade.

• Apart from custom, the altitude of Mexico City and its effect on your digestive system make it wise to eat your heaviest meal around midday.

• Around 5:00 P.M., expect *merienda*—a snack of tea, coffee, juices, pastries, and *pan dulce* (sweet bread).

Dinner: A late and light meal. In a home, dinner will be served between 8:00 and 10:00 P.M. There may be a soup, tamales, or beans with cheese. With the meal, people drink water or fruit juice; afterward, they have coffee.

• If a salad is served, expect it after the main course.

• Prepare to be offered a drink of *mezcal* (mehs-**cahl**), a liquor made from the maguey plant, after dinner. It is somewhat like aquavit, grappa, or brandy. Don't be surprised to see a worm in the bottle. When they polish off the bottle, Mexicans often eat the worm!

• To drink tequila as the Mexi-cans do, follow these four steps (a dish of salt and a slice of lime will be served with the tequila): (1) put a pinch of salt on the back of your left hand, in the hollow between the thumb and index finger; (2) lick the salt; (3) with the right hand, take the glass of tequila and drink it all; (4) suck on the piece of lime.

• Note that popular beverages are coffee, often made with hot milk and cinnamon; chocolate; beer; and tequila, which is made from the maguey plant.

• If your beer bottle has an indentation in the bottom, it's to remove the top from another bottle.

Table Manners

• If you're invited to a home for a meal, expect drinks in the living room first—usually a choice of whiskey, Cuba libre (rum and Coke), or *tequila*. Hors d'oeuvres will probably be *chicharrón* (pork crackling with a piquant sauce), nuts, and guacamole with fried tortilla chips.

• If you decide to hold a cocktail party, remember that it's *very* important to have large quantities of hors d'oeuvres.

• If the meal is formal or semiformal, expect courses to be served one at a time. At a casual meal, all the dishes will be put on the table at once.

• Before a meal, say *"Buen provecho"* (bwehn proh-**veh**-choh), which is like "bon appetit," but actually means "May it benefit you."

• Don't be surprised to see people—especially in informal settings—using *tortillas* to scoop up food.

• To eat a *tortilla* plain, salt it, roll it up into a tube, and eat it with your fingers. If you want to put a filling into it, place the *tortilla* in your palm, add the filling, and then fold the *tortilla*. In homes and casual restaurants, people push food onto the fork with a *tortilla*.

• Note that people expect you to try some of everything when you're invited to a meal, but they will understand if foreigners don't care for certain dishes such as tripe or hot peppers (or if they can't eat them for medical reasons). There isn't in Mexico the European expectation that you finish everything on your plate.

• When eating spicy foods, relieve the burning sensation by having some rice or *tortilla*.

Eating Out

• Remember that most restaurants are open from 1:00 P.M. to 4:00 P.M. for lunch. The more elegant restaurants do not re-open for dinner until 9:00 P.M., but other restaurants re-open earlier.

• Note that a *cafetería* in Mexico is not a U.S.-style cafeteria; it offers different kinds of coffees. A *pastelería* serves European-style pastries, hors d'oeuvres, coffee, tea, and soft drinks. The familiar restaurant is a *restaurante* (rehs-tow-**rahn**-teh). *Cantinas* or *salones de cerveza* are bars, open from noon to 1:00 A.M. (closed on Sunday), where men drink. Women should never enter these bars.

• Choose from a wide variety of teas in most Mexican restaurants: *té de canela* (cinnamon tea), *té de limón* (lemongrass tea), *té de naranja* (orange-leaf tea), *té de pelo de elote* (corn silk tea), *té de yerbabuena* (mint tea), *té de manzanilla* (chamomile tea).

• Remember that the type of Mexican food familiar north of the border is a poor and monotonous cousin of the real thing; Mexico has a most varied native cuisine (see "Specialties"). In addition, Mexico City abounds in restaurants of many nationalities—French, Italian, British, German, Spanish, Argentine, and Asian.

• When making a reservation at an elegant restaurant, ask if they have a dress code. Very few places do, but it's best to be sure.

• Expect to be able to read a menu before you enter a restaurant. Sometimes it's posted outside and sometimes at the entrance.

• Note that some restaurants offer a *comida corrida* or *menú turistico* for a set price. It consists of six or seven courses served in sequence: cocktail, appetizer, salad, a main dish (beef, pork, or fish) with rice and beans on the side, dessert, and coffee or tea.

• Don't join strangers at their table, except in German-style restaurants, where you're expected to sit on long benches with others whom you don't know.

• Keep in mind that most elegant restaurants have a cover charge (*cubierto*), but it is usually small.

• Be sure to treat waiters as the professionals that they are. Don't make sounds to call them. You'll hear many people saying "Psst" to the waiter, but it's rude. Beckon with your finger or hand.

• Be prepared for slow service. Mexicans like to take their time at meals.

• Expect *tortillas* to be served with most meals. Feel free to ask for more, as there is usually no additional charge. Sometimes, if the staff realizes that you are a foreigner, they will bring you a French-type bread, thinking that you'll prefer it.

• Remember that imported drinks are extremely expensive in fashionable restaurants. To save money, order Mexican liquor (rum or tequila), beer, or wine.

• To order beer, ask for *"una cerveza"* (sehr-**veh**-sah) followed by *"clara"* (**clah**-rah) for light, *"oscura"* (ohs-**koo**-rah) for dark,

"semioscura" (seh-mee-ohs-**koo**-rah) for semi-dark, or *"de barril"* (deh bah-**rreel**) for draft.

• Don't be surprised if your empty beer bottles are left on the table. When you're ready to pay, the waiter will count them and charge accordingly.

• Be aware that the waiter will not bring the check until it's requested. Ask for *"la cuenta"* (lah **kwehn**-tah). Don't annoy the waiter by asking for separate checks.

• Expect an argument over the check, since one person always pays for the whole group. Not to show interest in paying for the group is very rude. In practice, however, the oldest person in the group almost always pays. (Paying shows how well he cares for others.) To show your appreciation for being treated to a meal, invite the person who paid to a meal and state in advance that you are treating since the other person treated last time.

• After paying, leave the small change on the table. A 15% service charge is included in the bill.

• Note that most restaurants in Mexico City—and many elsewhere—accept major credit cards.

Specialties

• You'll find some foods served throughout Mexico, while others are regional specialties. The national dish is *mole poblano de guajolote,* turkey in a sauce made with chiles, chocolate, herbs, and spices. *Sopas secas*—literally "dry soups"—refers to pastas or rice with sauce and is often served as a separate course following the soup course. *Guacamole* is mashed avocado with fresh coriander leaf, tomato, onion, and chile paste.

• Other dishes found throughout the country: *quesadillas,* tortillas folded like turnovers and filled with cheese; *chalupas,* fried flat tortillas covered with shredded chicken or pork, tomato sauce, onions, and white cheese; *tamales,* any of various fillings (e.g., chiles and cheese, *mole poblano,* or pork and sauce) rolled in cornmeal dough, wrapped in corn husks, and steamed; *huevos rancheros,* fried eggs with tomato and chile sauce; *cabrito,* roasted kid; *frijoles refritos,* cooked beans that are then mashed and fried (not really "refried" beans as commonly called).

• *Bolillos* are French rolls served all over Mexico.

• Dishes to try in northern Mexico (Monterrey, Chihuahua): *empanadas de picadillo,* minced beef turnovers with onions, potatoes, and spices; *machaca de Monterrey,* dried beef fried with onions, tomatoes, and chiles, mixed with scrambled eggs and all put into a flour tortilla.

• Along the East coast (Vera-

cruz, Tampico), look for: *jaibas en chilpachole,* crabs simmered in tomato broth and spices; *camarones a la plancha,* shrimp marinated in olive oil, parsley, and lime juice and then grilled; *carne asada a la tampiqueña,* grilled beef tenderloin with grilled zucchini, apples, onions and potatoes, served with enchiladas filled with white cheese and tomato sauce as well as *frijoles* and *guacamole; huachinango a la Veracruz,* red snapper with a sauce made of capers, tomatoes, onion, garlic, lime juice, and spices; *sopa de mariscos,* a seafood soup similar to bouillabaisse.

• Visitors to the Yucatán peninsula can look for these specialties: *huevos motuleños,* a popular breakfast dish consisting of corn tortillas with black beans, ham, fried eggs, and tomato sauce; *sopa de lima,* chicken and lime soup; *papadzul,* tortillas stuffed, rolled, and served with a pumpkin-seed sauce; *pámpano a la yucateca,* a fish, similar to flounder, marinated and broiled; *pollo pibil,* chicken marinated and grilled in banana leaves; *panuchos,* tortillas, filled with fried black beans and hard-boiled eggs, which are puffed during cooking; *coctel campechana marinera,* a cooked shrimp and raw oyster cocktail. In many dishes you'll find *achiote,* the seed of the annatto tree, used for both flavor and color; the hard seeds are soaked and usually made into a paste. Expect to find many meat and poultry dishes wrapped in banana leaves for steaming or baking.

• In the central highlands (Jalapa, Córdoba, Puebla, Cuernavaca, Toluca, and Mexico City), try: *sopa de calabaza,* squash soup with chicken stock, *chalupas de Puebla,* fried tortillas filled with pork and green chile sauce; *pollo borracho* (literally, "drunken chicken"), chicken fried in oil with a sauce of tequila, chiles, orange juice, and sausages; *postre de almendra,* cake filled with almond paste.

• If you travel to the South (Oaxaca, Mitla, San Cristóbal de las Casas), sample: *sopa de frijol negro,* black bean soup; *plátanos en rompope,* a dessert of bananas soaked in eggnog.

• The lakes area (Morelia, Guadalajara) offers: *sopa de albóndigas,* meatball soup; *chayotes rellenos,* a pear-shaped vegetable stuffed with white cheese, egg, and onion; *adobo rojo de lomo de cerdo,* pork loin in a sauce of chiles, spices, and garlic; *flautas de puerco,* pork in a tightly rolled, fried corn tortilla; *blanco de Pátzcuaro,* whitefish from Patzcuaro lake—deep-fried fish with onions simmered in oil and vinegar; *chongos,* rennet custard with cinnamon and vanilla.

• Along the southwestern coast (Puerto Ángel, Puerto Escondido, and Acapulco), you can eat: *ceviche,* marinated raw fish with onion, tomatoes, lime juice, chiles, and coriander; *sopa de aguacate,* avocado soup with chicken broth, sherry, and cream; *huachinango con ajo,* red snapper with garlic.

• Visiting the central west coast (Puerto Vallarta, Tepic, Mazatlán), sample: *pisto,* scrambled eggs with ham, zucchini, peas, and green onions; *huachinango en salsa de perejil,* red snapper in parsley sauce; *chilaquiles,* tortilla hash made with cheese, cream, and *salsa verde* (chiles, coriander, garlic, and green tomatoes).

• In the *Bajío* or lowlands (Guanajuato, San Miguel de Allende), expect these special dishes: *sopa de ajo,* garlic soup with a chicken broth base; *enchiladas verdes,* green enchiladas made with rolled corn tortillas with green tomatoes, chiles, chopped chicken, and cream; *flan,* caramel custard.

• Specialties of the northwest (Culiacán, Los Mochis, Hermosillo) are: *sopa de la cena,* a soup of pork spareribs, tomatoes, corn, chiles, bay leaf, onion, and oregano; *carne de res en chile colorado,* beef in red chile; *ensalada de nopalitos, nopal,* prickly pear cactus, onion, tomatoes, chile, coriander, and farmer cheese; *tortillas de harina,* white wheat flour tortillas, common in the north; *chimichangas,* deep fried *tortillas de harina* stuffed with beans, beef, chiles, and spices—and served with *crema* (sour cream) and *guacamole.*

HOTELS

• Book well in advance (at least a month) for the Christmas–New Year and Easter periods. February is the most popular time for resort areas.

• If you're driving, ask if your hotel charges for parking, since many in large cities do, while others offer free parking.

• If you have a reservation, and the clerk at the reception desk says that there are no rooms, wait patiently in the lobby. Don't show anger, but keep returning to the desk and saying something such as, "Have you found my reservation yet? I want to stay here. It's the most beautiful place I've ever seen."

• Bring a flashlight with you as electricity frequently goes off for a brief time. (Some hotels have candles in the rooms for such an emergency.)

• Note that in elevators *PB* (*planta baja*) means the ground floor.

• In better hotels, expect a small, well-stocked refrigerator.

You pay for the items used at the end of your stay. Usually they are very expensive. If you're staying in one place for a while, buy your own drinks and keep them in the refrigerator.

• Ask the concierge to get tickets if you wish to attend a bullfight. Seats in the shade are best, though they are also the most expensive. If you prefer to buy the tickets yourself, do so in advance.

• *Never* drink tap water or brush your teeth with it. Buy mineral water, called *agua mineral* (**ah**-gwah mee-neh-**rahl**), either carbonated, *con gas* (kon gahs), or noncarbonated, *sin gas* (seen gahs).

TIPPING

• Give porters and bellboys the equivalent of 50 cents (U.S.) for a load of two to three bags.

• Tip taxi drivers 50 cents.

• Tip chambermaids $1.00 per day.

• To ushers, gas station attendants, and washroom attendants, give 25 to 50 cents.

• Because of the high unemployment rate, people will approach you when you park and offer to watch your car, wash the windshield, etc. Give these car watchers 25 to 50 cents.

PRIVATE HOMES

• Keep in mind that Mexicans usually invite only close friends to their home.

• If you're invited to a meal in a home, plan to stay about 30 minutes after dinner on a weeknight, longer on a weekend. Note, however, that Mexicans don't measure a social engagement by time—if everyone is having a good visit, feel free to stay longer.

• Be reserved in admiring any object in a home. If you are very enthusiastic, your host may feel obliged to give it to you.

• If you're staying with a family ask about—and observe—the meal times. Be sure to get up and have breakfast with the family so that the servants don't have to serve you separately.

• When visiting a family, plan to go out for a few meals in order to lessen the imposition on them. Tell them the night or morning before, since most people buy fresh food every day. Or, you might invite the family to a restaurant to a meal.

• If you want the maid to do some task for you (e.g., your laundry), tip her about $2.00. Put the money in her apron or pocket, rather than handing it to her directly.

• When you leave, after staying with the family for a few days, tip the maid the equivalent of $1.00. Don't ask your hostess' advice about the amount or she'll tell you not to give a tip.

• Observe the way the family treats its servants, and act accordingly. In some homes the relationship is more formal than in others.

Gifts: When invited to a meal, bring European or American chocolates, imported wine or champagne, or pastries.

• If a business acquaintance invites you to dinner at home, send flowers ahead of time.

• Avoid marigolds, as they are used to decorate graves. Avoid giving red flowers, since they are used for casting spells.

• If you are invited to a fifteenth-birthday party for a girl, note that it's equivalent to a "sweet sixteen" party in the U.S. There is usually a large gathering at home or in a restaurant for male and female guests to celebrate the young woman's entrance into society. Appropriate gifts are jewelry or religious medals.

• Good gifts from abroad are U.S. cigarettes, lighters, silk ties, good quality "magic markers," and gadgets such as electric timers and electric can openers.

BUSINESS

Hours

Businesses: 9:00 or 10:00 A.M. to 1:00 or 2:00 P.M., and then 2:00 or 3:00 P.M. until 6:00 P.M., Monday through Friday.

Government Offices: 8:00 A.M. to 2:30 P.M., Monday through Friday.

Banks: 9:00 A.M. to 1:30 P.M., Monday through Friday. Some open again from 4:00 to 7:00 P.M. for limited services. (Many banks will not cash travelers' checks after 12:30 P.M.)

Shops: 10:00 A.M. to 1:00 P.M., and 3:00 to 8:00 P.M., Monday through Saturday; except in Mexico City, where there is no lunch-hour closing.

Currency

• Remember that the *peso* is divided into 100 *centavos*.

• Coins: 20 and 50 *centavos;* 5, 10, 20, 50 (this coin comes in two sizes, the smaller for use in public telephones), and 100 *pesos*.

• Bills: 50, 100, 500, 1,000, 5,000, and 10,000 *pesos*.

Business Practices

• Anticipate several trips to Mexico to complete your business satisfactorily. The first visit is a sort of "field trip," to secure contacts and make initial approaches to the companies with which you would like to deal.

• Don't plan business travel to Mexico between December 15 and January 6 or during Holy Week. If you'll be dealing with elected government officials, check to make sure that there's no upcoming election, during which they might be away from their offices campaigning.

• Before you initiate business, be in touch with the Commerce Division of the Mexican Consulate in the nearest large city to find out about Mexico's rather strict laws on foreign investment.

• When you make an initial contact, have your letter written in Spanish, but mention that you don't speak Spanish (if that is the case).

• Make your first contact with the top person in the company. The initial approach should be from a top manager in a foreign firm to a top manager in a Mexican firm. The foreign top manager should make the trip to Mexico accompanied by members of the firm's staff.

• Remember that it helps enormously to have a contact in Mexico or a letter of introduction. If you don't, write to your country's Chamber of Commerce in Mexico City. Other sources of contacts: your bank, which may have a correspondent in Mexico; the Confederation of National Chambers of Industry, to which most large businesses belong and which can tell you names of top managers in Mexican firms; your embassy in Mexico.

• Note that all of the country's major businesses have offices in Mexico City.

• Make appointments at least two weeks in advance; however, don't be surprised if government officials re-schedule appointments at the last minute.

• After setting up an appointment from abroad, let your Mexican counterpart decide the time and place of the meeting. He may suggest a breakfast, lunch, or dinner meeting.

• Plan to arrive a day or two before your first scheduled appointment to acclimate yourself to the altitude and to reconfirm appointments. To minimize difficulties from the altitude, eat lightly, and don't drink alcohol or smoke.

• On a business trip, be sure to stay at the best possible hotel. It is one element in enhancing your prestige in the eyes of Mexicans. They will also notice in what restaurants you eat, how you dress, what kind of watch you wear, and so forth.

• Be aware that business offices officially open at 9:00 A.M., but you probably won't find anyone there at that time.

• Try to make appointments for some time between 10:00 A.M. and 1:00 P.M. A second choice is late afternoon. In Mexico City, allow 30 minutes more than you think you'll need between appointments; there are constant traffic jams.

• Don't be surprised if people schedule appointments at uncommon hours—e.g., 8:30 P.M.

• Consider it a plus if a Mexican colleague suggests a breakfast meeting at 8:00 or 8:30 A.M. It will probably be at your hotel, the meeting will probably be short, and there won't be any drinking—so you won't suffer the effects of altitude on one who drinks or overeats.

• Note that executives and managers do not work on Saturdays, though many factories are open for half the day or all day.

• On the second or third meeting with Mexican businessmen, men should be prepared for an *abrazo*—an embrace accompanied by two or three pats on the back and a handshake. Such a gesture does not, however, mean that you can call the person by his first name. Don't use first names until your Mexican colleague initiates it.

• Be sure to use a person's title; it is a very important part of business protocol. Some common titles: *Doctor* (doc-**tohr**), *Profesor* (proh-feh-**sohr**), *Químico*—chemist (**kee**-mee-coh), *Ingeniero*—engineer (een-heh-**nyeh**-roh), *Arquitecto*—architect (ahr-kee-tek-toh). "Lic." (an abbreviation for *Licenciado*) following a person's name in writing means that he or she has a bachelor's degree.

• Always refer to a secretary as "Señorita," whatever her age or marital status.

• Expect the first and possibly second meeting to be a social discussion. Mexicans want to know about you and your background before getting down to business. In the first conversations, mention how much you like Mexico, how charming the people are, and what you plan to see in the country. If you work at building a personal relationship before discussing business, you will counter the stereotype of North Americans as too direct and aggressive.

• Never state that something is done better or more efficiently in your country. Never discuss religious or political topics, and avoid mentioning historic problems between Mexico and your country, if these exist.

• Women in business may not be accorded the same respect as a man. It's very rare to find a woman in a top management position in Mexico. A businesswoman should behave in an extremely professional manner.

• Expect Mexicans at the managerial level to be fluent in English. (Many also speak French.) If you need an interpreter, go to your country's Chamber of Commerce in Mexico City. You can also write to them in advance with questions or to arrange for an interpreter.

• Be on time for business appointments, but expect your Mexican counterpart to be 30 minutes to an hour late. Never complain about this tardiness. Bring work or a book for the waiting period.

• Be sure to show respect to people in high rank and to elders.

Mexican managers receive great respect because of their position, their age, or their influence.

• Realize that you'll be at a disadvantage if you aren't related to someone in the company with which you're dealing. Kinship is an important factor in Mexican business.

• Keep in mind that the buyer in a Mexican transaction is accorded very high respect—very much as in Japan.

• Remember that parties at a meeting first exchange business cards. Have your cards translated into Spanish. Be sure to have your university degree following your name, and also indicate your position with the company. Example:

John Smith, Ph.D.
Director, ———

Have your cards printed in the U.S., since it takes a long time in Mexico.

• Have proposals, catalogues, or instructions translated into Spanish in your own country. (Be sure to use professionals for this job.) Mexican businesspeople will appreciate your effort. In addition, people at different levels of the company may have to deal with the materials, and they may not know English well.

• Don't worry if you need extra photocopies of your materials. There are photocopy shops everywhere in Mexico City.

• When preparing your presentation, keep in mind that Mexicans are impressed with scientific appearance. Have computer printouts, charts, graphs. If appropriate, use three-dimensional models.

• To achieve your goals in a Mexican company, start at the top. Don't, however, be put off if you're sent to meet with a lower official. Such a suggestion may simply be an opportunity for you to speak with the company's expert in your field. Always arrange for a follow-up appointment with a top manager.

• During a business meeting, be prepared for many interruptions, such as telephone calls or people coming in. Never show irritation. Be patient. Mexicans believe that people are more important than time schedules. If a business associate or a visitor drops in, give her or him your full attention. Put aside whatever else you might be doing.

• Keep in mind that there is little long-range planning in Mexican businesses. They seek to make high profits in a short time. If you are proposing a project that will take years to complete, Mexicans may not be interested.

• Avoid direct questions when negotiating. People will never say "No; we can't do that" and may agree to do something impossible.

• Develop a strategy for getting a candid response, since businesspeople will often tell you what they think you want to hear. Avoid questions that will produce a "yes" or "no" answer, as in:

Foreigner: What do you think of this product?
Mexican: I think it's wonderful.

To get the candid response, your next question should be, "Are there any small changes you think should be made?" Ask questions in different ways, and ask three or four follow-up questions to obtain the candid response. Skill at this tactic comes with experience.

• Be flexible regarding deadlines. People do not usually meet deadlines, even those to which they have agreed. If you need something in a month, say you need it in two weeks, and you *may* get it on time.
• Don't agree to a proposal quickly. Haste in decision-making is considered unbecoming. Say that you will think the arrangement over.
• Try to appear strong and confident (but not aggressive) to gain the respect of Mexican workers. Mexicans at all levels tend to believe that *gringos* are naive.
• Remember that Mexicans tend to stand very close to others and to make physical contact. If you

withdraw physically, you may unintentionally establish a social or emotional distance.
• If you're going to Villahermosa, the oil center, book well in advance, as there aren't many first-class hotels.
• If you're doing business in Monterrey, expect a mixture of U.S. and Mexican business styles; most senior executives there have had training in the U.S.

Business Gifts: Good business gifts: a clock for the office, calculators, a gold pen, a gold cigarette lighter, Scotch, cognac, art books.

• On a second trip to Mexico, bring a gift, e.g., perfume, for the secretaries of important persons. Say, "My wife sent this to you." If you're a businesswoman, you can also give an article of clothing, e.g., a blouse.
• Note that government secretaries who help you in any way—typing, arranging an appointment with an important person—expect a gift of, say, the equivalent of 50 cents or a dollar.
• Never give gifts of silver, which is considered appropriate only for tourists.

Business Entertaining: Realize that breakfast or lunch are the best meals at which to discuss business. During the negotiating process, mutual invitations are essential. Business breakfasts may start at 8:00 A.M. Lunches often start at about 2:00 P.M., and last for over two hours. Always reciprocate these invitations.

• Don't expect to do business at dinner. This time is for socializing. Remember that most fine restaurants don't start serving dinner until 9:00 or 9:30 P.M., so have a snack in the afternoon.

• Don't be surprised if younger executives suggest meeting at about 7:00 P.M. Such an invitation usually involves drinks and snacks after business.

• If a Mexican businessman invites you to dinner at home, send a bouquet of flowers to your hostess ahead of time. Impress on the florist that the flowers must arrive on time. If you know that the family has children, bring gifts for them, e.g., electronic toys or candy. Always arrive 30 minutes late for dinner. Compliment the family on their home, the meal, and so forth. Don't be too effusive about any specific object or your host may feel obliged to give it to you.

• If you are a single man doing business in Mexico, don't invite your counterpart's spouse to a meal. If your spouse accompanies you, then you can include your counterpart's.

• A foreign businesswoman should never make business dinner appointments with her male counterparts unless they are accompanied by their spouses.

• A businesswoman who wishes to entertain Mexican businessmen at lunch should arrange for the meal to be in her hotel's restaurant so that the check may be added to her bill and not presented at the table. If it is, men will not allow her to pay.

• Be sure to entertain Mexican businesspeople at a prestigious restaurant. Suggest three or four of the best, and ask your guests to choose.

HOLIDAYS AND SPECIAL OCCASIONS

Expect banks, offices, and many shops to be closed on the following days since they are national holidays. Individual localities sometimes celebrate additional holidays. Consult the tourist office to find out about holidays in the region you'll be visiting.

Holidays: New Year's Day (Jan. 1); Epiphany (Jan. 6); Constitution Day (Feb. 5); Flag Day (Feb. 24); Birthday of Benito Juarez (March 21); Holy Thursday, Good Friday, and Easter; Labor Day (May 1); Battle of Puebla (May 5); National Holiday (Sept. 1); Independence Day (Sept. 16); Columbus Day (Oct. 12); Anniversary of the Revolution (Nov. 20); Christmas Day (Dec. 25).

• Keep in mind that there are 175 additional holidays celebrated in Mexico, most of them religious. Be sure to show respect for these celebrations. Don't drive your car through a procession.

• If a holiday falls on a Tuesday or Thursday, be aware that the adjacent Monday or Friday is often a day off also.

• Note that September has two important holidays. On September 1, the President goes on radio and TV to discuss his accomplishments of the past year. On September 15, at 11:00 P.M., the President appears on the balcony of the Palacio Nacional in Mexico City and recites Father Hidalgo's revolutionary cry for independence. This is followed by the ringing of church bells and by fireworks. The next day features bullfights and general merriment.

• Expect celebrations on the Feasts of All Saints and All Souls—November 1 and 2 (they are religious holidays; offices and shops are open). Incorporating the pre-Columbian feast of the dead, All Souls' Day (*Día de los muertos*) is an occasion for family picnics in cemeteries, decorating graves with marigolds to cheer the dead. People give one another cookies in the shape of skeletons or other symbols of death. Engaged couples give each other coffins made of sugar with the names of their loved ones on them. To enter the spirit of the occasion, give friends chocolate skulls with their names inscribed on them.

• Anticipate major celebrations for another religious festival, the Feast of Our Lady of Guadalupe, on December 12.

TRANSPORTATION

Public Transportation

• When you arrive at Mexico City's airport, go to the transportation desk, where you can book a taxi or arrange for a shared minibus that stops at individual hotels.

• Consider taking the subway in Mexico City as an alternative to buses and taxis; the traffic in this city is often horrendous. To find it, ask for the *metro*. Avoid the subway during rush hours (8:00 to 10:00 A.M., and 5:00 to 7:00 P.M.); during those times certain cars are reserved for women and children. Ask for subway maps in subway stations, at information booths, tourist offices, and some hotels. Pay for your fare at a booth, and use small change, since the ticket seller won't be able to change large bills. The fare is the same, no matter what your destination. Guard purses and wallets from pickpockets.

• In general, buses in cities are for the more hardy and adventuresome visitors, as they are *very* crowded. Enter at the front and exit at the rear. Pay in small change; however, you don't need exact change. Again, beware of pickpockets.

• Note that *colectivos*, sometimes called *peseros*, are taxis (usually green and white) which take as many passengers as will fit and travel on designated routes. You have to flag them down on the street. Sometimes drivers hold fingers out the window to show how many places are available. The fare is based on the distance traveled. State your destination when you get in, and pay when you get out.

• Look for salmon-colored taxis, which cost a bit more than the *colectivos* but are more reliable. The meters in these taxis don't show the actual fare, but a price on a fare schedule. Ask to see the fare schedule to be sure that you haven't been overcharged.

• There are various inter-city bus companies. And they fall into different categories. Some are first-class, express buses, where a ticket assures you of a seat; others are second- or third-class, and have no reserved seats—they stop at all the towns and villages, and pick up as many people as can get in. Ask your hotel concierge for advice on which bus to take. If you do take the bus, you must buy your ticket at the bus terminal. Some buses have bathrooms, but they are usually in bad shape. If there isn't a bathroom, the bus will stop every three to five hours for a bathroom break. You might want to bring your own food and drink with you. The restaurants at which buses stop are not always very appealing.

• Note that trains cost less than buses and are usually a better choice for long distances (e.g., between Mexico City and Monterrey, Guadalajara, or Oaxaca). On popular routes, during busy travel periods such as holidays, make reservations well in advance. Since train travel is so inexpensive, take *primera especial*, also called *turismo*, which is first class. You'll have a spacious private compartment with your own bathroom. In second class, *gabinetes,* there are bunk beds for two to four people and a shared bath. Third class, *sección,* offers approximately 30 bunk beds separated from each other by curtains and with a shared bathroom. Though all these classes have air conditioning, don't be surprised if it doesn't work.

• Buy your ticket well in advance, if possible; however, on some routes tickets aren't available until an hour before the train arrives at the station.

• Be careful about getting off the train before you reach your destination. Sometimes it's hard to tell when the train will take off again.

• You may bring your own food and drink, although in many first-class trains there are dining cars where you are likely to get safe food.

• If you're traveling at night, whether by train or car, bring a flashlight.

Driving

• Try not to drive in Mexico City. Traffic is extremely congested at all times.

• Don't drive at night. It's especially dangerous because of robberies, people on bicycles, potholes, and so forth.

• Note that no one obeys posted speed limits. Drive with the flow of the traffic.

• Be aware of the "Watch for Cattle" signs. Livestock are a major cause of automobile accidents in Mexico.

• If your car breaks down, raise the hood as a signal for help. If you break down on a tourist route, look for the *Auxilio Turístico*— sometimes known as "Green Angels"—in green pickup trucks (marked "Tourist Assistance" in English and Spanish) equipped to handle breakdowns. They patrol tourist routes between 8:00 A.M. and 8:00 P.M. daily except Tuesday mornings. They often make repairs on the spot and can handle simple medical emergencies.

• If you return to your parked car and find the license plate missing, realize that this means you have parked illegally and that a local policeman has taken the plate. To get it back, go to the local police station where you will have to pay a fine.

• Don't park in "No Parking" zones even when you see that many other drivers have. (The cars probably belong to people of influence, e.g., politicians, journalists, doctors.)

• When crossing borders between Mexican states, driving into Mexico City, or arriving at a military checkpoint, you may be stopped. In order to go on, you may have to pay a bribe; if you're not allowed to proceed, offer money—discreetly.

LEGAL MATTERS, SAFETY, AND HEALTH

• Be sure to get a tourist card before you enter Mexico. It is available from travel agents, Mexican consulates, or at the border. Keep it with you at all times. You have to present it when you leave the country. Note on it any expensive items you're bringing with you into Mexico, e.g., cameras and watches.

• Dress conservatively when you cross the border into Mexico by land. Don't dress like a hippie or you may be taken aside for a long period of questioning.

• Don't try to bring videotapes into the country.

• Realize that "sexy" magazines will be confiscated at the border.

• Be aware that nude bathing is illegal and is also *very* offensive to Mexicans.

• Women should not go out at night unless with an escort or on a tour. Never go to a bar alone. Before you go out, ask at your hotel which city areas are not safe.

• If you're planning to swim, ask locals which beaches are safe; some have treacherous undertows.

• For information on medicine and hygiene products, see "Legal Matters, Safety, and Health" in the Introduction.

PANAMA

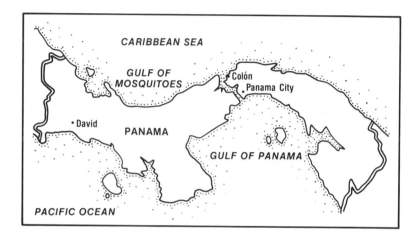

Robert McCulloch called his book about the Panama Canal *The Path Between the Seas*. And indeed most of us associate Panama with the 50-mile path between the oceans dug and hacked out of the jungle by men of many races and nationalities.

The construction of the canal had several side effects. Members of the many peoples that worked on the canal—of Caucasian, Black, and Oriental origin—have remained in Panama and lived there together in reasonable harmony through this century. And since the U.S. retained administration over the canal for so many years, most Panamanians are bilingual in Spanish and English.

The canal itself offers visitors a wondrous sight as the locks are flooded to enable ships to move through (often with a margin of only inches on either side of the ship) from one ocean to another.

GREETINGS

CONVERSATION

Language: Panama's official language is Spanish, although English is widely spoken.

• When people are introduced (whether men or women), they shake hands.

• Note that women friends kiss on one cheek in greeting and departing. Men and women shake hands or kiss on one cheek, and men shake hands with other men.

• At large parties, don't expect your host to introduce you individually. Go from group to group and introduce yourself.

• Remember that titles are important: *Licenciado* (lee-sehn-**syah**-doh) for someone with a B.A.; *Doctor* for a Ph.D., lawyer, or medical doctor; *Arquitecto* for an architect; and *Ingeniero* for an engineer.

• Be sure not to say anything that could give offense, since there is some anti-American feeling in Panama.

• Good subjects: family, common friends or acquaintances, interests and hobbies, basketball and baseball.

• Ask people for suggestions on what to see and where to dine.

• Avoid discussions of local politics, the former Canal Zone, and race.

• Don't discuss your possessions. Panamanians, in general, are not so interested in status and money as people in other countries.

• Don't get confused when talking to locals. They refer to Panama City as simply *"Panama."*

TELEPHONES

• You will find public phones on the street and along highways. Look for them also in shopping malls, or ask if you can use the phone in a shop. To make a local call, dial the number, and then deposit ten cents (American or Panamanian) when the party answers.

• To make long-distance calls, go to an ENTEL office. You can make collect calls there, but you can also make them from a private home or hotel.

IN PUBLIC

• Remember that Panamanians and Americans stationed in Panama tend not to mix.

• When you go shopping, feel free to use English; many clerks speak it.

• Be sensitive to people's feelings about being photographed. Many Cuna Indians, especially older ones, don't like it. Younger ones may expect payment. Ask first.

• Expect to find public bathrooms only in public buildings, hotels, restaurants, and bars.

DRESS

• For casual wear jeans are acceptable for men and women, but neither sex should wear shorts on the street.

• Women should not wear revealing clothing.

• If your business is with general managers of a corporation or with someone in banking, stocks, or accounting, expect them to wear suits. Low-level managers and those in retailing or manufacturing wear *panabrisas,* a shirt (like the *guayabera*) worn over pants, not tucked in. A foreign businessman should always wear a dark suit on his first visit but may later wear a *panabrisas*, if that's what his counterpart is wearing.

• For business, women should wear a dress or a skirt and tailored blouse.

• When invited to a home for the first time, men should wear a dark suit and women a dress or dressy pants.

MEALS

Hours and Foods

• Note that Panamanians eat three hearty meals a day, usually prepared by a maid.

Breakfast: 7:00 or 8:00 A.M. A typical one might be liver, onions, and garlic sauteed in oil; deep-fried, thick corn tortillas; *queso blanco,* a white cheese made with cow's milk; fresh bread or soft rolls. In Panama City, people sometimes have eggs in addition to one of the above. Coffee is the usual beverage.

Lunch: Noon. The meal may begin with soup, followed by steak or chicken with rice and plaintains (fried or baked). There will always be beans—*guandú* (pigeon peas) or red kidney beans—cooked together with rice. A salad is served with the main course.

Dinner: 7:00 P.M. You'll probably have meat (chicken or steak) prepared with a sauce and served with rice, and a salad.

• Note that pork is not a popular choice of meat in Panama.

• Don't be surprised to be served potato salad and rice at the same meal. Rice is an important part of all meals.

• Expect dishes to be spiced with *cilantro* (fresh coriander leaves) and other herbs and spices.

• Note that the most common dessert is fruit. Sometimes, however, there will be cake, pie, cheesecake, or chocolate mousse.

Beverages: Everyday beverages are water, soda, lemonade, fresh fruit juices (guava, papaya, strawberry, mandarin), or beer. On very special occasions there will be wine.

• Common drinks before dinner are Scotch on the rocks, rum and Coke, gin and tonic, and vodka and orange juice.

• After dinner comes coffee, usually espresso.

Table Manners

• Note that for company, drinks are served before, during, and after meals.
• While there is usually no appetizer course, expect snacks of *ceviche* (marinated raw fish) or cheese and crackers.
• Anticipate food service by a maid. At an informal meal she will place platters on the table from which you may help yourself. At a more formal meal she will serve each person at the table.
• Note that the father sits at the head of the table. The guest of honor usually sits at one end of the table.
• Remember that you'll please your hostess by eating everything on your plate, but if you really don't like something, it's okay to leave it.
• To signal that you have finished, place your knife and fork vertically and parallel on your plate.

Eating Out

• Expect a wide variety of restaurants in Panama City: French, Spanish, Italian, South American, Japanese, and Chinese, as well as those serving only Panamanian food.
• Note that a *restaurante* is a restaurant, a *panadería* offers bread

and rolls to take out, a *pastelería* sells pastry (primarily to take out), and a *bar* is a more elegant bar than a *cantina,* which is a drinking place usually in a lower-class neighborhood. (Unaccompanied women do not go into *bars* or *cantinas.*)
• Summon the waiter by saying *"Mozo"* (moh-soh) or *"Señor"*; call the waitress *"Señorita."*
• Remember that the person who invites also pays.

Specialties

• For appetizers, try *ceviche,* marinated raw fish; or *carimañola* —boiled, mashed *yuca* (cassava) wrapped around ground beef with spices, and then deep fried.
• Some special meat dishes: *ropa vieja* (literally "old clothes")— shredded beef, green pepper, and spices served with plaintains and rice; *empanadas*—fried meat pies; *lomo relleno*—steak stuffed with herbs and spices.
• Also sample: *arroz con coco y titi*—rice with coconut and small dried shrimp; *sancocho*—a stew of chicken, *yuca,* onions, potatoes, corn, and coriander leaf.
• For desserts, consider *arroz con cacao*—chocolate rice pudding, and *buñuelos de viento*—fritters served with syrup.
• Remember that seafood, such as lobster and shrimp, is consid-

ered special and is usually eaten only in restaurants.

• There are many varieties of fish. The most popular is *corvina* (sea bass), prepared in many different styles.

HOTELS

• Besides the luxury hotels in Panama City, consider *apartoteles,* residential hotels that provide kitchens with stove and refrigerator, sitting room, and maid service.

TIPPING

• Give porters at airports and hotels $1.00 per bag.

• Note that restaurants and hotels don't include service in their charges. Add 10 to 15% to the bill—15% in better restaurants.

• Give taxi drivers a 10% tip.

• If gasoline attendants check the oil, the air in the tires, and wash the windshield, give them 25 to 50 cents.

PRIVATE HOMES

• Feel free to drop in on people. They won't be offended.

• After having a meal in someone's home, feel free to stay until 1:00 or 2:00 A.M. Panamanians love parties.

• If you're invited to a party, don't arrive on time. In fact, you can be up to two hours late and no one will mind. Etiquette is somewhat different for a dinner party. If there will be many guests, arrive up to an hour late. If you (or you and your spouse) are the only guests, appear about 30 minutes late.

• When staying with a family, remember that everyone *always* eats together. Ask the times of meals, and be sure to be on time.

• If you make long-distance calls from a home, offer to pay for them.

• Check with your hostess to see if the bath water has to be heated. Feel free to take one or more daily baths, since Panamanians do.

• Ask your hostess where to do your laundry; she will probably tell you to leave it out for the maid to wash.

• If the family has a maid (and most middle- and upper-class families do), don't offer to help clear the table or do the dishes. If there is no maid, offer to help.

• After staying a week, you might want to tip the maid. Give her about $5.00. Don't ask your hostess about tipping; she may not like the idea.

• If you stay with a family for several days or a week, consider inviting them to a meal in a restaurant. A woman may make previous arrangements with the maître d' to pay with a credit card, so there won't be a conflict over the check.

Gifts: Note that you don't need to bring a gift if you're invited to dinner. It's polite to reciprocate by inviting your hosts to a restaurant. If you can't do that, bring a bottle of good wine or of Scotch.

• From abroad bring wine, CD's, chocolates, fancy bed linens and towels.

BUSINESS

Hours

Businesses: Monday to Friday, 8:00 A.M. to 5:00 P.M.

Government Offices: Monday to Friday, 8:00 A.M. to noon, and 12:30 to 4:30 P.M.

Banks: Monday to Friday, 8:00 A.M. to 1:00 P.M.

Shops: Monday to Saturday, 8:00 A.M. to noon, and 2:00 to 6:00 or 7:00 P.M.

Currency

• Note that Panama has no paper money of its own. They use U.S. bank notes, which are called *Balboas*.

• Panama's coins are the same size and shape as U.S. coins, but the engraving is distinctive. Coins are 10 *Balboas,* 50 cents (called a *peso*), 25, 10, and 5 cents (called a *real*), and 1 cent. Panamanian coins are used interchangeably with U.S. coins.

• Use credit cards, if you wish, in Panama City and in large shops and hotels in other areas. Outside the capital, use travelers' checks or cash.

Business Practices

• Make appointments from abroad at least two weeks in advance.

• Don't start talking about business immediately. Panamanian businesspeople want to get to know you first.

• To make the best impression, have any materials you'll be using translated into Spanish.

• Note that Panamanian women are moving into higher managerial positions, so foreign businesswomen shouldn't have any problem.

• Foreign businesswomen should not attempt to treat a Panamanian businessman to a meal in a restaurant. He will never allow her to pay the bill.

HOLIDAYS AND SPECIAL OCCASIONS

The following are national holidays on which you'll find businesses, banks, government offices, and many shops and restaurants closed. Check with the tourist office to learn if there will be any local festivals or religious celebrations during your visit.

Holidays: New Year's Day (Jan. 1); Day of National Mourning (Jan. 9); Carnival (four days preceding Ash Wednesday); Good Friday through Easter Sunday; Labor Day (May 1); Panama City Day (Aug. 15); National Anthem Day (Nov. 1); All Souls' Day (Nov. 2); Independence Day (Nov. 3); Flag Day (Nov. 4); First Call of Independence (Nov. 10); Independence from Spain (Nov. 28); Mother's Day (Dec. 8); Christmas (Dec. 25).

• Be aware that crowds are very unruly during Carnival. Attend the festivities only with a Panama-nian.

TRANSPORTATION

Public Transportation

• Look for corners with marked signs for *chivas,* the buses that go along regular routes in cities. Pay when you exit. When the bus nears the stop at which you want to get off, say *"Parada"* (pah-**rah**-dah).

• Note that most people fly or drive between cities. There are public buses, but it is not a recommended choice.

• Keep in mind that taxis don't have meters. Agree on the fare in advance. Cost is generally based on distance traveled and number of passengers. Larger taxis are more expensive than smaller ones, and taxis in front of large hotels are more expensive than those you hail in the street.

• Consider taking the train for the one-and-a-half hour trip between Panama City and Colón.

Buy your tickets at the station or on the train.

• Expect regularly scheduled flights and reasonable fares for service between Panamanian cities. Book these in advance.

Driving

• Note that road conditions are variable.

• If you're stopped by the police, and they keep talking and won't let you go, offer them $10.00.

LEGAL MATTERS, SAFETY, AND HEALTH

• Remember that you can bring in only one each of items such as calculators, cameras, and radios. If you have more, you will have to pay duty.

• Be very cautious in Panama, where violence is common. Colón, on the Atlantic coast, is considered the most dangerous city in the hemisphere. If you must drive there, keep doors locked and windows closed.

• Note that there may be curfew regulations in Colón.

• Don't go out walking after dusk.

• Don't get in a taxi with two or more people.

• Don't wear expensive jewelry or watches.

• Women should not go out unaccompanied, and should be especially careful of purse snatchers.

• Women should always take taxis after dark. If you're staying with a family, ask someone to drive you to your destination and pick you up.

• Realize that you can safely drink the water in Panama City; the same water supply serves the Canal Zone. Outside that city, drink only bottled water.

• For advice on medicine and hygiene products, see "Legal Matters, Safety, and Health" in the Introduction.

PARAGUAY

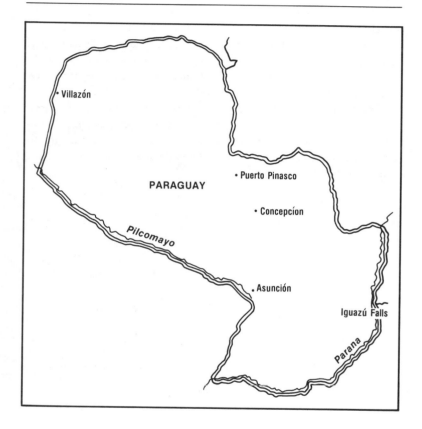

Paraguay and neighboring Bolivia share the distinction of being the only South American countries without coastlines.

If you saw the Jeremy Irons/Robert De Niro movie *The Mission,* you will recall the attempts of Jesuit missionaries to build utopian communities with the native Indians. The Jesuit experiments took place in several spots in South America, but most notably in Paraguay. Though most of the many missions constructed by the Jesuits and the Indians have been destroyed, travelers can visit a few remaining ruins in such towns as Itapúa.

portant. Greet a medical doctor, a Ph.D., or a lawyer as *Doctor,* and a person with a college degree as *Licenciado* (lee-sehn-syah-doh). Other titles are *Profesor* and *Arquitecto* (architect).

GREETINGS

Language: The official languages of Paraguay are Spanish and Guaraní. The use of Guaraní, the language of the native Indians, is very generalized. Government officials *must* be able to speak Guaraní. In the countryside, you'll find that most people will speak only Guaraní, not Spanish.

People will be very impressed if you, as a foreigner, learn a few words of Guaraní.

• When introduced, men shake hands with other men and with women. Two women introduced by a mutual friend may kiss each other on both cheeks; otherwise, they shake hands.

• Among good friends, women kiss other women, men and women who are related kiss (if not related, they shake hands), and men shake hands with other men or embrace.

• At parties, shake hands with everyone when you arrive and *especially* when you leave.

• Remember that titles are im-

CONVERSATION

• Be aware that people will stand very close to you while conversing. Don't back off.

• Discuss family, sports, and current events. Paraguayans are very proud of their hydroelectric dams, so you can make a good impression by asking about them.

• Avoid any political discussions. Before offering any opinions in such a conversation, try to feel out the Paraguayan's political views. People who are in the "wrong" political group often encounter problems.

TELEPHONES

• Note that there are few public phones. To use one, deposit 50 *guaranies,* for which you'll get an unlimited time. If you can't find a phone booth on the street, ask to use the phone in a small shop or restaurant.

• For long-distance or international calls, go to ANTELCO, the central telephone office. You can make collect calls from there or from your hotel, but check first to see whether the hotel imposes a surcharge on such calls.

IN PUBLIC

• Some gestures to note: (1) crossing the index and second fin-

gers (the North American "good luck" sign) is offensive; (2) the American "okay" sign (thumb and index finger in a circle) made with wrist dropped and fingers pointing toward the ground is obscene; (3) tilting the head backwards means "I forgot"; (4) flicking the chin with the top of the index finger means "I don't know."

• To be polite, ask permission when photographing people. They usually enjoy being photographed, but the picture will be posed. For candids, bring a telephoto lens.

• Don't photograph anything associated with the military or the police.

• Feel free to bargain in markets and in places that are half shops and half stalls. Don't bargain in established shops.

• Expect to find public bathrooms only in hotels and restaurants. In very rural areas, facilities are extremely simple. In the countryside, public bathrooms are almost always unclean and unsanitary; in the larger towns, the level of sanitation varies. Bring tissues as there probably won't be any.

DRESS

• When planning your wardrobe, consider the climate in Paraguay. There may be sudden changes from warm to cold during much of the year. From December to March, temperatures range from 77 to 110° F.; from the end of March to June the nights are cool; and from June through September the temperature is usually mild with some cold days.

• For casual wear, jeans are acceptable for both men and women. Don't wear shorts in cities.

• Women should not wear short skirts or revealing attire.

• For business, men should wear a conservative dark suit and tie and women should wear a suit, dress, or skirt with jacket or blouse.

• If invited to a meal in a home, women should wear a dress or skirt and blouse. Men should wear pants with shirt and sport jacket.

• Note that formal dress is worn only for a reception in a private social club, or to the opera, theaters, and weddings. The invitation will indicate if the dress will be formal. In that case, men should wear a dark suit and women should wear a dress or a Chanel-style suit.

MEALS

Hours and Foods

• First, a word of caution. Don't eat raw vegetables or fruit that can't be peeled. Drink only bottled water. Don't use ice cubes.

• Note that in the cities, Paraguayans eat two large meals a day, and they usually eat meat twice a day.

Breakfast: 7:00 A.M. Coffee with milk or *cocido con leche (yerba maté* with milk) are the usual beverages. This is accompanied by *galletas* (a kind of roll) or *chipas* (a very gritty bread made of corn flour, cheese, *mandioca* starch, and eggs) or *sopa paraguaya* (a type of pudding, made with mashed corn, milk, eggs, cheese, and onion— eaten with the hands as bread is, or with a knife and fork).

Lunch: 12:30 P.M. Some alternatives: *Milanesa* (fried breaded veal cutlet often served with an egg on top) and sometimes a lettuce and tomato salad; or *so'yosopý* (a Guaraní word meaning beaten meat), a hearty soup made with cornmeal, beef, oregano, and garlic and served with *sopa paraguaya* or, in the countryside, with *chipas.* *So'yosopý* soup is usually accompanied by *mandioca* (cassava, a rather bland tuber) which has been boiled in salted water. Lunch may be followed by a dessert: usually ice cream, but sometimes *dulce de guayaba* (guava paste) served with a white cheese called *queso blanco.*

Dinner: Sometimes a barbecue in the back yard, similar to an Argentine *parrillada* (barbecued beef). Outside the cities, people may have a light evening meal, perhaps just soup and bread.

Beverages: With meals the beverage will be a fresh fruit juice. It is usually simply squeezed fruit. In that case it's okay to drink it, but don't have any if water or ice cubes have been added.

• One of the most popular beverages is *maté,* the drinking of which is a social event. Dried, crushed *yerba maté* leaves are put into a cup made out of a gourd. Boiling water is poured over the *yerba maté,* and the gourd is passed around, and everyone takes a sip from it. You have to acquire a liking for the bitter taste of *maté.* The last person in the group hands the cup to the person with the kettle, and the gourd is refilled. This ritual may last for hours. When you've had enough, say *"Muchas gracias."* If you don't want any at all, say, "I have *'gringo'* taste," or "I'm not used to it." *Maté* made with cold water is called *tereré* (teh-reh-**reh**).

• Note a popular activity after lunch: men (and now women also) sit around and drink *tereré,* passing it from one person to another. In Asunción (the capital), it's safe to drink it, but not elsewhere, where it's best to avoid unboiled tap water.

• Other beverages: *Caña* is a kind of rum. And there are several brands of beer and wine made mostly by German immigrants.

Table Manners

• Don't expect drinks before dinner, but beer or wine will be served at a formal meal and juices at everyday meals.

• If you're the guest of honor, anticipate sitting at the head of the table. There is no rigid rule about seating, however.

• In upper-class homes expect a maid to put food onto individual plates in the kitchen and then serve it. As soon as you finish, more food will be offered or the next course will appear.

• Realize that your hosts will expect you to eat a great deal and to finish everything on your plate. More sophisticated people won't "push" food as much as others may.

• Don't expect vegetables with your meals. Paraguayans don't care for them.

• During the week, stay about one hour after dinner; on weekends feel free to stay two hours or more. People enjoy chatting, listening to music, and drinking after dinner.

Eating Out

• Realize that there are a variety of places to get food:

Parrilladas serve barbecued beef along with innards, and wine, beer, and soft drinks.

Copetines are like convenience stores with tables. You'll probably find a blackboard listing the day's specials. There will be four or five tables, where you can have *empanadas* (turnovers filled with meat or cheese), sandwiches, soda, and beer. You can also buy food to take out. To find a *copetín,* look for a lighted Pepsi-Cola sign.

A *bar,* higher class than a *copetín,* is a snack bar where you can buy

sandwiches, *empanadas,* coffee, or alcoholic beverages to eat there or to take out.

A *cafetería* is not a U.S.-style cafeteria; it's a place to buy coffee beans in bulk.

For bread and rolls go to *panaderías.*

Finally, expect to find many Chinese restaurants.

• Note that restaurants usually serve lunch between noon and 2:00 P.M., and dinner from 8:30 to 11:00 P.M.

• Look for menus in restaurant windows. Some restaurants post them.

• To summon the waiter, say *"Mozo"* (**moh-soh**).

• Realize that some dishes such as hamburgers and veal cutlets are served with a fried egg on top. If you don't want the egg, say *"Sin huevo"* (seen **weh-**boh).

• Don't expect a main course to be "garnished" with potatoes, rice, or vegetables. You must order them separately. Sometimes *mandioca* is served. Eat it with knife and fork.

• Expect beef to be plentiful in Paraguay, although it can be somewhat tough.

• When ordering beer, remember that it comes in large bottles— more than a pint.

• Note that the person who asks for the check usually pays it. Offer to pay your share, but you'll probably be refused. Reciprocate by inviting your host to a meal.

Specialites

Some special dishes from Paraguay: *so'yosopý*—a soup made of ground beef, cornmeal, garlic, and herbs; *bori-borí*—a soup made of vegetables, meat, cheese, and corn balls; *asado*—beef grilled over an open pit; *parrillada*—mixed grill of steak, sausage, and innards; *croquetas*—croquettes of pork, chicken, or beef; *surubí*—catfish, a delicacy prepared in a variety of ways; *palmitos*—hearts of palm, another delicacy.

HOTELS

• Be sure to make reservations well in advance for the high season—June through August.
• Note that inexpensive hotels don't accept travelers' checks.
• If you're on a budget you may consider one of the less expensive small hotels, which are quite com-

fortable. They are clean. Sometimes you'll have a private bath; at others, baths are shared. Usually there is constant hot water. Breakfast may be included in the room's price. If you need laundry service, ask the maid to do it (for a small fee).
• At breakfast, expect toast or bread rolls, butter, jam, and one pot of hot coffee and another of hot milk. If you like eggs for breakfast, ask for them.

TIPPING

• Give porters 75 *guaraníes* per piece of luggage.
• Tip taxi drivers 10% of the fare.
• Note that a service charge is not added to the check at restaurants. Leave 10 to 15% of the bill.
• Give doormen, attendants, and others who perform small services 25 *guaraníes*.
• U.S. bicentennial quarters or Kennedy half dollars will please very much when given as a tip.

PRIVATE HOMES

• Feel free to drop in on people, but if you don't know someone well, phone in advance. You'll find phones only in the homes of the upper classes, however. Never drop in on people from 12:30 to 3:00 P.M.—afternoon meal and siesta time.

• Offer to pay for any long-distance calls you make from a private home. It isn't necessary to pay for local calls.

• Note that some homes have constant hot water, while others have no hot water at all, since Paraguay is very warm during most of the year. Ask your hostess if there is hot water.

• Don't feel obliged to tip the maid if you've stayed with a family.

Gifts: Note that a gift isn't expected if you're invited to dinner, but flowers, wine, or whiskey will be welcome.

• From abroad bring small appliances, e.g., transistor radios, small tape recorders, pocket calculators with memory, or photographic books of your area.

• For young people, bring a Walkman or cassettes or records of American pop music.

• Because Paraguay's economy is based on contraband, realize that you can purchase items from all over the world at a cost lower than in the country of origin. You might want to wait until you get to Paraguay before making purchases.

BUSINESS

Hours

Businesses: Monday to Friday, 7:30 to 11:00 or 11:30 A.M., and 2:30 or 3:00 to 5:30 or 6:00 P.M.

Government Offices: Summer hours are Monday through Saturday, 6:30 to 11:30 A.M. Winter hours are 7:30 A.M. to noon.

Banks: Summer hours are Monday through Friday, 7:00 to

11:00 A.M. Winter hours are 7:00 to 11:30 A.M.

Shops: Monday through Friday, 6:30 or 7:00 A.M. until noon, and then from 3:00 or 3:30 until 6:30 or 7:00 P.M. Saturday, 7:00 to 11:30 A.M.

Currency

• Note that the currency is the *guaraní*—plural, *guaraníes*. Coins: 1, 5, 10, and 50 *guaraníes*. Bills: 100, 500, 1,000, 5,000, and 10,000 *guaraníes*.

Business Practices

• Plan business trips from June through October. Business vacations in Paraguay are usually taken December through February, and in May during the Independence Days holidays. Avoid the week before and after Easter, and the two weeks before and after Christmas.

• Realize that most business is conducted in Asunción, the capital.

• Try to make appointments in the morning. That's the time when you're most likely to find people, especially government officials, in their offices.

• Be sure to make appointments in advance with people in business and government. From abroad,

make arrangements two to four weeks in advance.

• Bring business cards printed in English on one side and in Spanish on the other. Have any sales literature available in Spanish.

• To make a good impression, compliment Paraguayans on the country's hydroelectric dams. The dams were built in conjunction with Brazil and Argentina.

• Cultivate patience. Decision making is a slow process. Decisions are made by an organization's top people.

• Realize that being a woman may have its advantages in doing business, since Paraguayan men don't like to confront or offend a woman.

• Note that most businesspeople eat the noon meal at home and then have a siesta. Business entertaining therefore usually takes place at night at one of the large hotels.

• If you want to give a businessperson a gift, offer a wristwatch with alarm or calculator or an electronic calculator. For a "super gift," bring a video cassette recorder.

• Don't be surprised at the sound of firecrackers everywhere on New Year's Eve.

HOLIDAYS AND SPECIAL OCCASIONS

Expect most banks, offices, shops, and many restaurants to be closed on the following national holidays. Check with the tourist office to learn about any local festivals that may occur during your visit.

Holidays: New Year's Day (Jan. 1); Feast of San Blas, patron saint of Paraguay (Feb. 3); Heroes' Day (March 1); Holy Thursday; Good Friday; Labor Day (May 1); Independence Days (May 14 and 15); Corpus Christi (the Thursday after the eighth Sunday after Easter); Chaco Armistice (June 12); Founding of Asunción (Aug. 15); Constitution Day (Aug. 25); Victory of Boquerón Day (Sept. 29); Columbus Day (Oct. 12); All Saints' Day (Nov. 1); Feast of the Virgin of Caacupé (Dec. 8); Christmas (Dec. 25).

TRANSPORTATION

Public Transportation

• Note that there are no subways.
• Pay when you get on a local bus. You don't need exact change. Keep the ticket you'll receive in case an inspector gets on the bus for a check. Carry your passport with you, as soldiers may board the bus to check passengers' identification. When you want the driver to stop, whistle or yell. Exit at the rear.
• Be aware that long-distance buses are extremely inexpensive. First-class buses have reclining seats, footrests, and a bathroom. Buy your ticket a day or two in advance, since all seats are reserved.
• During business hours in Asunción, consider taking trams

—yellow trolley cars. Pay as you get on; there's one fare for all distances. You don't need exact change.

• Note that taxis are very inexpensive, and you'll find 24-hour taxi stands in Asunción. Some taxis have meters, and others don't. Agree on the fare before you get in.

• Don't expect to take a train. There is a very slow and outdated system used only for freight. Paraguayans don't use trains as a means of transportation.

Driving

• Don't drive. Many roads are unpaved; on country roads, you'll find cattle, who won't respond to a tooting horn—you have to wait until they move. There are few road signs. In the countryside most people speak only Guaraní. They may understand you if you speak Spanish, but they'll respond in Guaraní, so it will be difficult to get directions if you get lost.

LEGAL MATTERS, SAFETY, AND HEALTH

• Remember that you can bring *one* of various items into the country, e.g., one camera, one Walkman, one tape recorder. If asked about the item, say that it's for your personal use.

• Be aware that it's illegal to take colonial antiques (items from the time of the Spanish conquest in the 1500s and 1600s) out of the country.

• Never publicly criticize the government. You could end up in prison.

• Women alone won't be harassed but should expect to be questioned about being alone, and as to the whereabouts of their husband. To avoid lengthy explanations, say that your husband is joining you on the following day.

• If you're taking any medication, bring an adequate supply because brand names and dosages may differ.

• Note that contraceptives for males are available over the counter.

• For further advice on medicine and hygiene products, see "Legal Matters, Safety, and Health" in the Introduction.

PERU

Nothing will more vividly show the difference between the Spanish and Incan cultures than visits to Lima and Machu Picchu.

When Francisco Pizarro founded Lima in 1535, he insisted on a city with no influences of the Incas, whom he had recently defeated. Though the city now has many skyscrapers (and a great deal of smog), colonial Spanish architecture is still plainly evident.

Shrouded in the clouds, Machu Picchu was unknown to Europeans until 1911. Machu Picchu, a great Inca center, is now a famous site, which writer Lynn Meisch described as "beautiful beyond words, an absolutely magical place."

To get to Machu Picchu, you will probably go through Cuzco, the oldest continuously inhabited city in the Americas. A stop there sometimes brings on a bout of altitude sickness, but hotels start you off with a complimentary cup of *maté de coca* (coca leaf tea) which will alleviate its effects. Because of the thinness of the air in the Cuzco area, you will find colors much more intense—the red-tiled roofs, the Indians' clothing, the sky.

If your appetite for Indian cultures isn't sated by Machu Picchu, you can also visit several places along Peru's coast identified with the many pre-Incan cultures.

GREETINGS

Language: Spanish is Peru's first official language; Quechua, the language of the Incas, is the other official language.

• Note that men and women shake hands in greeting and parting. Men embrace close friends or pat them on the back. Women kiss one another on the cheek. Sometimes when two women are introduced, they will kiss one an-other. The same is sometimes true of men and women.

• Greet officials or elders with their title plus last name. Principal titles are: *Doctor, Profesor, Arquitecto* (architect), *Ingeniero* (engineer).

CONVERSATION

• Expect people to discuss family and occupation as soon as they meet you.

• Expect people to stand much closer to you when speaking to you than they would in North America. Don't back away or others will feel offended.

• Organize your ideas on your country's government and on technology. People will ask you about them.

• Ask advice on sights to see and places to eat.

• If you're chatting with women, bring up fashion, a subject that interests most Peruvian women.

• Avoid discussing salary, how much you paid for something, or Peruvian government and politics.

• Don't make any remarks about Peru's government, even if you hear complaints and criticisms of it.

• Don't make any negative remarks about the appearance of Lima, which has changed dramatically since the well-to-do began moving to the suburbs.

• Never ask people about their ancestors. Peruvians feel more comfortable being associated with their Spanish colonial heritage than with their Indian heritage.

TELEPHONES

• Note that you'll find public phones only in major cities—and not many there. Buy tokens (called *rin*) at newsstands or stores or from lottery vendors. At the end of three minutes you will hear a signal; deposit another token, or you'll be cut off.

• If you can't find a public telephone, ask a restaurant or shop owner if you may use the phone. Most will allow you to make a local call.

• To make a long-distance call in Lima, go to the telephone office, Compañía de Teléfonos. Outside Lima, go to ENTEL-Perú for long-distance calls, either within Peru or abroad, as well as for telegram and telex services. (Smaller towns will have only phone service, not telex or telegram.) You leave a deposit, for which you get a receipt. At the end of the call, any money you have overpaid will be refunded. ENTEL offices are open from 8:00 A.M. to 10:00 P.M., Monday through Friday. Some are open from 9:00 A.M. to noon on Saturday. They are closed on Sunday.

• Remember that you can make collect calls from Peru only to certain countries. (The U.S. is one.) Check at the ENTEL office about the country you wish to call.

• Note that you can make long-distance and overseas calls from your hotel, but be sure to check first to find out whether there is a surcharge for such calls, and if so, how much.

• When making a long-distance call from a private home, tell the operator to call you back with the charges for the call. You don't need to pay for local calls made from a private home.

IN PUBLIC

• Anticipate a warm welcome in Peru. Foreigners are considered very special people.

• If you need directions, expect to ask several people before you find where you're going. Even if they don't know the correct direc-

tions, people will pretend that they do—to save face.

• Always offer cigarettes to others when you light one for yourself.

• Don't be surprised to see women walking arm in arm with other women or men with men, and don't be surprised if a person of the same sex takes your arm.

• To beckon someone, wave your hand back and forth while holding it vertically, palm facing out.

• Don't bargain in boutiques or government-owned craft shops, called *Artesanías del Perú*. Try bargaining in other craft shops and in markets. You'll find it easier to get a lower price if you offer cash and/or U.S. dollars.

• Be discreet in photographing Indians. Some object to having their picture taken, and some may become angry if you don't offer a tip.

• Don't photograph airports, military installations, or industrial plants.

• If you need a bathroom, go into a restaurant. It doesn't matter that you're not a customer.

• Realize that toilets in the countryside may be portable toilets or perhaps just a hole in the ground. Bring tissues.

• Don't put used toilet paper in the toilet, because it may overflow when you flush. Put it in the receptacle next to the toilet.

fun of them, and others will think you odd.

• Women should avoid wearing what is considered men's clothing—e.g., a poncho or a man's hat.

DRESS

• For casual attire, men can wear slacks and a polo shirt, and women a skirt or pants and a blouse.

• For business in winter men should wear dark wool suits and in summer dark lightweight suits or blazers and slacks. Women should wear a dress or a skirt, silk shirt, and a jacket.

• When invited to a meal in a home, men should wear a sports jacket and tie and women a dress or skirt and blouse. To a party in a home, men should wear suit and tie and women a dress or skirt and blouse.

• If an invitation says that dress is formal (as it often is for official government parties or private, elegant parties), men should wear tuxedos, and women should wear cocktail dresses.

• Because nights are cold in the highlands, bring a warm jacket or heavy coat for a visit there.

• Don't wear Indian clothing. Indians will think you are making

MEALS

Hours and Foods

• First, a word of caution. Don't drink tap water. Don't eat raw vegetables or fruits that can't be peeled. Avoid raw shellfish. When you order a drink, always say *"sin hielo"* (seen **yeh**-loh), which means "without ice."

Breakfast: 7:30–9:00 A.M. A simple meal: rolls with ham, cheese, or jam and *café con leche* (coffee with milk).

Lunch: 12:30 or 1:00 P.M. to 3:00 P.M. The meal usually begins with a pasta course, followed by steak, chops, chicken, or fish with salad and rice. Finally there will be fruit and demitasse. Infusions of herbs (e.g., *yerba Luisa*) are popular rather than coffee. With the meal, you'll drink wine, lemonade, or soft drinks. Many people mix wine and water.

Tea: 6:00 P.M. People have cake and cookies with tea.

Dinner: 8:30 or 9:00 P.M. The first course may be a soup with noodles, followed by a *guiso* (vegetables pureed with spices) served with rice. The meal ends with coffee or an herb tea (e.g., chamomile).

Beverages: Popular drinks before dinner are *pisco* (grape brandy) or a *pisco* sour (grape brandy, lemon, sugar, and beaten egg whites), which is much stronger than its sweet taste would lead you to believe; also popular are campari and whiskey.

• With meals people drink beer, wine, fruit juices, Coke, Inca Cola (a yellow carbonated soft drink that tastes like bubble gum), and *agua mineral,* bottled, carbonated mineral water.

• Another common beverage with meals is lemonade. Many people boil water before making lemonade, but if you're embarrassed to ask if they have, ask for a bottled soft drink.

• Remember that beer in Peru has twice the alcoholic content of U.S. or European beer.

• Expect coffee to be more popular in the jungle areas, where it is grown, than in other parts of Peru.

Table Manners

• Note that people never have more than one drink before dinner or before the midday meal on Sunday. If invited to dinner, you'll be served a drink with appetizers: olives, peanuts, pâté, cheeses, or huge Peruvian corn kernels on toothpicks with a dipping sauce—either one of avocado or one called *a la Huancaína* (white cheese with evaporated milk, hot peppers, onions, salt, and pepper).

• If invited to a meal, arrive 30 minutes later than the invitation states. Most dinner invitations are for 9:00 P.M. Dinner probably won't be served until 10:30 P.M., so it's a good idea to fortify yourself with a snack before setting out for the dinner party.

• Note that the table is set with forks to the left of the plate, knives to the right, and dessert and coffee spoons above the plate.

• Remember that the host and hostess usually sit next to one another. A male guest of honor sits to the right of the hostess and a female guest of honor to the right of the host.

• Anticipate one of two types of service: the maid may serve food directly onto your plate, or food may be served family style.

• If fish is served, use the fish knife and fork provided. A fish knife looks rather like an oversized butter knife, while a fish fork has one oversized tine.

• Don't be surprised to be served rice and potatoes at the same meal. Potatoes are considered a vegetable, not a starch.

• If beer is served in large bottles (about 64 oz.), serve yourself and then pass the bottle to others in your group.

• Don't be surprised if someone pours a glass of beer without asking if you want any. If you don't want it, be *very* firm.

• Realize that people eat enormous quantities of food at meals. (They don't snack between meals as North Americans often do.) Your hosts may press you insistently to eat more. Don't give in if you're full.

• Don't feel obliged to finish everything on your plate—in fact, it's polite to leave a little food— but do at least try everything or you'll offend your hosts. Leaving a bit shows that you're "stuffed" and satisfied.

• Keep your hands above the table. Don't put your hands on your lap.

• To indicate that you have finished eating, place your utensils either diagonally across the plate or vertically on the plate.

• Stay about 30 minutes after the meal ends. Your hosts may press you to stay, but they're usually just being polite. Leave anyway.

Eating Out

• Look for *pastelerías* (pastry shops): some offer places to sit and eat your pastries with tea or coffee; others sell pastries to take out.

• Men who want drinks or a light meal can visit a *picantería*. It will offer beer and native meals such as *ceviche, chicharrón* (pork crackling), *papas a la Huancaína,* and *olluquito con charqui* (potato with dried meat).

• Note that *chicha* describes two kinds of drink. One is made from fermented corn and is alcoholic; the other is a soft drink made from corn. There is really no way to distinguish the two unless you say, "the one that makes you drunk" or "the one that doesn't make you drunk."

• Don't expect to find the menu posted in a restaurant's window.

• Take advantages of the special menus some restaurants offer. At lunch you may find a *menú* or *menú fijo* (both terms mean the same thing), a fixed-price menu at a reasonable price.

• If you're eating in a nice restaurant, don't be surprised to find two or three waiters hovering at your table—though they are never intrusive. With subtle touches they make you feel pampered, e.g., even bringing a woman a little table on which to place her handbag.

• Be aware that if you ask for *té con leche* (tea with milk), you'll get a cup of hot milk with a tea bag in it.

• Keep in mind that the person who issues the invitation to a meal expects to pay.

Specialties

• Some fish and seafood specialties: *ceviche*—raw fish marinated in lime juice with onions and spices; *corvina*—sea bass, the best Peruvian fish; *chupe de camarones*—shrimp stew; *causa a la limeña*—a potato puree mound with shrimp salad, typical of Lima.

• Meat specialties: *anticuchos*—skewered beef hearts, marinated and grilled; *sancochado*—meat, legumes, and vegetable stew with garlic and spices; *lomo saltado*—chopped steak fried with potatoes, onions, and tomatoes, served with rice.

• A popular potato dish: *papas a la Huancaína*—potatoes with spicy cheese and chile sauce.

• Avocados are the base for several specialties: *palta rellena*—avocado stuffed with chicken salad; *palta a la jardinera*—avocado stuffed with vegetable salad.

• For dessert, try *suspiro a la limeña* (condensed milk, eggs, sugar, cinnamon, lemon juice, and Port wine) or *mazamorra morada* (a purple gelatin dessert made from purple corn).

HOTELS

• For accommodations other than the massive, anonymous hotels in central cities, seek out *pensiones* or *hostales* (oh-**stah**-lehs). They are small, family-run hotels in suburbs, and they are usually clean, comfortable, and very reasonable in price.

• If you enjoy a drink before dinner or a nightcap in your room, buy a bottle of duty-free liquor when you leave your country. Imported alcoholic drinks are very expensive in Peru.

• Planning to stay at youth hostels? Remember that you need a membership card from your country, though some hostels in major cities don't enforce this requirement.

• Keep in mind that the cheapest hotels may not have hot water at all hours. In addition, some hotels charge extra for hot showers, and some don't even have showers. Ask when you arrive.

• When under the shower, don't touch anything metal, or you may get a nasty shock. The shower head is hooked to an electric heating element. Be sure to dry yourself carefully before turning off the shower.

• Note that even the least expensive hotels can arrange to have your laundry done. At better hotels, the charge for this service may be very high.

• If you're traveling on business and will need to communicate with your home office, stay at a first-class hotel, where you'll be able to send a telex.

TIPPING

• Give porters the equivalent of $1.00 (U.S.) for all bags.
• Don't tip taxi drivers.
• Restaurants add a 10% ser-

vice charge. If the service is outstanding, add 5% or leave the equivalent of 25 or 50 cents extra.

• If gas station attendants perform extra services—e.g., checking the tires, filling the radiator, or cleaning the windshield—give them the equivalent of 25 cents.

PRIVATE HOMES

• Note that the typical time for visiting is at tea time—6:00 to 8:00 P.M. After tea, people go home to dinner.

• Phone before visiting.

• If you have a letter of introduction from a Peruvian, anticipate a warm and fulsome welcome.

• Offer to pay for long-distance calls both within Peru and to other countries.

• If you're staying in a middle-class home, feel free to take a daily bath or shower. There will be a constant supply of hot water. Be sure to ask for instructions about operating the shower. Turning things on in the wrong order could lead to electric shock.

• Don't feel obliged to spend all your time with family members. They won't mind if you go sightseeing on your own.

• Compliment the maid on the food she has prepared.

• If you stay with a family for several days, give the maid the equivalent of $4.00 to $5.00. Hand the money to her, or put it in her pocket.

Gifts: When invited to a meal, bring wine, liquor, or chocolates if you wish. Your hosts won't expect anything.

• If you give flowers, give roses. Other flowers are so inexpensive that they don't seem like a gift. You can send roses ahead. There is no delivery charge.

• Bring perfume, scarves, elegant neckties, or costume jewelry (many people don't wear real gold for fear that it will be stolen).

• Don't give clothing made of nylon or polyester. Peruvians prefer natural fabrics.

BUSINESS

Hours

Businesses: Monday to Friday, 8:30 A.M. to 12:30 P.M., and 3:00 to 6:30 P.M.

Government Offices: April to December: Monday to Friday, 8:00 A.M. to 2:00 P.M. January to March: Monday to Friday, 8:00 A.M. to 1:00 P.M. and 3:00 to 6:00 P.M.

Banks: April to December: Monday to Friday, 9:15 A.M. to 12:45 P.M. January to March: 8:30 to 11:30 A.M.

Shops: Monday to Saturday, 9:30 A.M. to 12:30 P.M. and 4:00 to 7:00 P.M.

• Be aware that everything is closed from 1:00 to 3:00 P.M. There isn't a siesta as such, but people usually return home for lunch during those hours.

Currency

• Remember that there are *two* major units of currency—the old one, the *sol,* consisting of 100 *centavos,* and the *inti,* introduced in 1986, and consisting of 1,000 *soles.*

• Coins: 50 *centavos* and 1, 5, 10, 50, and 100 *soles.*

• Bills: 5, 10, 50, 100, 500, 1,000, 5,000, and 10,000 *soles.*

• Remember that *sol* and *inti* bills of the same color and size are interchangeable. For example, the 10,000 *sol* bill is blue as is the 10 *inti* bill; both have the same value.

• The *inti* is divided into 100 *céntimos.* There are coins of 5, 10, and 50 *céntimos,* which look like the 50, 100, and 500 *sol* coins. A coin of 5 *céntimos* is worth a 50 *sol* coin; a 10 *céntimo* coin is worth a 100 *sol* coin, and so forth. There is also a new 1 *inti* coin.

• Shop around for the best rates, especially when changing travelers' checks. Change money or travelers' checks at banks, at *casas de cambio* (exchange places), with street changers, or in first-class hotels, restaurants, and shops. Banks often charge a higher commission and limit the amount you can change. *Casas de cambio* are usually open from 9:00 A.M. to 6:00 P.M., with a few hours off for lunch.

• If you pay in dollars at hotels, restaurants, or shops, you'll get change in Peruvian currency. Stores that deal in imported goods will welcome dollars.

• Traveling through areas with small towns, keep in mind that U.S. dollars are often the only currency you can exchange.

Business Practices

• Keep in mind that many American companies placed a moratorium on business travel to Peru as of October 1987 because of the many random kidnappings of executives. Kidnappers look for well-dressed white men carrying briefcases.

• Don't plan business trips to Peru during January to March, when most businesspeople vacation. Also avoid the two weeks before and the week after Christmas, and the week before and after Easter.

• Be aware that it's important to have contacts in Peru. See the "Business" section of the Introduction for suggestions on acquiring them. Contacts in the diplomatic world are especially valuable. They can arrange invitations to embassy parties at which you can gather valuable information.

• From abroad, make business appointments at least two weeks in advance. Don't consider arriving in Peru and making impromptu calls at business or government offices.

• Try to schedule appointments in the morning.

• To enhance your image, stay in the best hotels. It isn't necessary, however, to eat at the best restaurants.

• Have business cards printed in both English and Spanish. If you haven't brought a supply, you can have them made locally in two to three days.

• Realize that Peru's recent economic difficulties have made the country eager for foreign investment. You will be welcomed and business may proceed fairly quickly.

• Note that a morning appointment may produce an invitation to lunch, so it's wise not to make a second morning appointment at another company.

• Be as subtle as Peruvians in negotiating. Don't confront people directly. Ask many, many questions, but avoid questions that would produce a "Yes" or "No" response, since Peruvians will tell you what they think you want to hear rather than what they really believe.

• Don't suggest an appointment between 1:00 and 3:00 P.M., as many businesspeople take their lunch break during that time. However, a Peruvian may suggest lunch. More businesspeople now go out to eat in restaurants instead of returning home, so the lunch period may be shorter.

• Be punctual, though Peruvians usually aren't. Foreigners are expected to be on time.

• To impress Peruvian businesspeople, include charts and visual aids in your presentation.

• Realize that private enterprises are usually more reliable in time estimates and contracts than government offices.

• Women should realize that it will be *very* difficult for foreign businesswomen to succeed in Peru. Upper-class Peruvian women—if they work—have "second-economy" jobs. For example, they may hire goldsmiths to make jewelry and then sell it from their homes, or they may have knitters working in their garages and then sell the sweaters from their homes. Married women can't open a bank account without their husbands' consent.

• For business gifts, bring inexpensive cameras, calculators, or good pens (e.g., Cross or other major brands).

• Note that lunches are more appropriate for discussing business while dinners tend to be social.

• When planning to entertain for a business discussion, invite only those with whom you have been negotiating directly. When a deal is completed, feel free to invite everyone who has been involved in a project.

• Remember that Peruvian businesspeople like to be entertained at luxurious restaurants. Ask either the secretary of a top person in the Peruvian firm, or call the tourist office to get the names of the restaurants that cater to luxury dining.

• Include Peruvian wives in an invitation to a strictly social function, even if you are alone. If you have a co-worker whose wife has accompanied him, invite her, or ask the Peruvian businessman to invite someone else from the company with his wife. Do this so that the women can talk together.

Independence Days (July 28–29); Saint Rosa of the Americas (Aug. 30); National Heroes' Day (Oct. 8); All Saints' Day (Nov. 1); Immaculate Conception (Dec. 8); Christmas (Dec. 25).

HOLIDAYS AND SPECIAL OCCASIONS

Expect to find banks, offices, and many shops closed on the days listed below. Many local areas have holidays. Check with the tourist office to learn what they are.

Holidays: New Year's Day (Jan. 1); Easter; Labor Day (May 1); Sts. Peter and Paul (June 29);

TRANSPORTATION

Public Transportation

• When you take a local bus, pay when you get on. You don't need exact change. The fare is the same for all destinations within city limits. When you want to get off, yell "Baja" (bah-hah).

• Note that there are three types of taxis. Hotel taxis are black sedans. They are more expensive than others but they are also more reliable. They have set fares. Most taxis don't have meters. Ask at your hotel what the fare should be, and negotiate in advance.

• If you're in Lima, consider taking *colectivos*. They are small cars, accommodating about five passengers, that run along set routes and that are faster than buses. Fares are based on distance. They'll stop whenever you want to get off.

• Remember that there are many long-distance bus companies, each with its own terminal. Buy your ticket in advance, if possible, so that you'll be assured a seat. Keep your luggage with you, and keep an eye on it. Buses that travel the Pan-American Highway have reclining seats.

• Be aware that heating on buses doesn't always work. If you're traveling at a high altitude it can become *extremely* cold. Bring warm clothes and maybe even a blanket. Air-conditioning doesn't always work either; if you're traveling in the lowlands, it can get very hot.

• Expect buses to stop for three meals a day. If you want to be sure your food is safe, however, bring your own.

• On better buses, look for toilets, but be aware that they often don't work.

• Realize that trains have several classes. First class has compartments (no heat) with two bunk beds and a sink, a dining car, and a bathroom, which everyone shares. Better than first class is Pullman class, where the cars are heated, the sleeping compartments have bathrooms, and the food tends to be of better quality. Second class is crowded and uncomfortable.

• Avoid night trains, because of the prevalence of thieves.

• Buy train tickets a day in advance.

• If you take the train from Cuzco to Machu Picchu on your own, be one of the first to get off the train. There aren't many small buses going up the mountain to Machu Picchu, so you'll have to walk if you don't get one.

• If you hire a car and driver to take you around the country for several days, agree in advance whether you are responsible for paying for his food and hotel room or whether it's included in his price.

• Realize that air travel within Peru is inexpensive. Try to take a morning flight; they tend to be more punctual than later flights. Be sure to reconfirm flights. Be at the airport at least an hour before the flight, since weather conditions sometimes cause flights to leave *early*. Remember that there are no separate sections for smokers and that some flights have seat assignments but others do not.

Driving

• Realize that driving in Peru is very difficult. Rental cars are often not in good condition. Most streets don't have signs, and there are no signs for roads leading out of the city. Roads are full of potholes, and there are very few gas stations.

• Expect an on-the-spot fine if you are stopped for a traffic violation. Police may expect a bribe.

• When you stop for gas, get out of the car to make sure that the gauge on the pump is set at zero. Gas is measured in gallons.

LEGAL MATTERS, SAFETY, AND HEALTH

• Note that you'll receive a tourist card on arrival in Peru. There is no charge. Guard it carefully, because you'll have to hand it back when you leave the country.

• Always carry your passport and your tourist card, because there are often random checks on public transportation. If you don't have your documents, you could be subject to arrest.

• Remember that coca leaves for chewing or making tea are legal, but cocaine is not.

• Keep in mind that Peru's drug laws are *extremely* harsh. People can spend weeks in prison waiting for a trial and then serve a long jail sentence.

• Be aware that in Lima there is a *strict* curfew from 1:00 A.M. to 5:00 A.M. If you're visiting a friend, be sure to be back at your hotel before 1:00 A.M. If you arrive in Lima by plane during the curfew hours, you'll be given a safe-conduct pass. You'll have to pay the taxi driver *much* more than the normal fare to take you to your hotel.

• Be aware that Peru has a small but active and violent guerrilla movement, Sendero Luminoso, which means "Shining Path." This Maoist group is known to stage bombings in the city and is often responsible for power outages. Avoid the area around Ayacucho, which is more prone to Sendero Luminoso bomb attacks.

• Note that June 19 is the anniversary of the 1986 prison massacres. Many of the victims were members of Sendero Luminoso. That day may be violent in Lima, with blackouts and bombings caused by that organization. The blackouts usually last from one to two hours.

• Be very careful when crossing the streets. Cars do not respect the rules.

• Beware of pickpockets; try to avoid crowds where they can easily disappear. Carry most of your money in travelers' checks.

• Don't wear gold jewelry or expensive watches, or robbers may rip them off.

• When traveling to high altitudes, spend the first day resting. Avoid alcohol and cigarettes, and eat very lightly. On your second day, don't rush—walk slowly. If you get true altitude sickness, ask at your hotel (even if it is a small one) if they have a supply of oxygen. The only real cure is to descend to a lower level. Many hotels serve guests *maté de coca* (tea made with coca leaves), a brew that is supposed to ameliorate the effects of altitude sickness.

• Bring sunscreen from abroad. The type made in Peru is not effective.

• Contraceptives are also available in major cities, but the choices are limited.

• For information about medicine and hygiene products, see "Legal Matters, Safety, and Health" in the Introduction.

URUGUAY

Huddling next to gigantic Brazil, Uruguay, South America's small-est country, makes up for its size with some impressive qualities. It has the highest literacy rate in South America, not to mention the longest life expectancy on the continent.

Uruguay has a European culture and quiet style of life, and an extensive welfare system. Up until the sixties, it was often likened to Switzerland for its political stability and social and economic progressiveness. Eco-nomic setbacks have eroded the country's standard of living, however, and some once affluent families now search for bargains when they shop.

Unlike landlocked Switzerland, Uruguay boasts 250 miles of beaches, including one of the continent's playgrounds for the rich, Punta del Este, Uruguay's South American Riviera, which continues to fill with vacationers—and the good life goes on.

GREETINGS

Language: The official language of Uruguay is Spanish.

• When young people are introduced, note that girls kiss girls and boys kiss girls, while boys shake hands with other boys. When adults are introduced, the custom is to shake hands with members of both sexes, unless they are good friends. In that case, they greet one another as young people do.

• Remember that titles are important. Use *Doctor* for university graduates other than engineers (*Ingeniero*) or teachers (*Profesor*).

• When you leave a party, feel free to say one "good-bye" to the group, unless you've had a long conversation with someone. In that case, say an individual "good-bye."

CONVERSATION

• Good subjects for first conversations are sports—especially soccer—and international politics.

• Ask for suggestions about places to visit, interesting sights, and good restaurants.

• In a first conversation, don't discuss family.

• If you're a young person talking to other young people, prepare for a "one-upmanship" game about the courses you're studying.

TELEPHONES

• Buy tokens, called *monedas para teléfono* at shops, bars, or restaurants. To make a local call, deposit one token for a three-minute call. After that time, a tone sounds, and you must add more tokens.

• To make a long distance call, go to ANTEL, the telephone company, which has many offices throughout the country.

IN PUBLIC

• Gestures to remember: (1) thumbs up with other fingers closed means okay; (2) touching all the fingers and thumb of the right hand together signals doubt.

• Don't feel obliged to write a thank-you note for an invitation or a favor. People don't expect them.

• If you're a gambler, note that there are many casinos. Don't change money in one, however, because the exchange rate isn't very good.

• Try bargaining in small shops and markets but not in large department stores.

DRESS

• Casual wear for men is a sports jacket, shirt, and pants, and for women pants. Women shouldn't wear shorts or jeans though men can wear shorts for sightseeing.

• For business, men should wear dark suits and ties and in winter three-piece suits. Women should wear a skirt, blazer, and good shoes. In winter, women should wear a fur coat if they have one. During the winter, wear nylons; they aren't necessary in the summer.

• To a formal occasion (e.g., a

wedding, a girl's fifteenth birthday party, the theater), men should wear a dark suit and women a cocktail dress.

• In choosing your wardrobe, remember that Uruguayans don't usually wear bright, splashy colors for everyday dress. Bring clothes in subdued colors.

MEALS

Hours and Foods

Breakfast: 7:00 or 7:30 A.M. A light meal—usually toast with butter and cheese. The beverage will be coffee or tea.

Lunch: 1:00 P.M. A typical meal might be *churrasco* (steak— Uruguay is known for its excellent beef) with potatoes and salad, or veal cutlet *milanesa* with French fries. They would be followed by fruits or cake and coffee.

Dinner: About 10:00 P.M. A meal similar to lunch, but lighter. There might be *arroz con leche* (rice

with milk), chicken, or tortillas (made of eggs, cheese, and spinach, these tortillas are really omelettes, not Mexican tortillas).

Beverages: With lunch, expect wine, soda, mineral water, and juices. With dinner, wine and soda are the usual drinks. Before dinner, people drink whiskey and martinis. A popular drink between meals is *maté,* a kind of herb tea sipped from a gourd that is passed from person to person. Drink it only if it's hot, which means that it has been prepared with boiling water.

Table Manners

• Expect drinks before dinner to be accompanied by small appetizers, e.g., chips, nuts, or—at an elegant meal—caviar. Drinks and snacks are usually served in the living room.

• If you don't want an alcoholic beverage before dinner or with your meal, ask for a soda.

• Expect beef to be featured at almost all meals.

• Don't feel obliged to finish everything on your plate, but do try a little of everything.

• To indicate that you've finished, place the knife and fork vertically on your plate.

• If you're invited to dinner in someone's home during the week, leave after coffee. On weekends, you can stay later. Use your judgment on how the conversation is going, and leave when your host and hostess seem tired.

Eating Out

• *Confiterías* are tea shops. *Coctelerías* are places for cocktails and hors d'oeuvres. *Parrilladas,* the most common restaurants in Uruguay, are grills where beef is the main dish. *Heladerías* serve ice cream. A *bar* is a sidewalk cafe where you can have soft drinks, beer, and sandwiches.

• Remember that imported whiskey is expensive; local whiskies cost only half the price.

• If you order a *copetín* (coh-pehteen) you'll get a drink made with whiskey, and a selection of appetizers will be included in the price of the drink.

• Note that dinner hour at restaurants is from 9:00 P.M. to midnight. Some informal restaurants begin serving at 7:30 P.M.

• Don't expect to find menus posted in the windows of elegant restaurants.

• To get the waiter's attention in an elegant restaurant, simply raise your hand. In an informal restaurant, say *"Mozo"* (**moh**-soh), which means "waiter." Though you'll see some people making a kissing sound to attract the waiter's attention, don't do it—it's rude.

• If you're dining with people of the upper classes, expect one person to pay for the group. Among the lower classes, people usually pay individually.

Specialties

• Try some of Uruguay's beef dishes: *asado*—barbecued beef; *puchero*—beef with beans, bacon, sausages, and vegetables; *lomo*—the best cut of steak.

• Other meat specialties: *milanesa*—veal cutlet breaded and fried; *chivito*—a sandwich with meat, lettuce, egg, melted cheese, and olives; *choripań*—sausage baked in dough; *morcilla dulce*—a sweet blood sausage made with orange peel, raisins, and walnuts; *buseca*—a spicy soup with oxtail, beans, and peas; *carbonada*—a stew of meat, rice, peaches, pears, and raisins.

• Sweets include: *yemas*—crystallized egg yolks; *chajá*—a dessert made of sponge cake with cream and jam; *dulce de membrillo*—a quince preserve; *espuma de mar*—angel cake with whipped cream; *dulce de leche*—milk simmered with sugar and vanilla.

HOTELS

• If you're planning to visit Uruguay between December and April, book your hotel well in advance. Thousands of South Americans vacation in Uruguay during those months.

• Note that hotels in beach areas lower their prices after April 1, but some of them close their dining rooms. During Carnival week, hotel prices go up 20%.

TIPPING

• Give taxi drivers 5% of the fare.

• Tip porters 20 new *pesos* per piece of luggage.

• Leave waiters 10% of the check.

• Tip gas station attendants 10 new *pesos*.

PRIVATE HOMES

• Never drop in on people you don't know well. Always telephone in advance.

• Don't be surprised if people entertain you with a meal in a restaurant followed by coffee in their home.

• If you're invited to stay with a middle-class family, remember that they have probably been going through hard economic times. Don't expect luxury.

• Don't be surprised to find that upper- and middle-class families have more than one maid. However, it's better to make your own bed, keep your room neat, and do your own laundry.

• If the home does not have a maid, offer to help set and clear the table and do the dishes. Your offer may still be refused.

• Expect constant hot water in

most upper- and middle-class homes. Ask your hostess if the water needs to be heated for a bath, a process that will take from 30 minutes to an hour.

• If you stay with a family, give the maid a small gift (e.g., costume jewelry—not money).

Gifts: When you're invited to a meal, bring roses, the choicest and most appreciated flower.

• From abroad, bring something unusual for the house, such as a clock that gives the time in different places around the world.

• For young people, bring tapes of American popular music. They also enjoy T-shirts or sweatshirts with insignia of U.S. universities.

• Bring older people tapes of classical music.

BUSINESS

Hours

Businesses: Monday through Friday, 8:30 A.M. to noon, and 2:30 to 6:30 P.M.

Government Offices: From mid-March through mid-November, Monday to Friday, 11:00 A.M. to 5:00 P.M. From mid-November to mid-March, Monday to Friday, 7:00 A.M. to 1:00 P.M.

Banks: Monday to Friday, 10:00 A.M. to 4:00 P.M.

Shops: Monday to Friday, 9:00 A.M. to noon, and 2:30 to 7:00 P.M.

Currency

• Remember that the currency is the new *peso,* made up of 100 *centésimos.*

• Coins: 10, 20, 50 *centésimos* and 1, 2, 5, and 10 new *pesos.*

• Bills: 50, 100, 500, 1,000, 5,000, and 10,000 new *pesos.*

Business Practices

• Plan business travel to Uruguay between May and November. Vacation period is January through April. Avoid the two weeks before and after Christmas, Carnival period, and the week before and after Easter.

• Have business cards printed in English and Spanish. You can have them printed locally in two or three days.

• Be sure to have sales literature available in Spanish as well as English.

• Expect to find very sophisticated businesspeople, most of whom are of Spanish, Italian, or German ancestry.

• Be aware that Uruguayans understand U.S. business methods better than people in other Latin American countries. They realize that North Americans are practical and straightforward and that they like to proceed quickly in business.

• Don't be surprised to find that an executive's workday in Uruguay is a very long one.

• Note that business lunches are more common for discussions that are strictly business. Business dinners are usually held in the restaurants of major hotels.

• If you are entertaining a Uruguayan, choose a Chinese, French, or fine Uruguayan restaurant.

HOLIDAYS AND SPECIAL OCCASIONS

Expect to find businesses, government offices, banks, and many restaurants and stores closed on the following national holidays. Check with the tourist office to learn if there are any local or religious festivals which will lead to closings.

Holidays: New Year's Day (Jan. 1); Epiphany (Jan. 6); Carnival (three days before Ash Wednesday); Holy Week; Day of the Landing of the 33 Easterners (April 19); Labor Day (May 1); Anniversary of the Birth of Artigas (June 19); Constitution Day (July 18); Independence Day (Aug. 25); Columbus Day (Oct. 12); All Souls' Day (Nov. 2); Christmas (Dec. 25).

• April 19 celebrates the beginning of the struggle for independence in 1825. Thirty-three Uruguayans who had started an expedition from Argentina returned to their country and began the struggle against Portugal. (Uruguayans call themselves *orientales,* "Easterners," in reference to their country's location, east of Rio de la Plata.)

• June 19 honors the birthday of Artigas, a leader in the fight for independence associated with Simón Bolivar.

• On December 24 and 31, expect firecrackers and fireworks to be set off throughout cities or towns.

• Be cautious during Carnival and wear waterproof clothing. Young people throw water at everyone.

• For long distances, consider taking a bus. Buses for long trips have reclining seats, air-conditioning, and bathrooms. Buses that make trips of 100 kilometers or less don't have such amenities.

TRANSPORTATION

Public Transportation

• If you take a local bus, look for small signs on corners to mark bus stops, and be prepared for pushing and shoving in line. Enter from the front. You'll be asked your destination because the fare is based on zones. Keep your ticket as inspectors frequently board buses to check them. Don't pull the cord (which usually doesn't work) before you want to get off; instead, say "psst" to the conductor.

• Note that there are taxis and *coches,* unmetered cars for which you should be sure to agree on a fare in advance. If you have a choice between a taxi (usually a black-and-yellow Mercedes) and a *coche,* remember that the taxi has a meter and is usually much cheaper.

• Look for taxi stands in Montevideo. You can also telephone for a taxi or hail one on the street.

• Realize that passenger train service has been discontinued in Uruguay.

Driving

• Be aware that Uruguayan drivers don't signal when turning and don't respect traffic signals. While there are no laws about drinking and driving, if you're in an accident and have been drinking, you're in serious trouble.

• Don't be surprised if police stop you and want a bribe. If you're delayed for no serious reason, offer some money.

LEGAL MATTERS, SAFETY, AND HEALTH

• Feel free to drink the water and eat fruits and vegetables in Montevideo. Outside the city, observe precautions.

• Women should not go out alone after dark. Take a taxi. Feel free, however, to eat alone in a good restaurant.

• For information about medicine and hygiene products, see "Legal Matters, Safety, and Health" in the Introduction.

VENEZUELA

CARIBBEAN SEA

Maracaibo

Puerto Cabello

Caracas

Valencia

Barquisimeto

Maturin

El Tigre

San Cristóbal

Ciudad Bolívar

VENEZUELA

Arriving in Caracas, you may think that there's been a mistake—that you're actually in a city in the United States. The skyscrapers, the fast-food chains, even the strong traces of English that have crept into the language all attest to the country's close kinship to the U.S. No country in South America exhibits greater North American influence than Venezuela.

Had you arrived at the beginning of the century, you would have found a country little changed since its discovery in 1498. But in 1914 came the great miracle—oil. In the span of some 70 years, Venezuela has whizzed through five centuries of growth.

Besides the wealth brought by oil, you'll also notice the reverence paid to the hero of South America's liberation, Simón Bolívar, who was born in Caracas in 1783.

GREETINGS

Language: The official language of Venezuela is Spanish.

• When you first meet someone, shake hands when meeting and leaving. After the first meeting, men touch one another's shoulders, while women kiss one another on the cheek.

• When men know one another well, they shake hands and embrace or pat one another on the right shoulder. Men and women who are good friends often kiss, and women kiss one another.

• Always accept or return whatever greeting is offered.

• Use titles. They are important to Venezuelans. Some common titles: Doctor (for Ph.D. and medical doctor); architect; engineer; lawyer; professor. (See "Key Words and Phrases" at the end of the book for Spanish equivalents.) Use the title with the last name.

• At large parties, introduce yourself. At small parties you will be introduced by the host or host-

ess. At either type of party, shake hands and say good-bye to each person when you leave.

CONVERSATION

• Be aware that people stand very close to one another when conversing. Don't back away.

• Good subjects for conversation: people's jobs; sights you should see; art and literature.

• Note that Venezuelans are very interested in a visitor's view of their country's economy. Don't initiate a conversation on the subject, but be prepared to answer questions.

• Don't discuss politics—especially Venezuelan politics—or tell political jokes.

• Don't bring up the problem of illegal aliens from Colombia.

• Don't ask whether a person is married, has a family, and so forth. You should know someone fairly well before you ask personal questions.

TELEPHONES

IN PUBLIC

• Look for public telephones in pharmacies, subway stations, and in gray phone booths on the street.
• Recall that a local call costs 1 *bolívar*. There are slots in the phone for 25 *céntimo,* 50 *céntimo,* and 1 *bolívar* coins. For a local call, you have unlimited time. For a long-distance call, look for the timer, which will keep clicking and will show how much time you have left. When the timer reaches zero, deposit more money to continue talking.
• To get small coins go to a kiosk on the street, the Metro, or a pharmacy.
• For long-distance calls, go to the telephone office, called CANTV (kahn-teh-**veh**).

• If you see someone clenching the fist with the thumb between the index and middle finger, he is wishing good luck.
• Always say *"Buenos días"* when entering a shop or office. Usually everyone will respond. When leaving, say *"Adios."*
• For taking pictures, note that Venezuelans are not terribly concerned about privacy and won't mind being photographed.
• Don't take pictures near embassies.
• If you shop at places frequented by tourists, ask if there is a discount for paying cash.

DRESS

• Prepare to find people dressed very formally in cities. Even for a visit to a pizza parlor, men usually wear jackets. Stylish jeans are acceptable on the street in cities, but don't wear shorts except on the tennis court, at the beach, or at home.

• In elegant restaurants men must wear a jacket and tie. Women may wear fancy cocktail dresses to elegant restaurants in cities. Many theaters also require men to wear jackets and ties in the evening.

• For business, men should wear a suit, white shirt, and tie. Women may wear a suit, a dress, or a skirt and blouse.

• Venezuelan women rarely wear stockings, but do wear them when you want to make a good impression, e.g., for a business meeting.

• Note that men wear tuxedos only to large balls, such as the ones held for a girl's debutante ball when she has her fifteenth birthday. The invitation will state that tuxedos should be worn. For formal occasions, women should wear cocktail dresses.

MEALS

Hours and Foods

Breakfast: Families with children breakfast early (about 6:00 or 6:30 A.M.), since children must be at school by 7:00 A.M. Families without children usually eat between 7:00 and 8:00 A.M. The usual meal is scrambled eggs, *arepas* (see "Specialties") and butter, and coffee with milk. In other families, the meal is lighter: bread and rolls (which the maid buys fresh each morning) with strong coffee, similar to espresso. With either type of morning meal, there will be fresh fruit juices.

Lunch: Noon to 2:00 P.M. The main meal of the day, lunch features several courses: soup, salad, meat and vegetables, fruit, and desserts (often European pastries such as cream puffs, tortes, and fruit tarts). Beverages might be beer, mineral water, lemonade, or a soda.

Dinner: About 9:00 P.M. Usually a light meal, e.g., soup and a sandwich, or *arepas,* or *empanadas,* or bread and eggs. Beverages would be the same as those at lunch. Because of the large noontime meal, many people don't eat dinner.

Beverages: Before dinner the most common drink is whiskey with ice and water. Also popular are rum, wine, sangria, and beer.

• Note that most women in Venezuela don't drink beer or strong liquor.

• Expect coffee to be available in a great variety of ways: *guayoyo,* a large cup of mild black coffee; *negro,* a large cup of strong black coffee; *negrito,* a demitasse of strong black coffee; *marrón,* a large cup of strong coffee with a little milk; *marroncito,* a demitasse of strong coffee with a little milk.

• Another popular beverage is hot chocolate, which people sometimes drink at breakfast or in the evening.

Table Manners

• Keep in mind that some dinner parties don't begin until 11:00 P.M. and sometimes last until

3:00, 4:00, or 5:00 A.M. Fortify yourself with a snack early in the evening. Even after a dinner that begins earlier, people tend to stay late—till midnight or 1:00 A.M.

• Note that the seats at the head and foot of the table are usually reserved for the mother and father. Wait for your host to seat you. If you're the guest of honor, you will probably sit next to the host or hostess.

• Unless you're at a large dinner, which is often a buffet, expect the maid to serve food onto individual plates.

• Always wait until everyone at the table has been served before beginning to eat.

• Don't feel obliged to finish everything on your plate, and don't worry that people will push you to have second and third helpings. They won't.

• To indicate that you have finished eating, place your utensils at an angle, with tips pointing to 10:00.

Eating Out

• Look for *cafés,* which serve sandwiches, pizza, pastries, coffee, juices, milk shakes, and beer (the only type of alcohol they offer).

• To purchase bread or rolls, head for a *panadería.*

• For pastries, look for a *pastelería.* In some, you can sit down and have coffee, orange juice, or a soft drink. You'll often find *panaderías* and *pastelerías* combined.

• Note that there are fresh-fruit stands (called *juguerías*) everywhere. Fresh fruits are put in a blender and mixed with ice and water. Don't buy juice from these stands, since the water may not have been boiled.

• When ordering a drink, realize that imported whiskeys are very expensive.

• For meals at better restaurants, be sure to make reservations.

• To summon a waiter, say *"Mesonero"* (meh-soh-**neh**-roh). To call a waitress, say *"Mesonera"* (meh-soh-**neh**-rah).

• If you see *muchacho* (which means "boy") on the menu, realize that it is a cut of beef.

• Note that beef is very good, and portions are large.

• To order beer on tap, ask for *lisa* (**lee**-sah). A bottle of beer is *tercio* (**tehr**-syoh).

• Don't be surprised if your party receives two checks—one for food and another for drinks.

• Remember that the person who suggests the meal pays. There is no such thing as a "Dutch treat." Note that if a man and woman go out, the man *always* pays.

Specialties

• Taste the national dish, *pabellón*. You will be served three separate dishes: black beans with white rice; shredded beef mixed with tomatoes, onions, and green peppers; fried plaintains.

• No Venezuelan party is complete without *tequeños*—small, bite-size pieces of white cheese wrapped in dough and deep fried. They are served as appetizers.

• Try *hallacas*, a kind of *tamal*—ground-corn dough with a filling of a meat and/or chicken mixture, all wrapped in banana leaves, and then boiled. To eat one, you unwrap it, discard the leaves, and eat the *hallaca*.

• Special soups are *hervido de gallina* and *sancocho*—hearty soups made of chicken, meat, or fish and vegetables.

• Two dishes based on corn: *bollos de maíz*—spiced corn puffs fried in deep fat; *arepas*—flat white corn flour pancakes filled with butter, meat, or cheese.

• Sample dishes made with plaintain: *tortas de plátano*—cakes of plaintains and cheese, spiced with cinnamon, and served with meat dishes; *tostones* (often served as appetizers)—slices of plaintain which are cooked in oil, pounded, and fried again until they're very crisp.

• Two popular desserts: *quesillo*—a flan which is steamed rather than baked; *bien-me-sabe de coco*—a cake topped with muscatel wine and coconut cream.

HOTELS

• Note that Venezuela can boast of several world-class hotels.

• If you decide to stay at a less than luxury hotel, be sure that the air-conditioning works and that there is hot water before you take the room.

• Note that some of the smaller, budget hotels are used for "trysts"—or for brothels.

TIPPING

• Give porters the equivalent of $1.00 (U.S.) total for a few suitcases.

• Don't tip taxi drivers unless they have carried luggage or have gone out of their way to do something special.

• Restaurants and hotels add a 10% service charge. If service has been very good, leave an extra 5%.

• Leave hotel maids 2 *bolívares* per day.

• Tip gas station attendants 2 *bolívares*.

PRIVATE HOMES

• Don't visit or phone people between 1:00 and 3:00 P.M., which is siesta time.

• Expect to be invited to a home only if you're a close friend.

• Try not to decline the offer of coffee when you visit. To offer a small cup of black coffee is a symbol of hospitality.

• Don't expect people to be fanatic about saving energy, as people in other parts of the world are. Venezuelans tend to leave lights and TV sets on, so you needn't be as conscientious about saving electricity as you would in other places.

• Feel free to take a daily shower.

Most middle-class homes have constant hot water. Don't, however, stay in the shower for a long time as there can be water shortages.

• Expect your hostess to ask if you need laundry done. She'll take it and give it to the maid (in middle-class homes). If your hostess doesn't inquire, ask where you should wash your clothes.

• If a family is taking you sightseeing by car, realize that they may not be able to drive you on a certain day of the week because of the number on their license plate. (The restriction is an attempt to relieve some of the traffic congestion.)

Gifts: Note that Venezuelans appreciate whiskey because its price in the country is exorbitant.

• Give women orchids (the national flower). Give men items—such as pens—for the office.

• From abroad, bring electrical gadgets, cameras, pocket calculators, fashion magazines, perfume (if you know someone well), bestsellers in English (if you know that the person reads English), or chocolates.

• Note that it's unlucky to give handkerchiefs.

BUSINESS

Hours

Businesses: Monday through Friday, 8:00 A.M. to 6:00 P.M., with a break at noon.

Government Offices: Open to the public 8:00 A.M. to noon, Monday through Friday. However, if you need an appointment with an official, make it between 2:00 and 5:00 P.M.

Banks: Monday through Friday, 8:30 to 11:30 A.M., and 2:00 to 4:30 P.M.

Shops: Monday through Saturday, 9:00 A.M. to 1:00 P.M., and 3:00 to 7:00 P.M.

Currency

• Note that the unit of currency is the *bolívar,* abbreviated as *Bs,* consisting of 100 *céntimos.*
• Coins are 5 *céntimos* (called a *puya* or a *centavo*), 25 *céntimos* (called

a *medio*), 50 *céntimos* (called a *real*), and 1, 2, and 5 *bolívares*. Five-*bolívar* coins are called *fuertes*.

• Be aware that in the eastern part of Venezuela, most banks will not change travelers' checks. Even in Caracas, some banks will change only one brand of travelers' checks (the brand will differ from bank to bank). You can change the checks in shops, where there is a poor rate of exchange, or at *casas de cambio* (cah-sahs deh cahm-byoh), money exchange bureaus.

• Realize that there is no black market in currency, and there is no limit on how much local currency one can import or export.

Business Practices

• As soon as you know that you'll be going to Venezuela for business, make appointments. It may take a long time to set up appointments, so begin arrangements as far in advance as possible. Make appointments from abroad at least two to three weeks in advance.

• Note that the best time for business in Caracas is January to June and September to November; in Maracaibo, it's March to June. Avoid the two weeks before and after Christmas and Carnival, as well as the three weeks before and after Easter. At Christmastime, many companies close entirely for

a few days, and government offices are open for limited hours.

• Use telephone and telex to make arrangements for your trip. They are more reliable than airmail to Venezuela. Major hotels have telexes, which may be useful for making living arrangements and for communicating with your home office while you're in Venezuela.

• Don't suggest a business meeting after 4:00 P.M. on a Friday.

• Be prepared to make several trips to accomplish your goals, particularly because Venezuelans may not meet deadlines.

• To make a good impression, stay at the best hotels.

• To ensure success, make initial contacts with the top people in the Venezuelan firm. Decisions are *not* made by teams.

• If you don't have contacts in Venezuela, try to find one through an international bank, the commercial offices of your embassy or consulate in Venezuela, the American Chamber of Commerce in Caracas, or the *Centro Venezuela-Americano* in Caracas.

• Should you need to hire an interpreter, check the ads in *The Daily Journal,* the English-language newspaper.

• As a foreigner, try to be punctual, but don't "work up a sweat" to be on time. The typical excuse for lateness at any time of the day or night is, "I was stuck in traffic."

• Have business cards printed in English on one side and Spanish on the other. If a Venezuelan businessperson doesn't offer you a business card, ask for it.

• Bring any materials and specifications you'll be using in your presentation in Spanish. To really impress people, bring audio-visual material, such as videotapes. If possible, have the audio on the tapes in Spanish.

• Remember that Venezuelans like to do business in person rather than on the telephone.

• If you have a morning appointment, don't make plans for lunch. While a businessperson usually goes home at noon, he or she may invite you to lunch, but may not ask you until you arrive for your appointment. A good strategy is to make an afternoon appointment with one company and then a morning appointment for the next day with another firm.

• Expect to be offered a cup of coffee or tea at a meeting. It's good to accept, even if you just sip a little.

• Remember that even when men have met only a few times, they greet one another with an *abrazo* (bear hug). Be prepared— and don't back off if someone initiates this gesture. Another important gesture that a man will make to show friendship for another man: he will put his arm around you or touch you on the forearm.

This gesture indicates that you've been accepted; never flinch.

• Don't anticipate a long period of socializing before business discussions begin. Venezuelans are much less likely to follow this practice than other Latin Americans. However, should negotiating sessions be long, never show impatience by pacing, tapping your pen, or other such gestures.

• Be aware of the rank of the person with whom you are dealing. Show respect for people in high rank and for elders. Let them precede you through doorways, and never interrupt them in a discussion. Always allow senior ranking officials to speak first at a group meeting.

• Anticipate dealing with businessmen who are well educated and sophisticated.

• Expect Venezuelans to be very direct. There will be no subtlety and no beating around the bush. They will say "No" when they mean "No"; they won't say what they think you want to hear. Reciprocate this directness.

• Don't be surprised if Venezuelan businesspeople complain about problems in the country. If you complain, they will join in with you. They are not much offended by any criticism about their country. Venezuelan businesspeople are willing to discuss their country's problems.

• If you want to keep in touch

with your home office, arrange for someone there to call you at pre-arranged times, since phoning out from Venezuela costs much more than a call in from abroad.

• Stay on the right side of the law. If you have a court case against you—whatever the reason—you will not be allowed to leave the country until the case is resolved.

• Note that business lunches are more common than business dinners. Fewer people observe the custom of going home at noon than in other Latin American countries.

• Don't invite a businessman's wife to a business dinner unless he asks if your wife will be coming—and she will.

• Entertain at a French restaurant. They are considered prestigious.

• Be careful of complimenting a business contact's wife or of giving the impression that you are interested in her. Venezuelans can be very sensitive in this regard.

• Don't expect to be invited to a businessperson's home. Such an invitation is very rare. Most business entertaining is done at a restaurant or club.

• To succeed, a businesswoman should be very proper and businesslike. Dress elegantly; wear jewelry, makeup, heels; never wear anything too revealing.

• Remember that "thank-you" notes are very important. People tend to use them much more than

telephone calls. Write such a note if someone has entertained you, if they have picked you up at the airport, or if they have arranged for your wife to be taken sightseeing.

HOLIDAYS AND SPECIAL OCCASIONS

The following are national holidays on which banks, shops, government offices, and many restaurants will be closed. Check with the tourist office to learn if the region you will be visiting has special holidays when offices will be closed in the area.

Holidays: New Year's Day (Jan. 1); Carnival (Monday and Tuesday before Lent); Holy Thursday; Good Friday; Labor Day (May 1); Battle of Carabobo (June 24); Independence Day (July 5); Bolívar's Birthday (July 24); Columbus Day (Oct. 12); Christmas Eve and Christmas (Dec. 24 and 25).

• Realize that many banks and businesses close on the following religious holidays: Feast of St. Joseph (March 19); Feast of the Ascension (the Thursday which occurs 40 days after Easter); Feast of Corpus Christi (the eighth Thursday after Easter); Feast of All Saints' (Nov. 1); Feast of the Immaculate Conception (Dec. 8).

• Be aware that many banks and businesses close on December 17, the anniversary of Bolívar's death.

• Note that when a holiday falls on a Tuesday or Thursday, an extra day is often added to the holiday to make a four-day weekend. This is called *hacer puente* ("to bridge").

• If you're in Venezuela during Carnival (before Lent), expect water fights, parades, and dancing in the streets. Statues of Simón Bolívar will be hung with wreaths and flowers.

TRANSPORTATION

Public Transportation

• Be sure to get specific information about your destination. People usually give their street address with *Calle* (cah-yeh), which means "street" and the number, but some people give their address by the name of two intersecting streets. Pin down the exact street name and the exact number as well as the intersecting streets.

• Take the subway (*Metro*) in Caracas. It's efficient, air-conditioned, and relatively quiet, as the cars are on rubber wheels. It runs from 6:00 A.M. to 9:00 P.M., Monday to Saturday; and 9:00 A.M. to 9:00 P.M. on Sunday. The fare is based on the length of the trip. Deposit money in a machine, and take your ticket. Keep the ticket because you will need it to leave the subway.

• If you take one of the large city buses, pay on the bus. There is one fare, no matter what the distance. Buses are uncomfortable and crowded.

• Look for small vans, called *carritos por puesto*. They are shared taxis, which stop on main streets. Pay either when you get on or when you get off. When you want to get off, tell the driver, "Donde se pueda" (dohn-deh seh pweh-dah), which means "Stop wherever you can let me off."

• Consider taking taxis. They are reasonable, and drivers always use their meters. At the airport, however, use the taxi stand, where you pay first and receive a receipt. Don't go with drivers who approach you independently.

• For a long-distance trip, take buses, which are fast and comfortable. (There are no railways of importance in the country.) All the country's main roads are surfaced, so travel is smooth. Book ahead for one of the frequent buses between major cities. Be at the station 30 minutes before departure. Seats are not numbered, so prepare to grab a seat as soon as possible. People with tickets for a later bus will try to squeeze on an earlier bus.

Driving

• Be wary about driving in Venezuela. People don't respect traffic laws. They pass on the right, exceed the speed limit constantly—and usually get away with it. Driving is a contest about who has the best reflexes.

• Realize that in Caracas an attempt has been made to regulate traffic. Cars with a license plate beginning with "1" cannot drive in the city on Monday, those with "2" on Tuesday, and so forth. Wealthy people, however, have bought more cars, so the problem hasn't eased.

• If you are stopped for a traffic violation, say "I don't speak Spanish" and hope that the policeman is nice. If a Venezuelan is stopped, he usually says, "Let's arrange it

ourselves" and gives the officer $10 to $20. Paying a ticket involves long waits in line and dealing with the bureaucracy.

• If you're renting a car, first find out what your needs will be. In some areas of the country, you may need four-wheel drive.

LEGAL MATTERS, SAFETY, AND HEALTH

• If you're walking, be careful. In their haste, motorcyclists often drive on the sidewalks.

• Don't walk at night. Always take taxis.

• Women should not wear jewelry. People pull chains off women's necks.

• Women should avoid or beware of the isolated beaches.

• For information about medicine and hygiene products, see "Legal Matters, Safety, and Health" in the Introduction.

Key Words and Phrases: Spanish

Following are some words and phrases we hope you'll find useful in Spanish-speaking Latin America. Remember that in Spanish, accents vary from country to country as widely as they do in English in the various places where it is spoken. If you're having trouble being understood or understanding another person, point to the word in the list of phrases. That, and possibly a little body language, should help.

Spanish is actually an easy language to pronounce; the spelling is fairly phonetic. Remember that *o* in Spanish does *not* carry the *w* sound with it, as it does in English (*grow, go, now*). The *e* in Spanish is pronounced similarly to the *e* of the English word *met.*

In the pronunciation section, note that *h* at the beginning of a syllable represents a hard *h* sound, similar to that of the English *hip;* when the *h* appears within a syllable or at the end, it represents only a slight aspiration (except of course for the case of *ch,* which is pronounced just as you might expect). The *r* in Spanish is always pronounced with some trill. In the pronunciation section, a single *r* represents a single trill (as in *throw*), and a double *r* represents a double trill. Note that the syllable stressed in a word is set in boldface.

How much is it?	¿Cuánto cuesta?	**kwahn**-toh **kwehs**-tah
It's too much.	Es demasiado.	ehs deh-mah-**syah**-doh
Where is ____?	¿Dónde está ____?	**dohn**-deh ehs-**tah**
Where are ____?	¿Dónde es- tán ____?	**dohn**-deh ehs-**tahn**

Is/Are there?	¿Hay?	ay (rhymes with *my*)
a bathroom	un baño	oon **bah**-nyoh
a restaurant	un restaurante	oon rehs-tow-**rahn**-teh
a hotel	un hotel	oon oh-**tehl**
the post office	el correo	el ko-**rreh**-oh
the bus station	la estación de	lah ehs-tah-**syon** deh
	autobuses	au-toh-**boo**-sehs
A bus to ____	un autobús	oon au-toh-**boos**
	a ____	
the train station	la estación de	lah ehs-tah-**syon** deh
	ferrocarrile	feh-rroh-kah-**rreel**
the market	el mercado	el mehr-**kah**-doh
a hospital	un hospital	oon os-pee-**tahl**
a doctor	un médico	oon **meh**-dee-koh
a bank	un banco	oon **bahn**-koh
a taxi	un taxi	oon **tah**-ksee
a telephone	un teléfono	oon teh-**leh**-foh-noh
the police station	la estación de	lah ehs-tah-**syon** deh
	policía	poh-lee-**see**-yah
the embassy	la embajada	lah ehm-bah-**hah**-dah
a bakery	una panadería	**oo**-nah pah-nah-deh-**ree**-ah
the gas station	la estación de	lah ehs-tah-**syon** deh
	gasolina	gah-so-**lee**-nah
a garage	un taller de	oon tah-**yehr** deh
	reparación	rch-pah-rah-**syon**
	de carros	deh **kah**-rros
the pharmacy	la farmacia	lah fahr-**mah**-syah
the church	la iglesia	lah ee-**gleh**-syah
the museum	el museo	el moo-**seh**-oh
the ruins	las ruinas	lahs **rruee**-nahs
the airport	el aeropuerto	el ae-roh-**pwehr**-toh
in front of	en frente de	en **frehn**-teh deh
near	cerca	**sehr**-kah
far	lejos	**leh**-hos

to the left	a la izquierda	ah lah ees-**kyehr**-dah
to the right	a la derecha	ah lah deh-**reh**-chah
straight ahead	directo	dee-**rek**-toh

At what time is ____?	¿A qué hora es ____?	ah keh **oh**-rah ehs
What time is it?	¿Qué hora es?	keh **oh**-rah ehs
At what time does it open?	¿A qué hora abre?	ah keh **oh**-rah **ah**-breh
At what time does it close?	¿A qué hora cierra?	ah keh **oh**-rah **syeh**-rrah

Yes.	Sí.	see
No.	No.	noh
Please.	Por favor.	pohr fah-**vorr**
Thank you.	Gracias.	**grah**-syas
You're welcome.	De nada.	deh **nah**-dah
I'm sorry.	Lo siento.	lo **syehn**-toh
Excuse me.	Perdóneme.	pehr-**doh**-neh-meh
Speak more slowly.	Hable más lentamente.	**ah**-bleh mahs lehn-tah-**mehn**-teh
I don't understand.	No entiendo.	no ehn-**tyen**-doh
I don't speak Spanish.	No hablo español.	no **ah**-bloh ehs-pah-**nyol**
Do you speak English?	¿Habla usted inglés?	**ah**-blah oo-**stehd** een-**glehs**

Glad to meet you.	Mucho gusto.	**moo**-cho **goos**-toh
How are you?	¿Cómo está usted?	**koh**-moh ehs-**tah** oos-**tehd**
I'm fine.	Estoy bien.	ehs-**toy** byehn
What is your name?	¿Cómo se llama usted?	**ko**-mo seh **yah**-mah oo-**stehd**
My name is ____.	Me llamo ____.	meh **yah**-moh

Good morning.	Buenos días.	**bweh**-nohs **dee**-ahs
Good afternoon.	Buenas tardes.	**bweh**-nahs **tahr**-dehs
Good evening/	Buenas noches.	**bweh**-nas **noh**-chehs
night.		
today	hoy	oy
tomorrow	manaña	mah-**nyah**-nah
Good-bye.	Adiós.	ah-**dyohs**
I would like	yo quisiera	yoh kee-**syeh**-rah
I have to	yo tengo que	yoh **tehn**-go keh
I need	yo necesito	yoh neh-seh-**see**-toh
I don't like (it)	no me gusta	noh meh **goos**-tah
Help! Police!	¡Socorro! ¡Policía!	soh-**koh**-rroh poh-lee-**see**-yah
a man	un hombre	oon **ohm**-breh
a woman	una mujer	ooh-nah moo-**hehr**
a child (*m.*)	un niño	oon **nee**-nyoh
a child (*f.*)	una niña	oo-nah **nee**-nyah
cold	frío	**free**-oh
hot	caliente	kah-**lyen**-teh
iced	helado	eh-**lah**-doh
Mr.	Señor	seh-**nyohr**
Mrs.	Señora	seh-**nyoh**-rah
Miss	Señorita	seh-nyoh-**ree**-tah
Doctor	Doctor, Doctora	dok-**tohr**, dok-**toh**-rah
Engineer	Ingeniero(a).*	een-heh-**nyeh**-roh (-rah)
Architect	Arquitecto(a).*	ahr-kee-**tek**-toh (-tah)
Attorney	Abogado(a).*	ah-boh-**gah**-doh (-dah)
Professor	Profesor(a).*	proh-feh-**sohr** (-**soh**-rah)
to eat	comer	koh-**mehr**
to drink	beber	beh-**behr**
to go	ir	eer

* Change the *o* to *a* to make it feminine.

| to see | ver | behr |
| to be | estar | ehs-**tahr** |

I am sick.	Estoy enfermo(a).*	ehs-**toy** ehn-**fehr**-moh (-mah)
I am tired.	Estoy cansado(a).*	ehs-**toy** kahn-**sah**-doh (-dah)
I am thirsty.	Tengo sed.	**ten**-goh sed
I am hungry.	Tengo hambre.	**ten**-goh **ahm**-breh
I am lost.	Estoy perdido(a).*	ehs-**toy** pehr-**dee**-doh (-dah)

AT THE HOTEL

one bed	una cama	oo-nah **kah**-mah
a double bed	una cama doble	oo-nah **kah**-mah **doh**-bleh
hot water	agua caliente	ah-gwah cah-**lyehn**-teh
a shower	una ducha	oo-nah **doo**-chah
a room	un cuarto	oon **kwahr**-toh
a (private) bath-room	un baño (privado)	oon **bah**-nyoh (pree-**vah**-doh)
air-conditioning	aire acondicionado	**ay**-reh ah-cohn-dee-syoh-**nah**-doh
a television	un televisor	oon teh-leh-vee-**sohr**

TELEPHONING

collect call	cobro revertido	koh-broh reh-vehr-**tee**-doh
"Hello" (on the phone)	aló *or* ¿quién habla?	ah-**loh**, kyehn **ah**-blah
credit card call	llamada con tarjeta de crédito	yah-**mah**-dah con tahr-**heh**-tah deh **creh**-dee-toh

* Change the *o* to *a* to make it feminine.

AT THE PHARMACY

deodorant	desodorante	deh-soh-doh-**rahn**-teh
toothpaste	pasta dentífrica	**pahs**-tah den-**tee**-free-kah
sanitary napkins	toallas sanitarias	**twah**-yahs sah-nee-**tah**-ryahs
antacid	pastillas antiáci- das	pahs-**tee**-ahs ahn-tee-**ah**-see-dahs
laxative	laxante	lah-**ksahn**-teh
anti-diarrheal medication	medicina para la diarrea	meh-dee-**see**-nah **pah**-rah lah dee-ah-**reh**-ah

RESTAURANT

the menu	el menú	el meh-**noo**
the check	la cuenta	lah **kwehn**-tah
the tip	la propina	lah proh-**pee**-nah
cover charge	el cubierto	el kooh-**byehr**-toh

large	grande	**grahn**-deh
small	pequeño	peh-**keh**-nyoh
a little	un poco	oon **poh**-koh
a lot	mucho	**mooh**-choh

a fork	un tenedor	oon teh-neh-**dohr**
a knife	un cuchillo	oon kooh-**chee**-yoh
a spoon	una cuchara	oo-nah kooh-**chah**-rah
a glass	un vaso	oon **bah**-soh
a bottle	una botella	oo-nah boh-**teh**-yah
a cup	una taza	oo-nah **tah**-sah
a plate	un plato	oon **plah**-toh

fried	frito	**free**-toh
boiled	hervido	ehr-**vee**-doh
broiled or roasted	asado	ah-**sah**-doh
baked	al horno	ahl **or**-noh

scrambled	revuelto	reh-**vwehl**-toh
well-done	bien cocido	byen koh-**see**-doh
medium	un poquito crudo	oon poh-**kee**-toh **croo**-doh
rare	crudo	**croo**-doh

MEATS AND FISH

steak	filete	fee-**leh**-teh
chicken	pollo	**poh**-yoh
fish	pescado	pehs-**kah**-doh
pork	cerdo	**sehr**-doh
ham	jamón	ha-**mon**
bacon	tocino	toh-**see**-noh
chops	chuletas	choo-**leh**-tahs
shrimp	camarones	kah-mah-**roh**-nehs
lobster	langosta	lahn-**goh**-stah
clams	almejas	ahl-**meh**-has
white bass	corvina	kor-**vee**-nah
squid	calamares	kah-lah-**mah**-rehs

VEGETABLES

corn	maíz	mah-**ees**
spinach	espinaca	ehs-pee-**nah**-kah
beans	frijoles	free-**hoh**-lehs
tomato	tomate	toh-**mah**-teh
avocado	aguacate, palta	ah-gwah-**kah**-teh, **pahl**-tah
potatoes	papas	**pah**-pahs
mushrooms	champiñones	chahm-pee-**nyoh**-nehs
plantains	plátanos	**plah**-tah-nohs

FRUITS

| pineapple | piña | **pee**-nyah |
| mango | mango | **mahn**-goh |

| banana | banana | bah-**nah**-nah |
| melon | melón | meh-**lon** |

OTHER FOODS

rice	arroz	ah-**rrohs**
bread	pan	pahn
butter	mantequilla	mahn-teh-**kee**-yah
sugar	azúcar	ah-**soo**-kahr
eggs	huevos	**weh**-bohs
a sandwich	un sandwich	oon **sahn**-dweech
soup	sopa, caldo	**soh**-pah, **kahl**-doh

BEVERAGES

beer	cerveza	sehr-**veh**-sah
wine	vino	**bee**-noh
red	rojo	**roh**-hoh
white	blanco	**blahn**-koh
mineral water	agua mineral	**ah**-gwah mee-neh-**rahl**
tea	té	teh
coffee	café	kah-**feh**
with milk	con leche	kon **leh**-cheh
orange juice	jugo de naranja	**hoo**-goh deh nah-**rahn**-hah
pineapple juice	jugo de piña	**hoo**-goh deh **pee**-nyah

DAYS OF THE WEEK

Sunday	domingo	doh-**meen**-goh
Monday	lunes	**loo**-nehs
Tuesday	martes	**mahr**-tehs
Wednesday	miércoles	**myehr**-ko-lehs
Thursday	jueves	**hweh**-vehs
Friday	viernes	**byehr**-nehs
Saturday	sábado	**sah**-bah-doh

TIME

at 1:00	a la una	ah lah oo-nah
at 2:00	a las dos	ah lahs dohs
at 3:00	a las tres	ah lahs trehs
at 4:00	a las cuatro	ah lahs kwah-tro
at noon	al mediodía	ahl meh-dyoh-dee-yah
at midnight	a media noche	ah meh-dyah noh-cheh
at 2:15	a las dos y cuarto	ah lahs dohs ee kwahr-toh
at 2:30	a las dos y media	ah lahs dohs ee meh-dyah
at 2:45	a las tres menos cuarto	ah lahs trehs meh-nos kwahr-toh
a day	un día	oon dee-yah
a week	una semana	oo-nah seh-mah-nah
a month	un mes	oon mehs
a year	un año	oon ah-nyoh

NUMBERS

one	uno	oo-noh
two	dos	dohs
three	tres	trehs
four	cuatro	kwah-troh
five	cinco	seen-koh
six	seis	seis
seven	siete	syeh-teh
eight	ocho	oh-choh
nine	nueve	nweh-veh
ten	diez	dyehs
eleven	once	ohn-seh
twelve	doce	doh-seh
thirteen	trece	treh-seh
fourteen	catorce	kah-tor-seh
fifteen	quince	keen-seh
sixteen	dieciséis	dyeh-see-seis

seventeen	diecisiete	dyeh-see-**syeh**-teh
eighteen	dieciocho	dyeh-**syoh**-choh
nineteen	diecinueve	dyeh-see-**nweh**-veh
twenty	veinte	**bein**-teh
thirty	treinta	**trein**-tah
forty	cuarenta	kwah-**rehn**-tah
fifty	cincuenta	seen-**kwehn**-tah
sixty	sesenta	seh-**sehn**-tah
seventy	setenta	seh-**tehn**-tah
eighty	ochenta	oh-**chehn**-tah
ninety	noventa	noh-**vehn**-tah
one hundred	cien	syehn
two hundred	doscientos	doh-**syehn**-tohs
one thousand	mil	meel

NATIONALITIES

English	inglés(a).*	een-**glehs** (ah)
Welsh	galés(a).*	gah-**lehs** (ah)
Scottish	escocés(a).*	ehs-koh-**sehs** (ah)
Irish	irlandés(a).*	eer-lahn-**dehs** (ah)
North American	norteamericano(a).*	nohr-teh-ah-meh-ree-**kah**-no (ah)
from the United States	de los Estados Unidos	deh lohs ehs-**tah**-dohs oo-**nee**-dohs
Canadian (male or female)	canadiense	kah-nah-**dyehn**-seh

* Change the *o* to *a* to make it feminine.

Key Words and Phrases: Portuguese

Following are some words and phrases you should find useful in Brazil. Of course, Brazilian usage is given, which is not always the same as in Portugal.

There are nasal sounds in Portuguese that are made by passing the breath through the mouth and the nose at the same time. A line above letters in the pronunciation section indicates that there is a nasal sound, e.g., o̅o̅ as in *soon*, nasalized; a̅u̅ as in *town*, nasalized; e̅e̅ as in *seen*, nasalized; oh as in *own*, nasalized. Note also that the syllable stressed in a word is set in boldface.

How much is it?	Quanto é?	**kwahn**-toh eh?
It's too much.	Isso é muito.	ee-soh eh **mooy**-toh
Where is ____?	Onde está ____?	ohn-dih es-**tah**
Where are ____?	Onde estão ____?	ohn-dih es-**ta̅u̅**
Is/Are there?	Há?	ah
the bathroom	o toalete	oh twah-**leh**-tih
a restaurant	um restaurante	o̅o̅ res-tow-**rahn**-tih
a hotel	um hotel	o̅o̅ oh-**tehl**
the post office	o correio	oh koh-**rray**-yoh
the bus station	a estação de ônibus	ah ihs-tah-**sa̅u̅** dih oh-nee-**booj**
a bus to ____	um ônibus a ____	o̅o̅ oh-nee-**booj** ah
the train station	a estação de trens	ah ihs-tah-**sa̅u̅** deh tre̅n̅s
the market	o mercado	oh mehr-**kah**-doh

a hospital	o hospital	oh aws-pee-**tahl**
a doctor	um médico	o͞o meh-dee-koh
a bank	um banco	o͞o **bahn**-koh
a taxi	um taxi	o͞o **tahk**-see
a telephone	um telefone	o͞o teh-lay-**fo**-nih
the police station	a delegacia de polícia	ah deh-leh-gah-**see**-ah dih poh-**lee**-syah
the embassy	a embaixada	ah ehm-bay-**zhah**-dah
a bakery	uma padaria	o͞o-mah pah-dah-**ree**-ah
a gas station	um posto de gasolina	o͞o **pohs**-toh dih gah-zoh-**lee**-nah
a garage	uma garagem	o͞o-mah gah-**rah**-zhay
a pharmacy	uma drogaria	o͞o-mah droh-gah-**ree**-ah
the church	a igreja	ah ee-**greh**-zhah
the museum	o museu	oh moo-**zeh**-o͞o
the ruins	as ruínas	ahs roo-**ee**-nahs
the airport	o aeroporto	oh ay-roh-**pohr**-toh
in front of	em frente de	a͞y **fren**-tih dih
near	perto	**pehr**-toh
far	longe	**lohn**-zhih
to the left	a esquerda	ah ihs-**kehr**-dah
to the right	a direita	ah dih-**ray**-tah
straight ahead	diretamente em frente	dee-reh-tah-**men**-tih a͞y **fren**-tih
At what time is _____?	A que hora é _____?	ah kih oh-rah ih
What time is it?	Que horas são?	kih oh-rahs sa͞u
At what time does it open?	A que hora abre?	ah kih oh-rah **ah**-brih
At what time does it close?	A que hora fecha?	ah kih oh-rah feh-**shah**
Yes.	Sim.	se͞e
No.	Não.	na͞u
Please.	Faça o favor.	fah-zih oh fah-**vohr**

Thank you.	Obrigado.	oh-bree-**gah**-doh
You're welcome.	de nada.	dih **nah**-dah
I'm sorry.	Desculpe.	dih-**skool**-peh
Excuse me.	Com licença.	koh lee-sen-sah
Speak more slowly.		
	Fale devagar.	**fah**-leh dih-vah-**gahr**
I don't understand.	Não compreendo.	nau kohm-**prein**-doh
I don't speak	Eu não falo	eh-oo nau **fah**-loo
Portuguese.	português.	por-too-**geish**
Do you speak	Fala inglês?	**fah**-lah een-**gleish**
English?		

Glad to meet you.	Muito prazer.	**mooy**-toh prah-**zehr**
How are you?	Como vai?	**koh**-moh vie
I'm fine.	Muito bem.	**mooy**-toh bay
What is your	Come é o seu	**koh**-moh eh oh **seh**-oo
name?	nome?	**noh**-mih
My name is ____.	Mey nome é ____.	**meh**-oo **noh**-mih eh

Good morning.	Bom dia.	boh **dee**-ah
Good afternoon.	Boa tarde.	**boh**-ah **tahr**-dih
Good evening/	Boa noite.	**boh**-ah **noy**-tih
night.		
today	hoje	oh-**zhih**
tomorrow	amanhã	ah-mah-**nyah**
Good-bye.	Adeus.	ah-**deh**-oos

I would like	gostaria de	gohs-tah-**ree**-ah dih
I have to	tenho de	**teh**-nyo dih
I need	preciso	prih-**see**-zo
I don't like (it)	não gosto	nau **goh**-stoh
Help!	Socorro!	soh-**koh**-rroh

a man	um homem	oo oh-**mehm**
a woman	uma mulher	oo-mah moo-**lehr**
a child	uma criança	oo-mah cree-**ahn**-sah

cold	frio	free-oh
hot	quente	ken-tih
iced	gelado	jeh-lah-doh

to eat	comer	koo-mehr
to drink	beber	bah-behr
to go	ir	eehr
to see	ver	vehr
to be	estar	ihs-tahr

I am sick.	Estou doente.	ihs-toh doh-en-tih
I am tired.	Estou cansado.	ihs-toh kahn-sah-doh
I am thirsty.	Estou com sede.	ihs-toh koh say-dih
I am hungry.	Estou com fome.	ihs-toh koh foh-mih
I am lost.	Estou perdido.	ihs-toh pehr-dee-doh

AT THE HOTEL

one bed	uma cama	oo-mah kah-mah
a double bed	uma cama de casal	oo-mah kah-mah dih kah-zahl
hot water	água quente	ah-gwah ken-tih
with a shower	com chuveiro	koh shoo-vay-roh
a room	um quarto	oo kwahr-toh
with a bathroom	com banheiro	koh bah-nyay-roh
air-conditioning	ar condicionado	ahr kon-dee-syo-nah-doh
a television	um televisor	oo teh-leh-vee-zohr

TELEPHONING

| collect call | uma chamada a cobrar | oo-mah shah-mah-dah ah koh-brahr |
| "Hello" (on the phone) | alô | ah-loh |

| credit card | chamada com cartão | chah-**mah**-dah k̄oh |
| call | de crédito | **car**-tāu dih **creh**-dee-toh |

AT THE PHARMACY

deodorant	um desodorante	o͞o dih-zoh-doh-rahn-tih
toothpaste	pasta de dentes	**pahs**-tah dih **den**-tihs
sanitary napkins	toalhas higiênicas	toh-**ah**-lyahs ee-zhee-eh-nee-kahs
antacid	anti-ácido	ahn-tee-**ah**-see-doh
laxative	um laxante	o͞o lah-**shahn**-tih
anti-diarrheal medication	medicamento contra diarréia	meh-dee-kah-men-toh kon-tra dee-ah-rray-ah

AT THE RESTAURANT

the menu	o menú	oh meh-**noo**
the check	a conta	ah **kohn**-tah
the tip	a gorjeta	ah gohr-**zheh**-tah
cover charge	couvette	coo-**vet**

large	grande	**grahn**-dih
small	pequeno	pih-**keh**-noh
a little	um pouco	o͞o **poh**-koh
a lot	muito	**mo͞oy**-toh

a fork	um garfo	o͞o **gahr** foh
a knife	uma faca	oo-mah **fah**-kah
a spoon	uma colher	oo-mah **koh**-lehr
a glass	um copo	o͞o **kaw**-poh
a bottle	uma garrafa	oo-mah gah-**rrah**-fah
a cup	um copo	o͞o **kaw**-poh
a plate	um prato	o͞o **prah**-toh

fried	frito	free-toh
boiled	cozido	koh-zee-doh
broiled or roasted	assado	ah-sah-doh
well-done	bem passado	bay pah-sah-doh
medium	medio	meh-dioh
rare	sangrento	sahn-gren-toh

MEATS AND FISH

steak	bife	bee-fih
chicken	galinha	gah-lee-nyah
fish	peixe	pay-shih
pork chop	costeleta de porco	koh-steh-leh-tah
		dih pohr-koh
ham	presunto	prih-zoon-toh
bacon	bacon	bay-koh
shrimp	camarão	kah-mah-rau
lobster	lagosta	lah-gohs-tah
codfish	bacalhau	bah-kah-lyau

VEGETABLES

corn	milho	mee-lyoh
spinach	espinafre	es-pee-nah-frih
beans	feijão	fay-zhau
tomato	tomate	toh-mah-tih
potatoes	batatas	bah-tah-tahs
mushrooms	cogumelos	koh-goo-meh-los

FRUITS

pineapple	abacaxi	ah-bah-kah-shee
mango	manga	mahn-gah
banana	banana	bah-nah-nah
guava	goiaba	go-yah-bah

OTHER FOODS

rice	arrôs	ah-**rrohs**
bread	o pão	oh p $\overline{au}$
butter	a manteiga	ah mahn-tay-gah
sugar	o açúcar	oh ah-**soo**-kahr
eggs	ovos	**aw**-vohs
a sandwich	um sanduíche	$\overline{oo}$ sahn-**dwee**-shih
soup	sôpa	**soh**-pah
ice cream	sorvete	sohr-**veh**-tih

BEVERAGES

beer	cerveja	sehr-**veh**-zhah
wine	vinho	**vee**-nyoh
red	tinto	**teen**-toh
white	branco	**brahn**-koh
mineral water	água mineral	**ah**-gwah mee-neh-**rahl**
milk	leite	**lay**-tih
tea	chá	shah
coffee	café	kah-**feh**
coffee with milk	uma média	oo-mah **meh**-dyah
small cup of black coffee	cafézinho	kah-feh-**zee**-nyoh
orange juice	suco de laranja	**soo**-koh dih lah-**rahn**-zha
pineapple juice	suco de abacaxi	**soo**-koh dih ah-bah-kah-**shee**

DAYS OF THE WEEK

Sunday	domingo	doh-**meen**-goh
Monday	segunda feira	sih-**goon**-dah fay-rah
Tuesday	terça feira	**tehr**-sah fay-rah
Wednesday	quarta feira	**kwahr**-tah fay-rah
Thursday	quinta feira	**keen**-tah fay-rah

| Friday | sexta feira | **sehs**-tah **fay**-rah |
| Saturday | sabado | **sah**-bah-doh |

TIME

at 1:00	à uma hora	ah oo-mah **aw**-rah
at 2:00	às duas horas	ahs **doo**-ahs **aw**-rahs
at 3:00	às três horas	ahs trehs **aw**-rah
at 4:00	às quatro horas	ahs **cua**-tro **aw**-rahs
at noon	ao meio-dia	au meh-yoh-**dee**-ah
at midnight	à meia-noite	ah meh-yah-**noy**-tih
at 2:15	às duas e quinze	ahs **doo**-ahs ih **keen**-sih
at 2:30	às duas e trinta	ahs **doo**-ahs ih **treen**-tah
at 2:45	às duas e quarenta e cinco	ahs **doo**-ahs ih cuah-**rehn**-tah ih **seen**-koh
a day	um dia	oo **dee**-ah
a week	uma semana	oo-mah seh-**mah**-nah
a month	um mês	oo meis
a year	um ano	oo **ah**-no

NUMBERS

one	um	oo
two	dois	doys
three	três	trehs
four	quatro	**kwah**-troh
five	cinco	**seen**-koh
six	seis	says
seven	sete	**seh**-tih
eight	oito	**oy**-toh
nine	nove	**naw**-vih
ten	dez	dehsh
eleven	onze	**ohn**-zih
twelve	doze	**do**-zih
thirteen	treze	**treh**-zih

fourteen	catorze	ka-**tor**-zih
fifteen	quinze	**keen**-zih
sixteen	dezesseis	dih-zeh-**says**
seventeen	dezessete	dih-zeh-**seh**-tih
eighteen	dezoìto	dih-**zoy**-toh
nineteen	dezenove	dih-zeh-**naw**-vih
twenty	vinte	**veen**-tih
thirty	trinta	**treen**-tah
forty	quarenta	kwa-**ren**-tah
fifty	cinqüenta	seen-**kwen**-tah
sixty	sessenta	se-**sen**-tah
seventy	setenta	se-**ten**-tah
eighty	oitenta	oy-**ten**-tah
ninety	noventa	no-**ven**-tah
one hundred	cem	sāy
two hundred	duzentos	doo-**zen**-tohs
one thousand	mil	meel

About the Authors

We have written two travel books—*The Travelers' Guide to European Customs and Manners* and *The Travelers' Guide to Asian Customs and Manners*—and, despite hours of airport delays, trips on rickety trains, and more than a few wrong turnings in rented cars, we've retained a love of travel and a curiosity about the people of other countries. (Note: Nancy is by far the more adventurous. *E.D.*)

Elizabeth Devine, a professor at Salem State College in Massachusetts, has written books and travel articles. Nancy L. Braganti has taught foreign languages in the U.S., Europe, and Israel.

Researching this book involved not only travel but also countless hours of interviews and reading. We interviewed dozens of people from the countries covered, as well as a great number of North Americans who have lived in and done business in those countries.

ELIZABETH DEVINE
NANCY L. BRAGANTI